Listening + quietly

D0434719

AGATHA CHRISTIE
AND THE ELEVEN MISSING DAYS

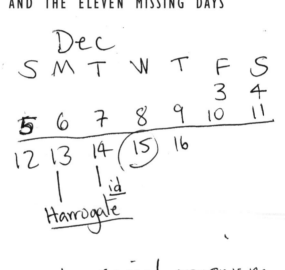

Dec

S	M	T	W	T	F	S
					3	4
5	6	7	8	9	10	11
12	13	14	(15)	16		

id

Harrogate

evil is not a social organism
deviation springing from the
heart of an individual

Jared Cade

AGATHA CHRISTIE
AND THE ELEVEN MISSING DAYS

PETER OWEN
LONDON AND CHESTER SPRINGS

PETER OWEN PUBLISHERS
73 Kenway Road, London SW5 0RE

Peter Owen books are distributed in the USA by
Dufour Editions Inc., Chester Springs, PA 19425-0007

First published in Great Britain 1998
Revised paperback edition first published 2000
Reprinted in this edition 2006
© Jared Cade 1998, 2000

ISBN 0 7206 1280 2

A catalogue record for this book is available from the British Library

Printed and Bound in Great Britain by
Short Run Press Ltd, Exeter, Devon

The front cover illustration shows Agatha Christie leaving the
Harrogate Hydro on 15 December 1926 after having been discovered.
(British Library Collection)

Acknowledgements

I should like to acknowledge the help I received in researching this book from the following people:

Ian Blair, Chief Constable of the Surrey Constabulary and Geraldine Phillips; Barbara Hick of West Yorkshire Police; Ruth Harris of West Yorkshire Archive Service; Maggie Bird of the Metropolitan Police Archives Branch; Susan Healy and Chris Bradley of Thames Valley Police (which now incorporates the Berkshire Constabulary); Dawn Smalley; Edith Butler; Nick Forbes of the Kew Public Record Office; Ralph Barnet of the Surrey County Council, who as an administrative ranger of Newlands Corner gave me a guided tour of the area and chalk pit into which Agatha's car almost plunged.

Richard Brotherton and Anders Ditlev Clausager of the British Motor Industry Heritage Trust; Mark Priddey of the Oxfordshire Archives; Detective Sergeant Christopher Roberts, formerly of the Camberley Police Force. Ian McGregor of the British National Meteorology Library and Archive; Bruce Hoag; Lisa Spurrier, Robert Hale, Elizabeth Hughes and Mark Stevens of the Berkshire Record Office; Patricia Willis of the Surrey Record Office; Eamon Dyas; R. M. Jones; Celeste Kenney; Althea Bridges; Colin Price; Bill Indge; Millie Bush; Tibby Kull; Jack Boxall; Eric Boshier and Wilfrid Morton, who as former police constables took part in the search for Agatha.

Gina Dobbs of Random House for permission to examine Agatha's business correspondence with the Bodley Head; Michael Bott of Reading University; Michael Rhodes, former keeper of Agatha's correspondence for the Bodley Head; Stuart Ó Seanóir of Trinity College Library; Glenise Matheson of the John Rylands University Library; Christopher Sheppard of the Brotherton Collection, Leeds University

Library; Catherine Cooke of Marylebone Library; Brigadier K.A. Timbers, Historical Secretary of the Royal Artillery Institution; Richard Bland of Clifton College; Roland Lewis; the staff of the British Library; Helen Pugh of the British Red Cross; Staff of the British Telecom Archives; Stewart Gillies and the staff of the Colindale Newspaper Library.

Kay Farnell of the Automobile Association; Margaret de Motte for access to the papers of the Watts Family of Abney Hall; Peter Berry; the Trustees of the Mountbatten Archive; Gwen Robyns; Kai Jorg Hinz; Jean Debny; Tim Raven; Christopher Dean, Barbara Reynolds and Phillip L. Scowcroft. Jacob Ecclestone; Jacqui Kanaugh of the BBC Written Archives; Mike Dolton of BBC Sound Archives; His Grace the late Duke of Northumberland; Michael Baxter; and Charles Ward.

Judith and Graham Gardner; Dame Felicity Peake; Christine Wilde; Marion and Ernest Chapel; Mr and Mrs David Tappin; Terrence Tappin; Patsy Robinson; Margery Campion; Richard D. Harris, Philip Garnons-Williams; Professor Donald Wiseman; Mrs Loram; and Jane Davies.

Shari Andrews of the Old Swan Hotel, formerly the Harrogate Hydro; Malcolm Nessam; Mr Stray of Harrogate Library; the staff of the Library of Congress; Mr T. Lidgate; St Catherine's House and Somerset House; Michael Meredith; the staff of Bristol University Library; the staff of Kensington and Chelsea Libraries; Sally Harrower of the National Library of Scotland. The late Kathleen Tynan, to whom I spoke before her death, and Leon Wieseltier, executor of her estate; Roxana and Matthew Tynan, who since then have helped to make it possible to view their mother's private research papers and other related matter; Mr and Mrs Wood for showing me around their home at Styles, Sunningdale.

Finally, special thanks is due to a small band of dedicated and knowledgeable Christie enthusiasts who kept me informed and whose modesty prevents them from being named here.

PREFACE

O N 3 DECEMBER 1926 a distraught woman mysteriously vanished
from her home in Berkshire, England. The discovery of her
abandoned car in Surrey led to fears for her safety. She was found a
week and a half later in a luxurious hotel in Harrogate, Yorkshire, reading newspaper accounts of the nationwide search for her. When her
extraordinary conduct was challenged, her husband intervened, claiming she was suffering from amnesia. The woman was Agatha Christie,
and the events of those eleven missing days would haunt her for the rest
of her life.

The disappearance was to prove a watershed in Agatha's life, and
her enduring reticence on the subject has posed a number of intriguing
questions: How could a woman who saw photographs of herself on the
front pages of newspapers have failed to realize she was the most talked-
about woman in Britain? What was the significance of the trail of letters
she left in her wake? And what prompted her husband to reveal that she
had previously spoken about the possibility of disappearing and, when
she was discovered, why was he approached to pay the bill for the police
search?

Although the disappearance made her famous, no previous account
of Agatha's life has fully explained the extraordinary circumstances
behind the disappearance and why she behaved as she did. I discovered
during the early stages of my research that most of the books written
about the authoress have amounted to little more than literary
critiques. All the writers have concluded that Agatha experienced some
sort of nervous breakdown and that the notoriety of the disappearance
lead to her becoming a recluse. In Britain there have been just two
actively researched biographies, and in their account of Agatha's long

life both writers have admitted difficulty in tracing witnesses. An unauthorized biography by Gwen Robyns in 1978 challenged the family's official explanation, while an authorized biography by Janet Morgan in 1984 drew a decorous veil over the disappearance, blaming much of what happened on press intrusiveness.

Both biographers maintain that Agatha never discussed the incident after she was found. This is factually wrong. Agatha did eventually discuss the disappearance, and her motive for breaking her silence was as instructive as her reasons for never publicly speaking of the matter again.

Intrigued by the story, I had a hunch that the explanations previously advanced for the most famous incident in the authoress's life contained too many discrepancies to be wholly credible. Restaging her journey proved that it could not possibly have occurred under the circumstances described by herself and latter-day theorists. So what had really happened? Fuelled by curiosity at the many unresolved questions, I embarked on a pilgrimage around England to find out more about the reclusive personality who had figured in her own bizarre real-life mystery.

As a child Agatha had delighted in *Alice's Adventures in Wonderland* and *Through the Looking Glass,* but it quickly emerged that the cover-up her family and others had perpetrated immediately following her disappearance demanded a greater suspension of disbelief than anything Lewis Carroll could have written. The Christie family's explanation left numerous questions unanswered and dozens of loose ends. For instance, what was the significance of the identity she created for herself during her disappearance, and why did the press hint broadly at deliberate design? Given that her bank accounts had been stopped by the police, how did she survive financially? Also, what was the intriguing significance of an inscription to a friend written on the flyleaf of one of her books three years after the disappearance?

In discovering the answers to these and other questions my own journey was no less labyrinthine than Agatha's, but I managed to trace a number of people with first-hand knowledge of the disappearance. The truth has emerged from an impeccable source following an inevitable weakening of the walls of silence that the writer built around herself in her lifetime, since her own prediction that she would be forgotten within ten years of her death has not proved true.

Nan Watts was Agatha's sister-in-law and life-long friend, and Nan's daughter and son-in-law, Judith and Graham Gardner, have confirmed the truth about the disappearance and other hitherto undisclosed details of Agatha's personal life. Judith and Graham knew Agatha intimately, and their knowledge of her together spans over eighty-five years. Their reason for confiding in me, in opening up their photograph albums and showing me private letters, is because I have read everything Agatha wrote, since, as they say, 'There's no short cut to Agatha. You have to read the books.' They have broken decades of silence and officially endorsed this biography in order to put Agatha's relationship with the Watts side of her family into perspective for her fans. I owe them an enormous debt of gratitude, as do Agatha's many admirers.

My decision to write this book arises from a life-long interest in the woman behind some of the most morally compelling crime fiction of our time. Her refusal to discuss the more painful aspects of her life has led some critics to dismiss her as an uninteresting recluse. Yet what she went through on the most traumatic night of her life led her to sublimate much of her experience into her fiction: in one instance she accurately reconstructed her departure on the night of her disappearance, and only the initiated knew.

The mystique surrounding the disappearance fascinates people to this day. What emerges is the compelling story of a woman driven by private torment to the edge of desperation who came back to become one of the best-loved story-tellers of the twentieth century.

ILLUSTRATIONS

(Between pages 136 and 137)

Abney Hall, Cheshire, home of the Watts family
Agatha and her sister-in-law Nan Watts, Princess Pier, Torquay, 1908
Archibald Christie's stepfather, William Hemsley
Archie in the early 1920s
Archie, Major Belcher, Mrs Hyam and Agatha during the British
    Empire Tour, 1922
Nan and her fiancé George Kon at Le Touquet golf course, France, 1925
George, Archie and Nancy Neele on Sandwich Golf Course, Kent, 1926
Nan's daughter Judith, aged ten at Brancaster, Norfolk, 1926
Map of Newlands Corner, where Agatha Christie's car was found
Map showing Sunningdale in relation to Newlands Corner
Berkshire Constabulary missing persons poster, 9 December 1926
Scenes from the 'Great Sunday Hunt', 12 December 1926, showing Deputy
    Chief Constable Kenward directing the searches
Front page of the *Daily Sketch*, 15 December 1926, after Agatha was found
London *Evening News* photograph showing Agatha *en route* to Abney Hall on
    15 December 1926
Front page of the *Daily Mirror*, 16 December 1926
Albert Whiteley of the Harry Codd Dance Band, who observed 'Mrs Neele' in
    the ballroom of the Harrogate Hydro
Rosie Asher, the hotel chambermaid who first identified Agatha
Superintendent Goddard of the Berkshire Constabulary
Flyleaves of some of the books Agatha personally inscribed to Nan
Nan's niece, Eleanor Watts, later Lady Campbell-Orde
Nan, Agatha's sister-in-law and life-long friend
Daily Express newspaper article, 24 January 1927, reporting Agatha's trip
    to the Canaries
Agatha's nephew Jack with his father Jimmy Watts, 1926
Agatha's secretary Charlotte Fisher, Agatha, Nan, Mary Fisher and Nan's
    daughter Judith outside Greenway, 1950
Agatha with Jimmy Watts, mid-1950s
Judith and Graham Gardner in the Middle East, 1962
Agatha with her second husband, the celebrated archaeologist
    Max Mallowan, 1967
Lady Mallowan, formerly Barbara Parker, Max's second wife, *c.*1988

Contents

PART 3: WHILE THE LIGHT LASTS

Prologue

GRANDFATHER'S WHISKERS

WHEN AGATHA CHRISTIE disappeared in December 1926 she was the toast of literary London with the publication of her sixth novel. *The Murder of Roger Ackroyd* was primarily a connoisseur's item when it first appeared, quickly selling 4,000 copies, but, as controversy raged over whether she had played fair or tricked her readers over the killer's identity and further reprints were destined to sell out, what no one realized was that it was set to become one of the most discussed detective stories ever written.

The debates about the novel confirmed Agatha's place as a rising star in the firmament of crime writers of the time. However, what should have been a happy period in her life was about to become the most traumatic. Shortly before the publication of the book her mother, to whom she was devoted, died. Not long after this her husband, Colonel Archibald Christie, a dashing flying hero of the First World War, told her that he had fallen in love with a young woman called Nancy Neele.

Then the unthinkable happened – Agatha vanished on the night of 3 December and the story became front-page news throughout Great Britain. News of marital discord came swiftly to the attention of the authorities. For a week and a half three police forces in the south of England competed to find her. Innumerable special constables, members of the public and the press assisted in the search. The revelation that the missing woman's husband had spent the night of the disappearance with his mistress led to whispers of suicide and murder.

The search came to an abrupt end on 14 December when Agatha was officially identified by her husband at a luxurious health hydro in Harrogate. The outcome, although dramatic, never fully explained how and why she had disappeared. Questions were asked about the extravagant lifestyle the missing writer had been leading, and the Colonel's explanation as to what had happened to her was considered by many to be far from convincing. He responded to public censure by calling in the family doctor and a consultant, and soon a carefully worded statement was released to the effect that she was 'suffering from an unquestionably genuine loss of memory'. He made a personal appeal to the press to let the matter drop, so that his wife could be restored to health and enjoy their married life out of the media spotlight.

It was, however, the end of the Christies' marriage, and the rest of the tragic drama that had briefly erupted on the public stage was played out resolutely behind closed doors. It was from this period that Agatha's revulsion of the press dated; it was later exacerbated by further headlines over her divorce from Archie and his subsequent marriage to Nancy Neele.

The public furore that erupted over the disappearance meant that Agatha went overnight from being a moderately well-known authoress to being a household name. After she was found she became the target of cartoonists, comedians and bar-room wits. Some members of the public were convinced that she must have experienced some sort of temporary mental breakdown. Others believed that her literary agent had organized the disappearance and spoke of it as a major publicity stunt.

The story soon vanished from the headlines, but a measure of the fame she achieved throughout Great Britain is attested to by a popular song which was sung each summer in the late twenties on a stage constructed on Bournemouth beach by Birchmore and Lindon's Gay Cadets. 'Grandfather's Whiskers' was altered thus to include their own explanation of the affair:

> Grandfather's whiskers, grandfather's beard!
> Never had it shingled, never had it sheared!
> Where did Mrs Christie go when she disappeared?
> Into grandfather's whiskers, grandfather's beard!

To this day the facts behind the disappearance have remained a mystery, and the incident has never been forgotten, despite the apparently normal and happy life Agatha led afterwards. Sadly, the stability she enjoyed following her second marriage was undermined by further shame and heartbreak which she hid from the public. When in later years she relaxed her guard and allowed the occasional journalist into her presence it was always on the condition that she was not asked questions about her private life or the disappearance. The few inter-viewers who were privileged to meet her seldom came away better informed: she had her stock answers and seldom deviated from them. The real Agatha was a complex woman who kept herself deliberately hidden from the public.

Despite the reverberations over her disappearance she gained more fans than she lost. An extraordinary example of how popular she became is a letter from a survivor of the German concentration camp at Buchenwald who wrote to her after the war telling her how the inmates had devised and performed a production of her novel *Ten Little Niggers*. Although it was one of her most macabre stories, in which all the characters are murdered one by one, the suspenseful plot, together with the underlying morality of the tale, had had the effect of lifting the prisoners' spirits.

Inevitably, there were honours: a CBE in 1956, a Doctorate of Letters in 1961 and the DBE in 1971. By then her readers had come to expect their 'Christie for Christmas'. When it seemed as if further fame and success were impossible, Sidney Lumet's faithful 1974 film version of *Murder on the Orient Express* marked the most successful adaptation of her work for the screen ever and resulted in a major film première. Although she savoured the evening and the widespread accolades, she never forgave the press for having intruded into her private life at a time when she had been at her most vulnerable. The emotional scars caused by the disappearance had never entirely left her. Her death two years later, on 12 January 1976, left such a void in the sphere of crime litera-ture that hers is one of the foremost names by which would-be detec-tive writers are compared.

The posthumous publication of her autobiography in 1977 was awaited eagerly. Would she finally reveal what had really happened during those eleven missing days? Far from comment on the disappearance, however, her memoirs made no reference to it whatsoever. Many of her readers felt cheated. Some commentators even wondered if it was an eccentric act of revenge on the press which had hounded her all those years before.

The tributes she still receives as a writer inevitably mention the disappearance, and so the one incident in her life which she would have preferred not to be dwelt on has continued to invite questions. To understand what happened it is necessary to examine her life from childhood, for it was here, surprisingly, that the seeds of her unhappiness were sown.

PART I
LOVE AND BETRAYAL

I

MAUVE IRISES AND EWE LAMBS

AGATHA WAS THE third child of the American-born Frederick Miller and his English wife Clarissa Boehmer Miller. Their marriage was such a happy one that Agatha confidently believed that the ideal husband for her would come along when she grew up and that love and happiness would be hers for ever.

Ashfield was a white villa on the outskirts of Torquay, a fashionable seaside resort spread over seven hills on the south coast of Devon. She was born there on 15 September 1890 and christened Agatha Mary Clarissa Miller – a much-loved 'afterthought' in the lives of her middle-aged parents. Frederick Miller was a genial and highly sociable gentleman, fussy in his health, and fond of all forms of theatrical activities. His cousin Clarissa, known to the family as Clara, had adored Frederick since she was a young child and theirs was a particularly loving and fulfilled marriage. Clarissa, who had long been fascinated by religion, was very mystical in outlook. Their love for Agatha, combined with their affluent lifestyle, would make for a secure and happy childhood that would leave Agatha insufficiently prepared for the blows life would offer.

The Millers' other two children were the gregarious and assertive Madge and Monty, who was charming but feckless. Madge was eleven years older than Agatha and would enthral her as she grew up by her ability to put on sinister voices and her love of dressing up. The ne'er-do-well Monty, who after a short-lived military career gradually faded out of his family's lives, was ten years older than Agatha and was apt to treat her in such a condescending and relentlessly teasing manner that she grew up relating more easily to the women in the family. Since Madge and Monty were away at school for much of this time Agatha was raised virtually as an only child. She never went to school as a little girl and was free to roam Ashfield, the family home, with playmates from her imagination.

The hub of her early universe was the nursery with its wallpaper with mauve irises, where Agatha was presided over by a caring nanny, a devout Christian, whose moral certitudes and conventional beliefs were conveyed forcefully to her adoring young charge. Agatha sometimes found it difficult to reconcile her nanny's strict morals and ideals with the ways of the world, but she never rebelled because of her compliant nature and the fact that her nanny's strictures, like those of the other adults around her, were instilled with love not fear.

Agatha was a hypersensitive child. In her memoirs she recalled her horror when she overheard her nanny confiding to a housemaid that young Miss Agatha had been playing again with her imaginary friends the Kittens. After this disturbing exposure of her privacy she vowed never again to let anyone know about her esoteric invented world.

The person on whom she came to depend most was Clarissa. There formed between mother and daughter a uniquely intuitive and loving bond. In times of misery Agatha found there was no one more understanding and supportive than Clarissa. Agatha also knew that when she was ill there was no one quite like her mother for restoring her vitality.

Agatha's dumpling face, with its heavy-lidded grey eyes and long blond hair, gave her a wraith-like appearance. As she grew older she developed an elusive manner, a defence against inquisitive probing; an unwelcome question was liable to glance off her like a spent arrow. When she did part with information she preferred to do so on her own terms. Silence for Agatha became a preciously guarded commodity, a cocoon for concocting fantasies, and in later life the two things she most hated were noise and large crowds.

Beneath the surface of her seemingly idyllic upper-middle-class childhood her dream of the Gun Man introduced an element of discord. This recurring nightmare originally involved a figure in some sort of military dress with a gun, only it was not his gun that frightened Agatha into waking up screaming but the moment when his pale blue eyes looked into hers. Later variations of the dream became more macabre: Agatha would be attending a tea-party or picnic with family and friends when she looked into a familiar loved one's face to see the dreaded blue eyes of the Gun Man staring back. To her greater horror she would see that stumps had replaced her loved one's hands. The dream perhaps reflected her caution and reticence before offering any object of her affections unconditional love.

Agatha's religious beliefs were derived mainly from her nanny. The child formed the opinion that, being virtuous, she was one of the 'saved' and dreamed of being addressed as 'Lady Agatha'. It came as a profound disappointment when her nanny told her she could be called Lady Agatha only if she was an aristocrat. Heaven, she thought, must be exactly like the beautiful meadows full of grazing lambs near Ashfield. Agatha's confused religious beliefs were revealed in her ambivalent feelings towards her father: for a time she feared that Frederick would burn in hell because he defied convention by playing croquet on Sunday afternoons and by telling light-hearted jokes about the clergy. Clarissa also played croquet, but Agatha's concern for her was less acute because her mother kept a copy of Thomas à Kempis's *The Imitation of Christ* by her bedside.

Shortly after Agatha's fifth birthday she went with her family for an extended holiday in France; included in their itinerary were Paris, Dinard, Pau, Argelès, Lourdes and Cauterets. Travelling was relatively inexpensive in those days. Ashfield was rented out because it was cheaper for the family to live abroad than at home, and Frederick was anxious to relieve the strain on his finances, which were being handled by a New York firm at this time. Later there were suspicions in family circles – though never any proof – that his fortune may have been embezzled by the US company.

The effect of Frederick's dwindling resources was to weaken his resistance to illness over the next six years, although doctors never managed to come up with a definite diagnosis. Frederick's finances and ill health formed a faint, almost imperceptible shadow over Agatha.

The decision for Agatha to be educated at home, after their return to Ashfield, was made by Clarissa, who was not afraid to try out new ideas. She had an exceptionally vivid imagination and this acted as a catalyst on her daughter. Clarissa was prejudiced against children learning to read before they were eight, but Agatha had already taught herself to read by the time she was five by learning to recognize the shapes of words, rather than the spelling. Her father taught her elementary mathematics and soon discovered she had a natural talent for the subject, and her ability to sort out complicated mental problems later proved invaluable when devising plots for her detective fiction. Her two grandmothers – one of whom lived in Bayswater, the other in Ealing – were firm upholders of Victorian values, and from them she gleaned many of the precepts that were to form the character of her spinster sleuth Miss Marple. Surrounded by so many forceful and extrovert adults, Agatha grew up believing herself to be 'the slow one' of the family. She was to realize only in her early twenties that her family had been abnormally bright and that she was more intelligent and able than she had previously thought.

Frederick's finances, strained by his eldest daughter's coming-out in New York, continued to dwindle and to perplex him. Around Agatha's eleventh birthday he sought employment in the City of London; a difficult prospect for a gentleman of fifty-five who had never worked and who had no qualifications. His inability to find a job in the City led to increased worry. The weather turned cold, and the chill Frederick caught turned into double pneumonia. On the afternoon of 26 November 1901 Agatha saw her mother burst out of the room in which her father was lying, and, without having to be told, she knew he was dead.

Frederick's death brought home to Agatha how things could suddenly change. Owing to the family's straitened circumstances it was thought that Clarissa would have to sell Ashfield. But following the entreaties of her daughters and a letter of protest from Monty – by now abroad serving with his regiment – Clarissa capitulated. Instead, rigid economizing enabled her to keep on the small estate. Agatha adored Ashfield so much that a recurring theme in several of her books would be her protagonists' overwhelming desire to retain the family home.

Fortunately, nine months after Frederick's death, an event took place that would reduce the isolation of mother and daughter at Ashfield. In September 1902 Agatha's sister Madge married Jimmy Watts, the eldest son of a wealthy Manchester manufacturer, James Watts Snr. Agatha approved of Jimmy, who was kind to her, always treated her seriously, refrained from making infantile jokes and, best of all, spoke to her as if she were an adult. Agatha's former jealousy at the attention Clarissa and Frederick had lavished on Madge's New York coming-out was forgotten, for she had her own part to play in her vivacious and witty sister's wedding.

The choral service was held in Torquay at St Saviour's Church, and Madge wore a gown of beautifully wrought silver embroidery and carried a prayer book instead of a bouquet out of respect for her father's memory. Agatha was one of six bridesmaids, including Nan Watts, the bridegroom's younger sister. They wore ivory white Louisine picture dresses, with petticoats, elbow sleeves and fichus of Alençon lace. Pinned on to the dresses were diamond and pearl brooches in the shape of marguerites, the gift of Jimmy, who also gave them bouquets of the same flower to carry as a floral pun on the name of the bride.

Although many deserted Agatha after the notoriety she acquired after her disappearance, Nan would stand by her for life. Initially, there was antagonism between the two prospective sisters-in-law. The brash fourteen-year-old tomboy Nan had been told that Agatha was an exceedingly demure and well-behaved twelve-year-old. Agatha had been given to understand that Nan was a polite but forthright child who always spoke up clearly for herself. The two girls met in mutual suspicion, but after the wedding they soon dropped their reserve and Ashfield's playroom echoed to their unruly games.

The relationship Madge forged with her new mother-in-law Anne Watts was not a happy one. Madge offended Nan's mother by being rude and demanding. Anne Watts never ceased to opine: 'Madge is the worst thing that's ever happened to this family.' Despite these tensions the good manners of Agatha and Clarissa ensured that they were always welcome in the Watts household; moreover, Anne Watts and Clarissa were already firm friends because they had been at school together in Cheshire as children.

Agatha's rich new in-laws had inherited a splendid Victorian Gothic pile called Abney Hall in Cheadle, Cheshire (now part of Greater

Manchester). Her regular visits there over the years provided her with the experience of grand living that she was to make use of in her future country house murders. Abney Hall had been in the Watts family since 1849, and in the past they had offered hospitality to Prince Albert and other famous aristocratic and political figures. Complete with gargoyles, it contained numerous corridors and passageways, ornate carved staircases, mullioned windows, suits of armour, marble busts and more than three hundred oil paintings, including ones by Holbein, Gainsborough and Ansdell; a stuffed lion that had once killed a missionary guarded the main hallway. Outside, the manicured gardens contained a small lake in front of the house and a larger one at the back. An archway with a clocktower opened on to the enormous walled kitchen garden where a Gothic-style ventilating shaft wafted warm air towards the fruit trees. Agatha considered Abney Hall 'marvellous', and it would later surface, lightly disguised, as the setting for a large number of her mysteries, including *The Secret of Chimneys* and *Hercule Poirot's Christmas.*

The straitened circumstances under which Agatha grew up at Ashfield had little effect on her as a teenager, since Clarissa ensured that their home remained a bastion of love and security. She also arranged for her daughter to take arithmetic and literature classes two days a week at a school run by a Miss Guyer in Torquay; Agatha was to attend for a year and a half.

Her religious beliefs received a jolt one day when one of her teachers insisted that every one of them would at some time in their lives face despair and that until that time they would not truly know what it was to be a Christian. The real test, she was told, was to know, as God did, what it was like to feel that all your friends had forsaken you, that those you love and trust have turned away from you. The teacher explained that the way to survive was to hold on to the conviction that this was not the end and to remember that if you love you will suffer and if you do not you will never know the meaning of a Christian life. Agatha never forgot this lesson.

An undoubted annual highlight of Agatha's rather staid life as a teenager was when Nan visited Ashfield. Agatha revelled in organizing their social activities. A favourite game was to cram themselves into a wardrobe packed with clothes and fall out of it. The fact that Nan was an heiress meant that Agatha often became the recipient of her sister-in-law's cast-off clothes.

Christmases were invariably spent at Abney Hall. Agatha and Nan liked to drink a mixture of milk and cream on the estate farm, where Nan once painted all the piglets green. It was an established routine for the Wattses and their guests to dress up for dinner, and a photograph exists showing Nan made up to resemble a Kentucky minstrel. Agatha and Nan were irrepressible together, and after dinner they often performed pantomimes in a room known as the Council Chamber. An enormous curtained alcove in front of the fireplace made an excellent stage and, on account of her porcelain features and dreamy manner, Agatha was nicknamed 'Starry Eyes' by the Watts family.

Years later, after the disappearance, Agatha developed agoraphobia, a nervous reaction to crowds and strangers that led many to suppose that she was pathologically shy. Yet those who knew Agatha before the incident remembered her as an extremely attractive young girl who, when she grew older, had no shortage of male admirers. Her reticence, which arose from her pleasure in observing others and her disinclination to part with information except on her own terms, meant that she was often mistaken by those who did not know her well as either aloof or shy.

Agatha made up for the general lack of excitement in her life by taking part in a number of amateur theatricals in Torquay. While performing in *The Blue Beard of Unhappiness* she met a young man called Amyas Boston, who became for a time the object of Agatha's affections and an ardent admirer. However, her passion was music, and when Clarissa sent her to finishing school in Paris she took piano and singing lessons and Amyas faded from her life.

Over the next two years finishing school awakened in Agatha the idea of making a career in the performing arts. Sadly, her dream was not matched by sufficient discipline or ability. Her teachers undermined her confidence, and she eventually concluded that she did not have enough talent to appear in public as a solo pianist. Once she realized that she did not possess the volume of voice needed for opera she gave up the idea of performing in public, since becoming a concert singer fell short of her musical ambitions.

During this period Nan was attending a finishing school in Florence. The former tomboy had turned into a demure, apple-cheeked brunette, whose mischievous sense of humour readily attracted would-be suitors. Agatha kept in touch with her sister-in-law by visiting the Italian city during her school holidays.

After Agatha returned from Paris Clarissa rounded off her education by arranging a coming-out season in Cairo. By now Agatha had developed into a highly attractive blonde of almost Scandinavian appearance: tall and slim, with a radiant smile and an oval face. The one feature that made her self-conscious was what she called her 'Roman' nose, and it has been said of her, unfairly, that she was never photogenic. In fact most of the best photographs taken of her as a young woman were informal ones taken when she was caught unawares or when she was enjoying herself in a group of friends. During her time in Cairo a series of enjoyable flirtations took the edge off Agatha's natural reticence. But her suitors were more ardent in their pursuit of her than she of them, for none of them had the adventurous qualities she craved, and so she returned to England.

Agatha recalled that she was 'gloriously idle' back at Ashfield, but the tranquillity was undermined by her growing feelings of restlessness. The life led by her sister-in-law seemed far more glamorous and exciting. Nan had recently become attracted to a highly undesirable suitor, and her parents had sent her on a round-the-world trip with her Uncle George and Aunt Helen to prevent the romance from developing.

On 4 January 1910 the unforeseen occurred. The steamer *Waikare*, on which Nan was travelling with her guardians, struck an underwater rock pinnacle in the Dusky Sound and they were shipwrecked without loss of life on Stop Island off the coast of New Zealand. The two-day ordeal of the 210 passengers and crew was relieved by the fact that they had managed to salvage food supplies, luggage and a grand piano before the ship went down. A cat that was rescued gave birth to four kittens, and Nan, unfazed by the incident, made use of her Kodak camera to photograph her fellow victims sheltering under the tarpaulins.

Unfinished Portrait

Years later Agatha would use the shipwreck in her story 'The Voice in the Dark'. The incident made front-page news in the *Otago Witness*, and Nan triumphantly bore copies of the newspaper back to England to show her disbelieving family. On the return sea voyage she became romantically attached to a man called Hugo Pollock, whom she would marry two years later, and she happily regaled Agatha with the details of their liaison.

Agatha was recovering from influenza one winter's day when her mother suggested that she follow in her successful sister Madge's footsteps and write a short story to alleviate her boredom; this and other stories that followed were rejected by publishers. With her mother's encouragement Agatha sought the advice of their neighbour, the celebrated author Eden Phillpots, who, after reading her first attempt at a novel, *Snow Upon the Desert,* suggested she should refrain from moralizing so much. It was some years before Agatha's literary promise would be recognized, for her romantic disposition and attractive looks ensured that her energies were taken up for the most part by courtships, in which she did all the rejecting.

The most serious of these was with the modest, kindly and happy-go-lucky Reggie Lucy, a major in the Gunners, who later became the model for Peter Maitland in her autobiographical novel *Unfinished Portrait*, which was published under the pseudonym of Mary Westmacott. Clarissa approved their engagement, and when Reggie Lucy returned to his regiment in Hong Kong their courtship continued by post.

Despite Reggie Lucy's lazy charm there was one thing he was unable to offer Agatha: she had a secret desire to be conquered by a stranger, 'the Man from the Sea', as she termed him in her autobiography. The need to be swept away by a stranger became a romantic obsession.

Reggie Lucy, despite his devil-may-care attitude, had missed out on many things in life, and his suggestion that Agatha should keep her options open gave her an escape clause. The romance and adventure that Agatha craved suddenly materialized on 12 October 1912 in the form of Archibald Christie, the man who would change her life for ever then break her heart.

2

THE MAN FROM THE SEA

AGATHA WAS JUST twenty-two years old when she met the dashing and assertive Archibald Christie at a dance given by Lord and Lady Clifford of Chudleigh at their home Ugbrooke House in Devon. Twenty-three years old, he was tall and handsome, with wavy fair hair, a cleft chin, an unusually upturned nose and intensely blue eyes. He had been born on 30 September 1889 in Peshawar in northern India.

Archie's Irish mother, Ellen Ruth Christie, was alive, but his English father, Archibald Christie Senior, a former divisional judge in the Indian civil service, had died some years earlier after falling from his horse following his return to England. Ellen Christie, known within family circles as Peg, later married William Hemsley a schoolmaster from Clifton College in Bristol, where Archie had been head boy. There was another son from the first marriage, Campbell Manning Christie, four years younger, who would end his military career as a major-general. He was a paler version of his brother, much more sensitive to the feelings and thoughts of others, with artistic leanings that would reach fruition after the Second World War when he would write a series of highly successful plays.

Archie had trained at the Royal Woolwich Military Academy after leaving Clifton and was a lieutenant stationed at Exeter in Devon. He encouraged Agatha to cut several partners so that she could dance with him on their first meeting, but Agatha wistfully assumed theirs had been a passing encounter. Much to her surprise he turned up at Ashfield several days later on a motor cycle.

Agatha was quickly drawn out of herself by Archie's charm, intelligence and impetuosity. Here was someone who promised romance and adventure in equal proportions and could challenge her reticence and seek out her hidden depths. Archie was that romantic figure of whom she had dreamed, her 'Man from the Sea'. His profession was as adventurous as it was exciting: he was one of a small band of qualified aviators who had joined the elite ranks of the recently formed Royal Flying Corps.

Archie, in turn, was mesmerized by Agatha's radiant attractiveness, as well as her femininity and her reticence, which made him feel even more decisive. A whirlwind courtship ensued. Archie tipped the scales in his favour and set Agatha's heart lurching two and a half months into their relationship when he said he wanted to marry her straight away. Despite recognizing they were poles apart in many ways, Agatha desperately wanted Archie to be her husband.

She knew that, in part, her fascination for him derived from the fact that he was still a stranger to her, and around this time she woke from a disturbing dream, distractedly murmuring: 'The stranger from the sea, the stranger from the sea . . .' She was so affected by this that she wrote a poem, 'The Ballad of the Flint', in which Archie was cast as the Leader of the Vikings whose fleet raids the peaceful inhabitants of Dartmoor in Devon. She cast herself as the Priestess of Dartmoor, and her feeling of helplessness over their circumstances was measured in the fact that after the Leader of the Vikings claims the Priestess as his own they both die tragically.

One person Archie was unable to win over completely with his confident manner and his charm was Agatha's mother. It was not just possessiveness of her much-loved daughter that led Clarissa to oppose the idea of their marrying straight away but the practical concern of how Archie might support a wife. Archie earned a modest subaltern's pay, and beyond this the only money he had was a small allowance from his mother. The £100 Agatha received each year from the legacy of her paternal grandfather, Nathaniel Miller, was clearly not a sufficient supplement to Archie's income.

Clarissa recognized, too, a certain ruthlessness in Archie's character which gave her forebodings; she knew also that her younger daughter's sensitive temperament made her vulnerable in the face of misery and hardship. Furthermore, Clarissa's instincts – which could at times amount to something like clairvoyance – told her that Archie would not be a faithful husband. But Clarissa loved Agatha too much to cause her pain, and confronted by her daughter's stubbornness she allowed the couple to become engaged.

Agatha plucked up the courage to write to Reggie Lucy to tell him their engagement was off. She would later ponder, after Archie had turned against her, that she might have been secure and happy with Reggie, although she knew she would never have loved him as much as she loved Archie.

Quite early in their relationship Archie made it clear to her that he could not bear it when people were unhappy or ill, and an adoring Agatha only appreciated the significance of this admission much later.

Their tempestuous engagement, which lasted a year and a half, was filled with ups and downs, with both Agatha and Archie often despairing as to whether their adverse circumstances would ever allow them to marry. No man in love, certainly not one of Archie's temperament, likes to feel he is playing second fiddle to his prospective mother-in-law, but Clarissa's precarious health was another reason the engagement was called off several times by Agatha.

Agatha's love for Archie continued to grow, because in some ways he remained a stranger to her. Everything he did or said seemed somehow exciting and unfamiliar, and he felt the same way about her, exclaiming once: 'I feel I can't get *at* you.' In moments of uncertainty Agatha had the feeling of 'wanting to go back', to have 'a safe foot on the shore'. But, where Archie was concerned, the lure of the 'Man from the Sea' was too strong, and she was aware that she had of her own accord swum out into deep water.

The advent of the First World War provided them with an incentive to grasp at happiness while they could. Archie was on three days' leave and they were staying with his mother in Clifton. The decision to marry was undertaken so precipitously that they had to apply for a special licence. Archie's stepfather, William Hemsley, proved fatherly and supportive as usual and helped the couple to finalize their plans.

The same could not be said of Agatha's future mother-in-law, Peg Hemsley, who had once been described by her other son, Campbell, as a dangerous woman, for hers was the sort of gushing affection that could rapidly change into hate. While at the beginning of their relationship she had warmly received Agatha into the family circle for Archie's sake, Peg had never considered Agatha a suitable spouse for her son. Agatha wore the new 'Peter Pan' collars – then considered very modern and daring – and Peg regarded her son's fiancée as 'fast'. Peg had consoled herself with the thought that Archie was too young to marry and that nothing would come of the unhappy alliance. She had not reckoned on her son's determination. There were many occasions when Peg alternated between demonstrating ostentatious displays of affection towards Agatha and making her antipathy clear to her future daughter-in-law. Agatha suspected rightly that there would be trouble from Peg over their decision to marry.

However, not even Peg's attack of hysterics and refusal to attend the ceremony at the parish church of Emmanuel, Clifton, could sway Archie or Agatha, who were married on Christmas Eve 1914. Agatha's initially angry and disappointed family only learned afterwards that she had become Mrs Archibald Christie. Thus the marriage got off to a bad start, and Agatha later recalled of their wedding day that all the people she and Archie were most fond of had been annoyed with them.

Two days later Archie was posted to France. Agatha returned to her mother. Ashfield's upkeep had become increasingly difficult for Clarissa, but a second source of income improved matters, since Agatha's aged and increasingly infirm grandmother from Ealing was now living with them. When Agatha was not helping with the running of the household she devoted her energies to the war effort as a Voluntary Aid Detachment nurse at the Torquay Town Hall Red Cross Hospital.

She found that reading detective stories eased her worries about Archie, for beneath the conventional elements of menace and sudden death there was always a comforting morality tale. Towards the end of the war Archie was prevented from flying in further combat owing to worsening sinus problems and he was given a desk job in France. Agatha passed her apothecaries' examination and went to work in the Torquay hospital dispensary.

Agatha's decision to write her first detective story was rooted in her complex feelings about Madge. Agatha both admired and felt a strong undercurrent of jealousy for the elder sister who was dubbed 'the clever one'. Madge had married into an extremely wealthy family, her looks and wit were widely praised, and she had travelled to such exotic places as the Italian Alps and St Moritz. While frequently argumentative, Madge could be highly entertaining. The fascinating stories she told about herself and others were often heavily embellished but always contained a grain of truth. Much to Agatha's awe and chagrin Madge had had a series of short stories published in *Vanity Fair*, making Agatha's own literary rejections even more disappointing and humiliating.

After this, around the time of Agatha's romance with Reggie Lucy, the sisters had got into a heated discussion on what made a good detective story. Madge had made a bet with her sister that she could not write a detective story where the reader was not able to guess who was responsible for the crime that had been committed, despite having the same clues as the detective.

Goaded by jealousy, Agatha planned *The Mysterious Affair at Styles* during idle moments in the dispensary. The ingenious murder method for her story was inspired by her newly acquired knowledge of poisons, while the many Belgian refugees proliferating in Torquay suggested to her the background of her little detective with the egg-shaped head, Hercule Poirot.

Her married life really only began in September 1918, two months before the war finally ended. Agatha gave up her war work in Torquay and moved to London to be with Archie. Her husband had been posted to the Air Ministry in Covent Garden where he served as Chief Technical Officer of the South-Eastern Area. He had returned from France a much decorated war hero, for in addition to having been mentioned in five dispatches he had received three medals: the DSO, the CMG and the Order of St Stanislaus Third Class with Swords. Archie no longer intended pursuing a career in the Royal Air Force, because he had become convinced there was no future for him in the armed forces, and he was determined to find a job in the City of London in order to make a lot of money.

Agatha's weekdays were lonely, and initially she avoided her well-off

friends in London. She was embarrassed by the financial gulf that separated her and Archie from them. Nan had recently moved to 10 More's
Gardens in Chelsea, and after Agatha had plucked up the courage to get
in touch she regretted not having looked up her sister-in-law sooner.

Nan's marriage to Hugo Pollock in 1912 was not a success. She had
borne him a daughter, Judith, four years later, but he had had no time
for the child and often told her to 'hop it' in Arabic. Shortly before
Agatha visited Nan he had gone off on a walking holiday and had not
bothered to return. Rather than brood, Nan had moved to London in
search of a more cosmopolitan lifestyle. Agatha was so impoverished
that one of her greatest pleasures when visiting Nan was to be invited
to examine the contents of her affluent friend's wardrobe.

It was while Archie was looking for the right opportunity to come
along in this difficult post-war period that Agatha discovered that she
was pregnant. Archie was subdued on hearing the news and he
expressed a desire for a daughter, saying he would be jealous of a son.
His reaction was not altogether surprising, for after their marriage much
of his boldness and audacity had evaporated to reveal a diffidence and
boyishness that met the child in Agatha. Archie also was very concerned that his wife should regain her physical attractiveness after the
birth. On 5 August 1919 they became the proud parents of a daughter,
Rosalind, whom they nicknamed Teddy.

That same year Archie resigned his commission when he received
an offer to join the staff of the Imperial and Foreign Corporation, deem-
ing this to be the stepping-stone for which he had been looking. In the
joy and excitement of being reunited with Archie and starting their life
together – in a succession of cramped flats across London – Agatha had
given up on *The Mysterious Affair at Styles*, which over the last few years
had been rejected by five publishers. When the Bodley Head publishers
wrote towards the end of 1919 requesting a meeting it seemed a promising omen.

Agatha met John Lane of the Bodley Head in January 1920 and,
after agreeing to alter the last two chapters, she eagerly – too eagerly –
signed a contract there and then to have her manuscript published.
What she did not realize was that the terms of the contract were very

much in the Bodley Head's favour. Nor did she take in the fact that she was obliged to offer her new publishers a total of five books.

After fulfilling her agreement to alter the courtroom setting of the book's denouement to a drawing-room bristling with tension, she received the rare distinction for a début novelist of having *The Mysterious Affair at Styles* serialized in the Friday supplement of *The Times Weekly Edition* from February to June that year. Agatha's real desire, however, was to see her story published in book form. The Bodley Head had advertised that the book would come out in August. When it had still not appeared by October Agatha was disappointed and frustrated. In a letter to her publishers she expressed the desire to see her book released before Christmas in order to coincide with the Greenwood trial. In November there was much press interest when the Kidwelly solicitor, Harold Greenwood, was acquitted of poisoning his wife. It was Agatha's hope that her tale with its poisoning and courtroom drama would strike a similar chord of interest in the public.

The Mysterious Affair at Styles eventually appeared in America at the end of 1920 and in Britain at the beginning of 1921 selling just over 2,000 copies, which was then considered a good sale for a first detective story. But since the contract she had signed was so much in her publishers' favour all she made was £25, which was her half-share of the serial rights.

Agatha's next book, *The Secret Adversary*, would earn almost twice as much and introduced an idealized version of Archie and herself in the characters of the recently demobbed Tommy Beresford and Prudence 'Tuppence' Cowley, two bright young things whose decision to place an advertisement in *The Times* hiring out their services – 'No unreasonable offer refused' – would lead them into an espionage conspiracy involving missing papers and a mysterious girl who eludes her enemies by faking amnesia.

Agatha was hoping to succeed at her writing to relieve the financial constraints of her married life and also because, once again, it had become difficult for her mother to maintain Ashfield on only one source of income following the death in 1919 of Agatha's grandmother from Ealing.

Once Agatha realized that the Bodley Head had taken advantage of her, she determined to fulfil her contract with them as quickly as possible so that she might find a new publisher. Her contract did not stipulate that the five books she owed the Bodley Head had to be detective stories, and she seized on this loophole, after delivering the manuscript of *The Secret Adversary*, to offer the Bodley Head a long mystical story she had written some years previously called *Vision*.

Agatha was quite rightly convinced that the company would not accept it, but because her publishers had treated her so unfairly she felt no compunction in the matter. *The Secret Adversary* was brought out by the Bodley Head in 1922 and fancifully dedicated 'To all those who lead monotonous lives in the hope that they may experience at second hand the delights and dangers of adventure', by which time the Christies had embarked on their own adventure.

Agatha accompanied Archie in his capacity as Financial Adviser on the British Empire Mission of 1922, which took them to South Africa, Australia, New Zealand, Canada and the United States, to promote the forthcoming British Empire Exhibition to be held in 1924 at Wembley on the outskirts of London. It was one of the most exciting experiences of their lives. Although the tour turned out to be an arduous publicity campaign that involved meeting numerous government officials from each country, it offered moments of respite such as when Archie and Agatha spent two weeks together in Honolulu, where their fascination for one another and their delight in surfing resulted in a mood of companionable playfulness all too often dampened by Archie's struggle to create a niche for himself in the business world. On the negative side, there was the irascible Major Ernest Belcher, whose fierce temper tantrums made him a volatile leader of the tour, and separation from their daughter Rosalind, who was being looked after by relatives. Their major problems, however, were to come on their return to England.

3

ADVERSITY AND PROSPERITY

As SOON AS the Christies returned to their London flat things started to go wrong. The Imperial and Foreign Corporation had not kept Archie's position open, and he found himself unemployed and unable to get a job. The couple had known before they started on the tour that it was highly likely that this might happen, but they had never believed in playing safe and had been determined to see the world and risk the consequences.

The beginning of 1923 saw the publication of *The Murder on the Links*, a new Poirot tale about a millionaire found stabbed on a golf course in France. Before the book's publication Agatha won a major row with her publishers, resulting in some ill feeling, over the proposed book jacket, which was to have featured a misleading illustration. Despite their continued financial hardship and Archie's dark moods Agatha was convinced he would eventually find the right job since he was fiercely ambitious and had a drive she had always admired.

A minor boost to their finances came in the second week of May when she won a small prize by correctly identifying the killer of Hugh Bowden in the seven-week-long newspaper serial *The Mystery of Norman's Court*. Had hers been the first correct entry received by the *Daily Sketch* the first prize of £1,300 would have resolved their financial difficulties, but it was not, and the second prize of £800 was divided among twelve runners-up, of whom Agatha was just one.

At this time, after many years' absence, her elder brother Monty had returned to England. In her autobiography Agatha does not reveal the secret shame concerning her brother and the reason her mother found it so difficult to cope with his erratic behaviour. In fact, Monty had become a drug addict. He had been expelled from Harrow because of his failure to apply himself to his studies and then served in the army in South Africa and India. He quickly squandered the legacy left to him by his paternal grandfather, Nathaniel Miller, and seems to have resigned his commission when his debts became too embarrassing. He moved to Kenya and took up farming and safari-hunting. His elder sister Madge eventually financed his ill-fated plans to run small cargo boats on Lake Victoria in East Africa, but this venture had to be aborted on the outbreak of war in 1914. He served in the King's African Rifles until he was discharged with a wound to his arm. The wound became infected and, although he resumed hunting, his health deteriorated. Finally, his doctors gave him six months to live because of the infected limb. Remarkably, however, he began to recover on his return to Ashfield. Like many charming people Monty was often economical with the truth, and it is not clear whether he became addicted to the morphine that would have been prescribed to relieve the pain of his injury or whether he became a habitual drug user for other reasons.

The worst of Monty's behaviour saw him firing pistol shots out of a window at visitors and tradesmen who called at Ashfield. His intention was not to hit or maim but to scare the wits out of his hapless victims. Incredibly, Monty bluffed his way out of the situation to the police by insisting that he was a crack shot and that there had been no real danger to his victims. The stress of dealing with her son's irresponsible behaviour put further strain on Clarissa's fragile health.

Agatha swiftly united with Madge to avert further scandal and distress to their mother. Their rather drastic solution involved installing Monty temporarily in a bungalow on Dartmoor, where he was looked after by a doctor's widow. Nan's daughter and son-in-law, Judith and Graham Gardner, recall that Madge's much put-upon husband, Jimmy – who thoroughly disapproved of Monty – paid his bills for the rest of his life.

Meanwhile, the strain of living with an unemployed husband became so great for Agatha that she contemplated taking Rosalind home with her to Ashfield or Abney Hall while Archie sorted himself out. Being sensitive to failure, he hated being unable to get a job. If Agatha attempted to take his mind off their worries by indulging in light-hearted chat she was accused of having no sense of the gravity of their situation; while if she was silent she was censured for not trying to cheer him up.

By November 1923 Agatha had completed *The Man in the Brown Suit*, a fast-moving, tightly plotted thriller inspired by her visit to South Africa. She injected her own feelings and experiences about marriage into the character of Anne Beddingfeld, the attractive and fiercely independent heroine. She says she would not dream of marrying anyone unless she was madly in love with him and insists that sacrifices are worth it for the man one loves. She claims that the reason so many marriages are unhappy is because husbands either give way to their wives all the time or else cause resentment in their wives by being utterly selfish. She maintains that women like to be mastered but hate not to have their sacrifices appreciated, while men do not really appreciate women who are nice to them all the time. She concludes that the most successful marriages occur where a man is able to get his wife to do precisely what he wants then makes an enormous fuss of her.

As if recognizing where her own recent subservience had landed her, Agatha has the heroine add defiantly that when she is married she will be a devil most of the time but will occasionally surprise her husband by behaving angelically. When the hero remarks what a cat-and-dog life she will lead, she assures him that lovers always fight because they don't understand each other and that by the time they do they aren't in love any more. The hero asks if the reverse is true, whether people who always fight each other are lovers? The heroine is lost for a reply.

This exchange suggests that, while Agatha had reason to feel unappreciated by Archie, she considered that discord and confusion were acceptable in a marriage because it indicated that the couple still loved each other and that the woman's suffering was all part of the greater, nobler cause of love.

Meanwhile Archie's professional difficulties had at last ended; he had found a job with a somewhat disreputable firm. While he knew that he would have to be careful not to get caught up in anything shady, he was finally able to smile again. Agatha was delighted in the change in him and was relieved to find her marriage back on a seemingly even keel.

By now the Bodley Head had recognized Agatha's commercial worth and suggested scrapping her old contract for a new one, also for five books but with more favourable terms. Agatha declined the offer without giving a specific reason.

She had reason to feel confident about her decision on account of the popular reception of some Poirot stories she had written for *The Sketch* and the accompanying star treatment she had received. The first series had appeared between March and May 1923 and had been heralded by a portrait taken by Boorthorn that showed a poised Agatha wearing a string of pearls. She had by now cropped her long blond hair into a stylish red-tinted bob and had been proclaimed by *The Sketch's* publicist, with reference to *The Mysterious Affair at Styles*, as 'Writer of the Most Brilliant Detective Novel of the Day'. In March another page of *The Sketch* had been devoted to photographs by Alfieri, taken at the authoress's home. Finally, 'A Family Study', in which Archie was conspicuously absent from Marcus Adams's charming studio photograph of Agatha and Rosalind, had appeared in April. The second series of Poirot stories appeared between September and December that year.

The Sketch's publicity had not gone to Agatha's head – she had given no personal interview to accompany the photographs – but the acclaim gave her a sense of self-worth that was conspicuously lacking in her increasingly combative dealings with the Bodley Head. Although Archie had encouraged her to write for money at the beginning of her career, he had begun to resent the attention she was starting to receive. He constantly undermined her, when she tried to engage him in conversation, by snapping: 'Must you always keep nattering on?'

Agatha was shaken by this but did not to let him see that he had upset her. Inwardly, however, she was upset when he put her down. She compensated by becoming increasingly high-handed in financial matters: what money she made was hers and hers alone, and she never ceased to remind Archie of this fact. It made her increasingly uneasy that he appeared to want a wife only as a lover and housekeeper, rather than a friend and confidante. As a result she sought to control him with her money. This exacerbated Archie's nervous dyspepsia and his growing feeling of being confined by his work. She received an unpleasant jolt from an inquiry from the Inland Revenue that year, which brought home to her the fact that her earnings could no longer be regarded as pocket money, and at that point she found herself a literary agent – Edmund Cork, a benign young man from the firm of Hughes Massie.

Throughout November 1923 Agatha wrote regularly to the Bodley Head urging the company to publish a collection of Poirot stories while the publicity from the second series that was appearing in *The Sketch* was still fresh in people's minds. She agreed that this collection of short stories was not to be considered as one of the books covered by her existing contract but insisted that the Bodley Head agree that *Vision* had been submitted as her third book. Had the Bodley Head agreed that this was the case, then *The Man in the Brown Suit* would have counted as Agatha's fifth book and she would not have been obliged by the terms of her five-book agreement to offer them any further novels.

But the Bodley Head now needed Agatha more than she needed them, and *Vision* became a bitter bone of contention between authoress and publisher. Both were on uncertain ground and a permanent state of stalemate could easily have followed, but Agatha capitulated over *Vision,* so *The Man in the Brown Suit* counted as her fourth novel instead of her fifth.

It was an annoying setback, but at least the London *Evening News* offered her the substantial sum of £500 to serialize *The Man in the Brown Suit* from November through to January 1924 under the rather improbable title of *Anne the Adventurous.* The cost of a Morris Cowley (half of all cars on the road at the time were Morris Cowleys) was £225, and she immediately acquired a four-seater model. Since Agatha's money had paid for the car she often annoyed Archie by reminding him that it belonged to her.

Archie's prospects improved when a friend of his, Clive Baillieu, returned from Australia and offered him a position on the board of directors with the City firm of Austral Ltd. He now felt his own man once again, back in control of his career and his abilities appreciated.

Control was one thing, freedom another. The feeling of confinement he had felt towards city life before the British Empire Tour had continued unabated on his return, and he had recently taken to relieving his frustrations by playing golf in East Croydon at weekends. Agatha, a competent player but with no real enthusiasm for the sport, had introduced him to the game and had begun to regret it. Golf was just the distraction Archie was looking for: an unimaginative man of action, he enjoyed the outdoor exercise, the camaraderie of male friends and the physical skills and challenges demanded of him. What Agatha had originally perceived as a mildly diverting distraction for her and Archie was now becoming an obsession with him.

Following the rise in their fortunes, Agatha unwittingly set the seal on their future relationship when she suggested they fulfil their dream of living in a cottage in the country. They finally seemed to have overcome adversity, but she was to discover, within a year, the downside of that dream.

4

CONFLICTING DESIRES

THE ROMANTIC IDEAL of a cottage in the country was one thing. The reality was another. Archie needed to be able to commute to London for work each day. He had recently been elected to the Sunningdale Golf Club, and he suggested that they move near by.

Sunningdale was stockbroker-belt territory, twenty-six miles out of London on the border of Surrey and Berkshire, and in January 1924 the couple moved into a rented upper-floor flat in a large Victorian house called Scotswood in the older area of Sunningdale known as Sunninghill. In the first flush of excitement of leaving crowded London it was easy to overlook the flat's constant plumbing and electrical problems.

On 27 January 1924 Agatha signed a three-book contract with Collins, which promised a lucrative £200 advance on each title and a generous royalty, even though she had one more book to deliver to the Bodley Head. When Agatha's literary agent Edmund Cork informed John Lane of the offer he grumpily responded that anyone who was prepared to pay that much for her work was welcome to it.

Agatha was now an established writer, but with success came new problems. Archie and Agatha constantly fought over money; she resolutely refused to share her earnings with him. The income from the books and the short stories had gone to her head – it was the first time she had an income of her own – and she turned Archie down every time he asked for money, unaware that it was leading to a rift between them. Agatha's financial independence led to her installing her mother in an adjacent flat in Scotswood. As Archie had always been secretly jealous of his wife's relationship with Clarissa this had the unintended effect of making him feel even more excluded from Agatha's life.

Clarissa was happy with the arrangement, since it enabled her to be near her granddaughter. Rosalind was an intelligent five-year-old, and her grandmother's pleasure in teaching revived. The new lease of life Clarissa experienced was not without its drawbacks, however, since she was as jealous of Archie's relationship with her daughter as he was with hers and she was becoming distinctly set in her ways. Agatha would later opine that living in close proximity to a mother-in-law is enough to wreck most marriages – it is unclear to which mother-in-law she was referring.

After the war Archie's mother had moved to the market town of Dorking in Surrey, just twenty-five miles from Sunninghill. His step-father, William Hemsley, now had a post as a schoolmaster at Rugby School. During term time he did not commute the 113-mile journey to his home every day, as he was required to live at the school. This led to Peg having a good deal of spare time on her hands, and Agatha found she coped best with her in small doses. Agatha's volatile mother-in-law was only too happy to tell other people their business and had never entirely rid herself of the belief that Agatha was not good enough for her eldest son. Relations between Peg and Agatha would undoubtedly have been more strained if the latter had been less tactful and outwardly compliant.

One activity that united Agatha and Archie was looking for a home of their own to buy, since Scotswood needed continual maintenance. House-hunting was always one of Agatha's great pleasures in life, and their protracted search for a suitable property had the effect of bringing them closer. But the stability of their union was illusory, as events would reveal. For all her meddling ways Peg was more clear-sighted than she was given credit for when she intimated to friends that her son and daughter-in-law were beginning to lead separate lives.

Following the publication in August 1924 of *The Man in the Brown Suit*, Agatha immersed herself in the world of the London theatre. At this time her sister Madge had a play, *The Claimant*, produced by Basil Dean at the Queen's Theatre. *The Claimant* opened on 11 September and ran for five weeks. When she heard of Madge's impending success Agatha confided her excitement in a letter to her mother and added that she would be 'furiously jealous' if Madge made it into films first with her writing.

Agatha contented herself that year by publishing, at her own expense under the imprint of Geoffrey Bles *The Road of Dreams*, a series of rather mystical love poems she had written, several of which were based on the mythical figures of the *commedia dell'arte*, which in the form of the china figurines on her mother's mantelpiece had fascinated her ever since she was a child. Although Agatha was never more than a pedestrian poet, publishing the collection enabled her to express the repressed romantic side of her nature she was unable to give rein to in her marriage. While she and Archie still took intermittent pleasure in shared activities – golf permitting – he had always been reluctant to reveal his innermost feelings. He considered discussing emotions to be indecent. This disinclination to confide his feelings, while initially surprising and hurtful to Agatha, had resulted in her attempting to repress her own feelings and had led her to conclude that Archie probably loved her more than she loved him, since he apparently needed less expression of love to satisfy him.

By March 1925 Agatha was hard at work on *The Murder of Roger Ackroyd*, unaware that Archie had been introduced at the golf course to a brunette typing clerk who worked at the Imperial Continental Gas Association in London. Nancy Neele was vivacious, had plenty of time for socializing and was down to earth and practical; more importantly, her passion for golf equalled Archie's. Romance blossomed.

Agatha remained in total ignorance of Archie's affair while she was busy writing. Given that her tastes were literary and Archie's sporting, Sunninghill was clearly not the place for them to regain what she believed was the temporary lost footing in their marriage. Somewhere altogether different was required. Following the completion of *The Murder of Roger Ackroyd* they went abroad in the summer of 1925 to Cauterets in the French Pyrenees. The holiday could not have come at a better time: Archie had stopped seeing Nancy because he was convinced their affair was sure to lead to further complications and unhappiness. It seemed Agatha and Archie might be able to unite their lives once again.

The decision to visit Cauterets was Agatha's, since she had happy memories of staying there with her family as a young child. At first, the couple found it disappointing. Their holiday soon acquired momentum, however, with walks up the mountains where they drank the sulphurous waters, which in a letter to Clarissa they described as *'la douche nasale'*. There were charabanc expeditions (Archie wrote scathingly about their fellow passengers to Clarissa) and games, including boule, before they moved on to San Sebastian, where they indulged in one of Agatha's favourite passions: bathing. The evenings were spent at the Kursaal, where Agatha found Archie sadly lacking in spontaneity. The cabaret show started at 10.30 each night, and Archie, who was used to going to bed early at home, duly retired at the first interval. Agatha, who took pleasure in being as impulsive and capricious as her mother, considered her husband was becoming rather stuffy. Their holiday ended on a more carefree, frivolous note when, having endured the outward journey to France sitting upright in a second-class train compartment all night for reasons of economy, they decided to travel home first class.

What Agatha was unaware of was that Archie's moodiness during the holiday was caused by his mixed feelings about Nancy, and soon after their return home Agatha began to feel like a golfing widow once more – and with good reason. The abandoned wife was more abandoned than she knew, for Archie was once again seeing Nancy.

Archie's preoccupation with furthering his career intensified, and this meant that Agatha was obliged to attend a number of business dinners, every minute of which she hated. When he came home from work in the evening he often immersed himself in a book or in business matters after dinner. By working so hard through the week Archie was deliberately contriving to ensure that his weekends were free to spend with Nancy.

Agatha loved him too much to displease him by complaining and looked forward instead to the weekends when she could reclaim him from his work. But the country walks and picnics Agatha and Archie had enjoyed earlier in their marriage had become things of the past. The strain of Archie's double life took its toll: he became tired and listless, the routine of City life dragged him down, and his work-day often began with him arriving at Sunningdale Station so late that he had to run across the lines in front of the approaching train to reach the far platform in order to catch it.

Increasingly the most vital link between the Christies was their daughter. Rosalind was now six. Archie's indifference to fatherhood before she had been born had been transformed into a special kind of mutual love, based on a shared practical outlook and sense of humour; this often left Agatha feeling excluded. Archie spoke to Rosalind as if she were an adult and expected her to respond in kind. When he gave her a task to perform, such as cleaning his golf clubs, he expected her to clean them properly, and Rosalind appeared to enjoy the challenge far more than her mother's imaginary games. Archie had developed into a wonderful father, happily playing games with pennies on the floor for the amusement of Rosalind and Nan's eight-year-old daughter Judith. The two young girls were virtually raised together, and Judith, a quiet, introverted child, developed quite 'a pash' on Archie and thought he had the most 'lovely blue eyes'.

Agatha's feelings for her daughter ran deep, and she was saddened to find that she had not been able to reproduce the same mother–daughter relationship that she, as a child, had enjoyed with Clarissa. Agatha's attempts to play make-believe games with Rosalind were undermined by the latter's practical nature, and she was disappointed to find that Rosalind did not share her enthusiasm for the activities and fairy books that Agatha had enjoyed as a child. Agatha found in Rosalind the same cool, judgemental qualities apparent in Archie and was secretly rather alarmed by her child.

June 1925 saw the publication of Agatha's last book for the Bodley Head, *The Secret of Chimneys*, a light-hearted thriller involving the murder of a prince in an English stately home. The novel included a crack at the Bodley Head's failure to adhere to its publishing schedules when she makes one of her characters observe of a book written by another character that it would be at least a year before it was brought out, as publishers sat on manuscripts and hatched them like eggs.

The publication of *The Secret of Chimneys* was eclipsed that same year by a more significant literary event. *The Murder of Roger Ackroyd*, the plot of which had been partly inspired by two similar suggestions put to her by her brother-in-law, Jimmy Watts, and a young fan, Lord Louis Mountbatten, first appeared in the London *Evening News* as a serial that ran from July to September under the title *Who Killed Ackroyd?*

The unsuspecting public was taken aback by the unexpected identity of the killer: what Agatha had done amounted to colossal cheek or nerve, depending on whether or not one approved of her audacity. Agatha had reached a significant artistic plateau in her career, for she now had the satisfaction of knowing she could write detective stories and that she could make money out of them.

But Agatha's success as a writer continued to overshadow Archie. The financial divide between them widened throughout 1925, and this led to heated arguments. Another factor contributing to the ultimate breakdown of their marriage was Agatha's battle with her weight, which had begun after Rosalind was born. Archie felt the slim young girl he had married was becoming matronly and loquacious, rather like his mother whose emotional excesses he preferred to ignore. Archie continually asked Agatha to lose weight, but she was unable to do so, and she become the victim of his cruel taunts about her figure.

Agatha's and Archie's marriage looked increasingly shaky, and at first it was easy to blame this on the confines of their upper-floor flat at Scotswood. Agatha was hoping to escape the obsessive golf and bridge fraternities in Sunninghill by moving further into the country, but the decision to buy a large house ten minutes' walk from Sunningdale Station was Archie's. He was secretly anxious not to move further from London because this would make it difficult for him to continue his clandestine relationship with Nancy Neele. But in their furtive affair the couple had been skating on thin ice for some time – and the ice was about to crack. Owing to an unexpected twist of fate Archie was to find himself under the same roof as his wife and mistress at the beginning of 1926, the year all three would look back on as the worst in their lives.

5

THE GUN MAN REINCARNATE

T HE SCENE FOR the tumultuous breakdown of Agatha's and Archie's marriage in 1926 was Styles, a large, mock-Tudor house ten minutes' walk from Sunningdale Station. The house had a reputation for being unlucky, since the last three owners had all come to grief in various ways. Styles had formerly been known as 'Sans Souci', not an apposite name, meaning, as it did, 'carefree'.

The move to Styles at the beginning of the year was not a happy one. Sunningdale society – conventional in its attitudes and with a strong emphasis on sporting and outdoor pursuits, especially golf – had become stultifying and restrictive for Agatha. Rosalind was now attending Oakfield, a private school, and Agatha found it impossible to escape golfing associations even when she took her daughter to dancing classes, because they were often held at Dormey House, an annexe of the Sunningdale Golf Club.

Agatha's loneliness increased, and Archie would sulk if she invited married friends down from London, because he was obliged to entertain the husbands – the only place he really wanted to be at weekends was on the golf course with his mistress. The one couple to whom Agatha could extend hospitality without incurring Archie's wrath was Nan Watts, recently divorced, and her second husband. George Kon was a distinguished cancer specialist and lecturer at the Imperial College in London, as well as a Fellow of the Royal Society of Medicine. He spoke seven Chinese dialects as a result of a passion for beetles which led him to travel to China on hunting expeditions. Both Nan and George were good at golf; they had won the Prince of Monaco Cup for mixed foursomes at Le Touquet.

Nan and Agatha would sit in the Sunningdale clubhouse, sipping their favourite drink of milk and cream, watching their young daughters play together as they patiently waited for their husbands to finish their game of golf. It was through George that Nan learned of Archie's affair with Nancy Neele. Nan instructed George to 'try to calm it down', but George instead provided an alibi for Archie. Nan said nothing to her friend, not wanting to be the bearer of such crushing news.

Most of the Christies' friends now knew about the affair, and Nan was becoming alarmed at Agatha's preoccupation with her fiction-writing, since she seemed to be losing contact with reality as her career really took off. A photograph that Nan took on the golf course at Sandwich in Kent of George, Archie and Nancy, in which the latter two gazed uneasily into the camera lens, was a portent of the deception to follow.

In an attempt to alleviate her loneliness Agatha unsuspectingly invited Nancy Neele to spend the weekend at Styles. Archie was appalled, being justifiably apprehensive at having his wife and mistress under one roof. It would have seemed odd for Nancy to have declined the invitation. She came down from London to Sunningdale every weekend to play golf, and they had mutual friends in Major Belcher and his Australian wife, with whom Nancy had stayed on holiday in France the previous year.

The tension at Styles was exacerbated by the fact that Agatha genuinely liked Nancy. Agatha admired her for many of the reasons that Archie did: she was cheerful and bright, a lively conversationalist, good at telling stories and capable of maintaining a companionable silence – a quality that Archie particularly admired in a woman. Nancy professed to be an admirer of Agatha's books, and, as Agatha gave an account of Belcher's irascible antics as leader of the British Empire tour, she was oblivious to the fact that she was offering her friendship and hospitality to the usurper of her husband's affections.

Agatha extended several irregular invitations to Nancy throughout the first half of 1926, and the other showed no hesitation in accepting. Archie, uneasy about this, told Agatha that having Nancy to stay spoiled his golf. When they went to a nearby dance, the twenty-seven-year-old Nancy thanked Agatha for acting as her chaperone, since her parents, who lived at Croxley Green in Ricksmansworth, would have been worried by her going out socially on her own.

Around this time Agatha suggested to Archie that they might try for another baby. Her request prompted him to do some serious thinking. He stalled for time by suggesting to Agatha that first of all they get another car, and he became the owner of a second-hand Delage.

That spring Archie turned down Agatha's proposal that they take a short holiday in Corsica together with the excuse that he could not get the time off work. Agatha went instead with her sister Madge, unaware of the opportunity she was offering her husband and his mistress. Agatha had begun *The Mystery of the Blue Train* and needed a break from work. She had reason to feel tired and drained, for her literary output in the previous six years had been phenomenal. She was by now more widely known to the magazine-buying public through her seventy-odd short stories than for her handful of novels. Agatha had long forgotten the advice her mother had offered before the British Empire tour about it being a wife's duty always to be by her husband's side, and she was set to suffer the consequences on her return.

The first crisis came when Clarissa fell ill with bronchitis at Ashfield a few weeks later. In her memoirs Agatha reveals that Madge removed their mother to Abney Hall in Cheadle. In fact Madge and Jimmy were living in Cheadle Hall next to the village church. The 72-year-old Clarissa appeared to get better, then took an unexpected turn for the worse. Agatha was sent a telegram but could not get to Cheadle Hall in time. Clarissa died on 5 April with Madge by her side. At the moment of death Agatha was travelling by train to Manchester when she was suddenly overcome by a feeling of cold desolation, and her strong sense that her mother had died was soon to be confirmed.

Agatha attended Clarissa's funeral without Archie, who was away in Spain on a business trip for Austral Ltd. Clarissa was laid to rest in the same burial plot in Ealing cemetery as her husband. Agatha needed Archie more than ever before and longed to be comforted by him. When he returned to Styles a week later he was ill-equipped to console her. Agatha felt as if the bottom had dropped out of her world, for Clarissa had always made her feel loved and able to deal with things, no matter what she said or did, and the certainty of her mother's uncon-ditional affection had enabled her to cope better with being the sen-sible, independent wife Archie required her to be.

Archie handled his reunion with Agatha badly. He awkwardly attempted to cheer up his grieving wife by appearing bright and cheer-ful, but his jollity had the opposite effect to that intended. Agatha was horrified by his apparent callousness and proceeded to berate him. Archie had further business to transact in Spain, and in her desire to come to terms with her grief Agatha turned down his suggestion that she should accompany him.

She was feeling no better by the time he returned, and she fell in with his suggestion of renting out Styles for the summer while she sorted out Ashfield. She needed time to mourn her mother, and she believed that Archie would find it hard to be around while she did. Archie escaped the pall of her grief by spending the summer months at his club in London, which made it easier than ever for him to see Nancy, frequently taking her out to dinner and to the theatre.

Under the terms of Clarissa's will, Agatha inherited Ashfield, and she stayed there with Rosalind. Charlotte Fisher, the secretary-cum-governess that Agatha had hired to help her take care of Rosalind, did not accompany them because she had been recalled home to Scotland since her father was thought to be seriously ill. Agatha asked her sister to help her clear out Ashfield, but Madge was too busy. The future of Ashfield was uncertain. Agatha was faced with the option of either renovating the house and renting it out or else selling it off.

Agatha came across a letter her father had written to her mother shortly before he died, telling Clarissa how much he loved her and how she had made all the difference to his life. Agatha kept it, still convinced that her own marriage was as loving and durable as that of her parents. Yet going over the past led her to contemplate her future. While she loved Archie and Rosalind unreservedly, Agatha felt that neither of them gave her the love she required. Archie's short emotional tether made it impossible for him to be as intimate with Agatha as his late mother-in-law.

Agatha felt stifled and misunderstood, her life dictated by the routine of Archie's work, and she longed to travel. But she still felt her future lay with her family.

Archie contributed to Agatha's loneliness by making excuses about being too busy at work to come down from London to Torquay at weekends. He used the General Strike, during which he drove a lorry to deliver essential supplies, as a further excuse to stay away.

The chore of sorting out Ashfield was alleviated by the knowledge that Agatha's latest book was her most successful to date: *The Murder of Roger Ackroyd* had been published by Collins in May. However, the marriage was put under further strain when Agatha proposed that she and Archie take a holiday in Alassio in Italy after Rosalind's seventh birthday on 5 August and then left Archie burdened with the task of making all the practical arrangements for the trip.

When Archie arrived at Ashfield Agatha was struck by the fact that he seemed a stranger to her. Her instincts told her something was wrong, and she became convinced he was holding something back.

Agatha asked him what was wrong and found her world turned upside down. Archie informed her that he had not booked their proposed holiday. He then explained that he had been seeing a lot of Nancy. Agatha responded by denying the obvious. 'Well, why shouldn't you?' she asked. He told her he had fallen in love with Nancy.

Agatha's shock and horror were compounded when Archie admitted that the affair had been going on for eighteen months. He said he wished to protect Nancy's reputation by making it appear that he had committed adultery with an unknown third party – since admitting adultery was the usual way of initiating divorce proceedings.

Agatha had previously admired Archie's strong desire to be considered respectable, but his wish to hush up Nancy's part in the break-up of the marriage made her see that there was a disturbing side to his conventionality. The man she loved so much, the man whom she had put on a pedestal, suddenly became the 'Gun Man' to her.

The two made a pretence of celebrating Rosalind's birthday, then Archie returned to his London club and a distraught Agatha attempted to carry on with her life. Madge, who had come to Ashfield to celebrate Rosalind's birthday, was shocked by what had happened.

She attempted to calm her sister down by insisting that Archie would come back to her, but nothing from Agatha's past experience had prepared her for the blow he had delivered and she could not be consoled.

Agatha felt totally alone. All she had left to cling to was the hope that Archie would return; she convinced herself that his liaison with Nancy was just a passing affair, inflated in importance because he had felt neglected in the months after Clarissa's death. Agatha determined to return to Styles to save her marriage.

On the way she stopped her car for a rest. To her horror her wire-haired terrier Peter wandered into the middle of the road and was knocked unconscious by the undercarriage of a hit-and-run vehicle. Agatha, presuming him to be dead, lifted him on to the back seat of her car and frantically resumed her journey. She failed to notice that by the time she reached Styles Peter was regaining consciousness. Agatha ran into the house crying out that Peter was dead. When Charlotte Fisher, who had returned from Scotland, reassured her that the dog was alive Agatha refused to believe her. In fact Peter made a full recovery and was his usual self within a few days. Agatha later incorporated aspects of Peter's accident in her stories 'The Edge' and 'The Man from the Sea' and in her novel *The Rose and the Yew Tree*.

A fortnight after his defection Archie returned. Agatha felt as if she had received a direct reprieve from God when Archie suggested that he had perhaps made a mistake and ought not to break up their marriage for the sake of their daughter. It had not been an easy decision for him to make, and Agatha was not only conscious of this but of her own needs as well. She wondered whether she could face the pain of further betrayal if he broke his promise to be faithful.

She felt they should keep their marriage going for another year to see how it went, but her husband would agree only to a three-month trial reconciliation. The one person who showed insight into Agatha's problems was her secretary Charlotte, who told her: 'He won't stay.' Rosalind, with the uncompromising candour of the young, was outspoken to her mother on the matter: 'I know Daddy likes me, and would like to be with me. It's you he doesn't seem to like.'

Agatha resorted to desperate measures and in October arranged a month-long trip for her and Archie to Guéthary, a tiny bathing village at the foot of the French Pyrenees between Biarritz and the Spanish border. Archie reluctantly agreed to go. The Pyrenees held memories of Agatha's happy childhood and her parents' perfect marriage, but a less-than-idyllic trip to the same region with Archie the previous year ought to have warned her that it was impossible to turn back the clock.

Away from Styles Agatha found it easy to imagine that their relationship was improving. But the couple were unable to establish the easy camaraderie of the early days of their marriage. They acted as though they were polite strangers, and, after all the recent strains, such an atmosphere seemed almost a relief. In fact, it was the lull before the storm that would destroy their lives for ever.

6

DESPERATE MEASURES

AGATHA HAD KNOWN the real test of her reconciliation with Archie would begin on their return to Styles in November 1926, but his absences immediately told their own story. Agatha found his sullen silences hard to bear, and ugly confrontations ensued.

Her torment was made worse by Archie's refusal either to commit himself to the marriage or totally break away from it. Agatha insisted that she would not give in to a divorce if Archie asked for one again, because she was convinced that their daughter would be stigmatized for the rest of her life. The fact that Agatha would physically throw things at Archie during their fights only made matters worse.

There were pressures, too, from outside the marital battleground. Her publisher Sir Godfrey Collins was delighted with the public's reception of *The Murder of Roger Ackroyd* and was anxious to know when he could expect delivery of her latest Hercule Poirot book. The popularity of Agatha's Belgian detective was attested to by the requests of the *Liverpool Weekly Post* and *Reynolds's Illustrated News* to serialize stories with the character. Although Agatha was persevering with *The Mystery of the Blue Train,* she clearly was not going to finish it in time for publication in early 1927. Owing to her productive short-story output, Sir Godfrey and her literary agent Edmund Cork exerted pressure on her to agree to release a series of Poirot tales under the title *The Big Four.*

These stories had already appeared as an ongoing serial in *The Sketch* from January to March 1924 under the title *The Man Who Was Number Four.* Agatha was reluctant to fall in with their wishes, because she recognized only too well that the collection would fall well short of her readers' expectations. The stories read like a parody of an Edgar Wallace thriller and, until Agatha produced *The Murder of Roger Ackroyd*, she was undecided as to whether she was a writer of thrillers or detective stories.

In her autobiography Agatha gives the impression that the twelve stories which make up *The Big Four* were put together during 1927 with the help of her brother-in-law Campbell Christie in order to give the appearance of a full-length book, since she claims the breakdown of her marriage had not left her well enough to attempt such a task by herself. *The Big Four* was in fact in production by Collins before her disappearance, and the alterations she alone instigated at this time amounted to no more than minor editing.

Furthermore, Agatha tells her readers that the reason why she was desperate to write following her marital breakdown was because 'I had no money now coming in from anywhere.' But nothing could be further from the truth. Clarissa's will, in which she had left everything to Agatha, had been probated on 29 June 1926, and after the deduction of death duties Agatha was the recipient of the handsome sum of £13,527 16s. 8d. It was enough money for Agatha and Rosalind to live on for several years, and Agatha's reason for claiming to be very poor at that time in her memoirs was to create the impression of a woman hounded into a mental breakdown during 1926. Her pre-disappearance decision to release *The Big Four* early the following year arose from her desire to put her one-book-a-year routine back on track.

Despite her new financial security Agatha was under considerable mental strain in the months before she went missing. She kept up appearances as best she could with friends she had made in Sunningdale. She looked forward to Christmas, when she could get Archie away from Sunningdale by taking him and Rosalind up to Abney Hall for the traditional family festivities. She also planned to take him abroad to Portugal in the New Year with some friends from Sunningdale, the da Silvas, in the feverish hope that by removing him to a different environment he would forget Nancy.

Meanwhile Agatha looked around for a suitable flat or house to lease in London in order to be closer to her husband's place of work.

She was determined to sell Styles, or at least rent it out, indefinitely if necessary, and she was aware that her daughter would have to change schools. But these were small sacrifices to ensure that she kept Rosalind's father.

Conscious of her approaching middle age Agatha felt unable to compete for her husband's attentions, and she duly vented the intense jealousy she felt towards her younger rival by writing 'The Edge'. This short story not only affirms Agatha's belief in the sanctity of marriage but sheds light on the one circumstance under which she might have forgiven Nancy for taking Archie from her.

The raw emotion that imbues 'The Edge' sharply contrasts with the usual mystery element to be found in Agatha's fiction and makes it one of her most compelling short stories. Interestingly, Agatha cast Nancy in the role of 'the wife', while she cast herself as Clare, 'the other woman' who has always loved her rival's husband but who has not stood in the way of their happiness. The turning point in the story comes when Clare stops off at a distant hotel for refreshments, after taking her dog to the vet following an accident in which he has been knocked over by a car. Clare's casual glance at the names in the hotel register leads to the discovery that her married rival has been having an affair. This discovery, after years of suffering and self-denial, unleashes Clare's jealousy and leads to a bitter confrontation on the Downs during which she threatens to expose the wife's infidelity. The pressure Clare applies to the wife is too great and, rather than face exposure, the wife jumps from the ridge to her death. The story ends with Clare being driven mad from the unforeseen consequences of her blackmail.

While the death of the Nancy Neele character was merely a gratifying literary whim on Agatha's part, Clare's resulting madness was in many respects symbolic of her creator's despair over her real-life marital problems. Agatha had never been an unfaithful wife to Archie; this would have been the one circumstance under which she might have been able to forgive Nancy for stealing her husband.

The story was finished shortly before Agatha became the most talked-about woman in the country. In those final days Agatha's obstinacy, the stubbornness that was also her greatest strength, drew her near to the edge of despair. What Agatha found especially hard to bear was that eleven years of marriage could have turned so swiftly on Archie's part to an ill-concealed dislike of her. Agatha felt worn down by the need to keep up appearances, as much for the servants' sake as to minimize Rosalind's anxiety. Her secretary Charlotte proved invaluable, taking over the running of the household at this time.

Judith recalls that her mother, Nan, was very anxious about Agatha; the visits Nan made to Styles helped to alleviate the strain between the Christies. One day, shortly before the disappearance, Judith and Rosalind were playing in a bedroom when they climbed on to the top shelf of a wardrobe and closed the door. Their mothers heard a loud crash and hurried upstairs. The wardrobe had toppled over, trapping the two girls inside. Nan and Agatha were relieved that their daughters were not hurt.

Agatha slept badly and ate little in the fortnight before she disappeared. It seemed to her that if Archie could betray her then nothing, not even God, could be trusted. God ceased to exist for her: her overriding thought was that Archie had betrayed her following her mother's death. She cast herself as the innocent victim and had no comprehension of how she had contributed to the breakdown of their relationship. There were endless rows, because he was still undecided as to whether or not to leave her for good. Agatha, failing to realize this, lost her temper completely and flung a teapot at him. It was the worst thing she could have done. It was Nan's opinion that if Agatha had not thrown the teapot she might have kept Archie.

Agatha withdrew into herself, enveloped in bitterness and misery. Her one solace at this time was her dog Peter, who gave her unconditional and unquestioning love. Husband and wife went through the motions of leading normal lives, but the atmosphere in the house grew increasingly acrimonious until Agatha's nerves were near breaking point.

On the morning of her disappearance the couple had their worst row ever. Charlotte, aware of the discord between husband and wife, had left early on a day trip to London, reassured by the sight of Agatha romping happily with Rosalind. During the row Archie made it clear that he had no intention of accompanying Agatha to Beverley in Yorkshire for the weekend, as she hoped he would. He then told her he could not stand the charade of their attempted reconciliation any longer.

Deeply shaken, she accused him of seeing Nancy behind her back. He admitted that he had made plans to spend the weekend with his mistress and that he had decided, once and for all, to marry her. Their argument ended with Archie storming off to work.

Agatha was extremely upset and, later that morning, she left Styles in her Morris Cowley without telling any of the servants where she was going. Although she was still feeling despondent after she returned to Styles for lunch, she drove with Rosalind to Archie's mother's house in Dorking for afternoon tea.

While she waited for her mother-in-law's kettle to boil Agatha sang songs and joked with her daughter. The subject of Nancy Neele was not raised in the little girl's presence, and Agatha told Peg she was going to Beverley for the weekend. Peg was aware that Clarissa's death eight months earlier had come as a great blow to Agatha, and when she commented on how well her daughter-in-law seemed Agatha agreed that she was feeling much better. A few minutes later Agatha appeared to become very depressed. Peg noticed she was not wearing her wedding ring, only her engagement ring. When Peg commented on this, Agatha sat perfectly still for some minutes gazing into space, then, issuing a hysterical laugh, she turned away and patted Rosalind's head. It was dusk by the time Agatha and Rosalind left at around five o'clock and began the hour-long drive back to Styles.

Agatha dined alone after Rosalind was put to bed and waited and waited for her husband's return.

When Archie failed to come home on the evening of Friday 3 December 1926 there was no doubt in Agatha's mind – or the minds of the servants – that he had left for good.

Unable to bear the strain of her situation any longer she got into her car at 9.45 that night, dressed in a fur coat and a velour hat. She knew by then that her marriage was irretrievably over and that nothing could bring her husband back. As Agatha drove away from Styles her plan was to spite Archie for his infidelity. Tragically, she was unaware that she was setting in motion the most widely publicized missing person's inquiry of the day. The consequences that rippled out from her actions that night would be far more devastating than any she had ever conceived in her fiction and would reverberate throughout the rest of her life.

Part 2

SUSPICION, SPECULATION AND UNCERTAINTY

7

DREDGING THE SILENT POOL

WHAT NO ONE could have predicted on the night of Agatha's disappearance from her home in Berkshire were the unprecedented steps the authorities would take to find her and the way the press would blow the incident up into a front-page sensation.

Agatha's absence was first noticed on the morning of Saturday 4 December 1926 through the discovery of her abandoned Morris Cowley near Newlands Corner, a local beauty spot frequented by motorists and tourists five miles from Guildford in the neighbouring county of Surrey. The car was three hundred yards below the plateau of Newlands Corner at the edge of a chalk pit by Water Lane, a rutted, twisting dirt track leading to the village of Albury in the gently sloping valley below. The situation was like a scene from one of Agatha's detective novels, and what was to follow in the next week and a half was more bizarre than anything she ever penned.

The headlights of the abandoned four-seater were first seen piercing the winter darkness around seven o'clock by a Chilworth cattleman, Harry Green, but as he was on his way to work he did nothing at the time. Almost an hour elapsed before Jack Best, a gypsy boy on his way to work for a shooting party, passed the spot and took a closer look. The person who actually brought the matter to the attention of the authorities, shortly after eight o'clock, was Frederick Dore, a car tester who worked in Thames Ditton, who subsequently recalled: 'When I found the car the brakes were off, and it was in neutral gear. The running board and the under part of the carriage were resting on the bush. From its position it appeared to me that the car must have been given a push at the top of the hill and sent down deliberately. The lights were off and I found that the battery had run right down. The lamps had evidently been left on until the current became exhausted. If anyone had accidentally run off the road the car would have pulled up earlier. There was no sign that the brakes had been applied. I looked for skid marks on the soft ground but could find none.'

A gypsy girl told Dore she had heard a car about midnight coming along the track on the top of the downs leading from Guildford. While there was no way of knowing whether the two incidents were connected the unusual discovery prompted Dore to take immediate action: 'I went to Mr Alfred Luland, who looks after the refreshment kiosk on the other side of the road, and asked him to take charge of the car, while I informed the policeman at Merrow.' Dore telephoned the police from the Newlands Corner Hotel, some five hundred yards away on the Clandon Road.

The first intimation Archie had of Agatha's disappearance was when her secretary Charlotte rang the home of his hosts, Sam and Madge James, at Hurtmore Cottage near Godalming to tell him that a policeman had turned up at Styles that morning to announce that Mrs Christie appeared to be missing. Archie was none too pleased at having his weekend with Nancy interrupted. He had no sooner terminated the telephone call and announced he had to leave because his mother had been taken ill than a police officer set the tongues of the Jameses' servants wagging by turning up on the doorstep.

Archie was escorted back to Styles. He insisted that he was unable to shed any light on Agatha's whereabouts, saying he had last seen her on the Friday morning before departing for work. He gave every indication of being completely baffled, but after surreptitiously reading the letter that Agatha had left for him on the hall table the previous night he burned it without telling the police of its existence or contents. He adjured Charlotte, who knew of the letter, to silence by telling her it had been written before Agatha had changed her plans to go to Beverley for the weekend.

News of the discovery of the abandoned car was relayed to the Surrey County Police Headquarters in Woodbridge Road in Guildford, but it was not until 11 p.m. that the matter came to the attention of Deputy Chief Constable William Kenward. The fifty-year-old recipient of the King's Police Medal had been involved two years earlier in the investigations which had led to the trial and conviction of the Frenchman Jean Vacquier in what was known as the Byfleet murder. The press had been riveted by the story, tailing the police twenty-four hours a day, often interviewing important witnesses before the police arrived. Deputy Chief Constable Kenward was not to know that the press would be even more enthralled by this new story.

He took a grim view of the affair from the very first: 'The car was found in such a position as to indicate that some unusual proceeding had taken place, the car being found half-way down a grassy slope well off the main road with its bonnet buried in some bushes, as if it had got out of control. In the car was found a fur coat, a dressing case containing various articles of ladies' wearing apparel and a driving licence indicating that the owner was Mrs Agatha Christie of Sunningdale, Berkshire.'

Several questions needed urgent answers. How, why and when had Agatha's car been abandoned? And why had her handbag, distinguished by its fashionable zip, been removed?

Another intriguing factor was the weather. On the night of the disappearance the temperature at six o'clock had been 41 degrees Fahrenheit, a quarter of the sky had been covered in cloud and there had been a westerly breeze. By midnight the temperature had fallen to 36 degrees, the sky had completely cleared of cloud cover and the breeze had swung round to the north-west. So why had Agatha's heavy fur coat been abandoned on the back seat?

Deputy Chief Constable Kenward's bewilderment was shared by his officers, including Tom Roberts, a 21-year-old probationary constable, who described the mysterious affair at Newlands Corner as 'the most sensational event that occurred whilst I was at Headquarters . . . The bushes were crushed and broken from the impact of the car, but they had prevented it from falling into the chalk pit.'

Curiously, there was very little damage to the car, which was found in an upright position with the glass windscreen intact. Furthermore, the folding canvas roof was still erect and the plastic side-screens in place, although the bonnet was slightly damaged, the speedometer cable was broken and one of the wings was a little bent. The car doors were closed, the brakes were off and the gears were in neutral. The spare tin of petrol, carried on the side step, appeared to have been knocked off when the car collided with the bushes and was found lying in the grass. By the time Deputy Chief Constable Kenward arrived on the scene the battery was flat, in accordance with Frederick Dore's observations.

The police officer's subsequent inquiries did not bode well: 'I immediately instituted inquiries, and found that the lady had left her home at Sunningdale in the car, late the previous evening, under rather unusual circumstances. I also learned that Mrs Christie had been very depressed and that just before leaving in the car she had gone upstairs and kissed her daughter who was in bed asleep.'

A pall of bewilderment and uncertainty hung over Styles. The police slowly gathered together the known details of Agatha's last week in the hope of finding a clue to her whereabouts.

Gradually, the pieces fell into place like a jigsaw – only Deputy Chief Constable Kenward discovered there were pieces missing. It transpired that on the Monday Agatha had played golf with her friend, Mrs da Silva. On Wednesday they had gone to London on a shopping expedition, and Agatha had stayed overnight at her club, the Forum, before meeting her literary agent on Thursday morning to discuss the impending publication of *The Big Four* and her difficulties over finishing her latest novel, *The Mystery of the Blue Train*. She had also been contracted to write six stories for a US magazine and had another two to complete. Agatha had returned to Styles on Thursday afternoon and later that night had gone dancing with her secretary at Ascot. Charlotte had last seen her employer on the morning of Friday the 3rd and said that Agatha had appeared in such good spirits, happily playing with Rosalind, that she had decided to take up her employer's offer of a day off and visit London.

But where exactly had Agatha driven to that morning before returning to Styles for lunch? If the police had thought to follow this up, the answer could have helped them find the missing writer, but they did not. The case's many other baffling features, along with other apparently promising leads, proved too distracting.

Charlotte had last communicated with Agatha when she had rung her employer shortly after six o'clock on the night of the disappearance to see if she was all right; Agatha had answered the telephone, sounding normal despite her earlier row with Archie, and had urged Charlotte to enjoy herself and return by the last train. The police were forced to ask themselves whether the writer's mood was of any special significance or whether she had merely been determined to keep her problems to herself.

After the ten-minute walk from Sunningdale Station Charlotte had arrived back at Styles at eleven o'clock. She told the police that she had been confronted by the parlour-maid and cook who expressed concern at the unusual manner in which Agatha had left the house at 9.45 that night. After leaving Rosalind's bedroom Agatha had come downstairs, kissed and patted Peter, placed him on the front hall mat and then driven off without telling her staff where she was going.

It transpired that Agatha had left behind a letter addressed to Charlotte, which the servants gave her as soon as she returned home. The letter asked the secretary to cancel rooms that had been booked for Agatha in Beverley for the weekend. Agatha implied that she was in great trouble and would contact Charlotte the next day to let her know her plans. The secretary admitted she had felt so uneasy about the letter that she had wanted to contact the police that night, because it included such sentences as 'My head is bursting. I cannot stay in this house', but she had not dared do so for fear of offending her employer. Early on Saturday morning, before news of the abandoned car had reached Styles, Charlotte had telephoned Ascot Post Office to arrange for a telegram to be sent to the boarding-house in Beverley: 'Regret cannot come – Christie.'

Agatha's disappearance led to increasing apprehension among her her family and friends. They were apparently at a loss as to the missing woman's whereabouts. The police took Charlotte and Archie to Newlands Corner on Saturday afternoon. A number of interested bystanders were already there, eager to find out what the police were doing. The secretary and the Colonel were shown the car but said they were unable to explain what had happened.

What appeared to have been a casual night drive had turned into something disturbing and inexplicable. As the police became aware of the disharmony between husband and wife they realized the importance of locating the writer in case her life was in jeopardy. Wilfrid Morton, one of the Surrey probationary police officers on the case, told me his instructions were: 'Find Mrs Agatha Christie as quickly as you can.'

Deputy Chief Constable Kenward's inquiries established that Agatha did not carry out her intention to travel north to the boarding-house in Beverley. Her last known journey on the day of the disappearance was to her mother-in-law's home in Dorking for afternoon tea. It was revealed that Agatha had visited her wearing the knitted green outfit in which she had gone missing later that evening. Peg told the police that the only plan Agatha had mentioned was to go to Beverley that weekend.

The police investigation was complicated by the fact that it was impossible to tell whether Agatha had driven directly to Newlands Corner. It was not known how much petrol had been in the tank at the outset of the journey. Nearly two gallons remained, and the spare petrol can of two gallons had not been used. There was plenty of water in the radiator, and when the car was hauled up on to the main road on the afternoon of Saturday the 4th the police had no difficulty in starting it. Although there were no signs of blood in or around the car it was kept overnight at the Guildford Garage on the Epsom Road.

One of the less disturbing theories considered by the authorities during the initial stages of the investigation was the possibility that on the Friday night Agatha had wandered away from the car after abandoning it and had got herself lost in the thick undergrowth. On the Saturday afternoon, accompanied by seven or eight regular police officers and a number of special constables, Deputy Chief Constable Kenward initiated a search of the surrounding area. The special constables were a group of registered men living throughout Surrey whose voluntary services were available to the county in the event of an emergency, and they were directly accountable to the Surrey Constabulary through their leader Captain Tuckwell and his deputy Colonel Bethall.

Did she wander off?

Deputy Chief Constable Kenward's interest in the Silent Pool, a quarter of a mile away from Newlands Corner at the bottom of the hill on the left-hand side of the A25 Dorking Road, captured the imagination of many, since it was rumoured that two people had already died there in tragic circumstances. According to legend, in medieval times a naked young woman had been spied bathing there and she had retreated to the deepest part of the pool to avoid the lascivious advances of King John. Her brother had drowned trying to save her, and their bodies had never been recovered. (Nowadays a car-park has been built by the side of the A25 near the shallow basin known as Sherbourne Pond. This is sometimes mistaken for the Silent Pool, which is higher up on the incline, shielded by a copse and overlooked by a bird-watching hut.)

As the news of Agatha's absence spread, civilian volunteers were quick to offer their services to the police. A statement that Agatha had been seen driving through Shere, a village two miles from Newlands Corner, at four o'clock on Saturday morning by a cow-man moving a herd of cattle was subsequently disproved, since the informant stated after being questioned a second time that the car he had seen had a square radiator. Agatha's Morris Cowley, like all the older models of this car, had a round radiator; the distinctive square radiators appeared for the first time in 1926.

By Saturday night Archie was growing increasingly agitated. He was filled with dread at the possible consequences of Agatha's disappearance. A minor accident, in which she had wandered away from her car alive and well, seemed increasingly improbable to the Colonel, and he began to worry that he might have driven her to suicide by telling her that their trial reconciliation was over. The two letters Agatha had left behind at Styles had not given any clue as to her proposed movements, and Archie had reassured their daughter by telling her that Agatha had gone to Ashfield to do some writing. Inquiries by the Torquay police, however, had revealed that Ashfield was uninhabited. What concerned the Colonel most was the fact that the longer Agatha remained missing the more likely it was that his relationship with Nancy would come out into the open.

On Sunday the 5th Deputy Chief Constable Kenward mounted an all-day search around Newlands Corner, unaware that a third letter, written by Agatha before she left Styles on the Friday night, had since been delivered by post to the London workplace of Archie's brother, Campbell Christie, an instructor at the Royal Woolwich Military Academy. The letter had been posted in London on the morning her car had been found abandoned. Campbell did not immediately pass on the information because he had yet to learn that his sister-in-law was missing.

3rd letter

One of the civilian helpers during the search on Sunday was eighteen-year-old Jack Boxall, a local gardener in Guildford. He vividly recalls the feeling of community spirit that prompted him, together with his father and a number of friends, to walk several miles from his home to Newlands Corner. He told me the police search parties were working in the direction of the Silent Pool and the village of Shere in the southeast, while his own party undertook to search that area in the northwest between Newlands Corner and Merrow known as the Roughs. It was an area very familiar to his father, a house painter, who in his spare time played golf in the open spaces on the Roughs. Despite their diligent efforts to locate Agatha, there was no sign of the missing woman as dusk fell, and the group was forced to admit defeat. Jack Boxall recalls that this did not discourage a veritable posse of police officers from continuing the search by lamplight.

On Sunday night the police visited the village of Albury on receiving a report from a hotel there that a woman had been seen who answered the description of the novelist. They searched the wood at the back of Albury but drew a blank. Later that evening a missing persons notice was circulated to the fifty police stations nearest the village:

DESCRIP

Missing from her home, Styles, Sunningdale, Berkshire, Mrs Agatha Mary Clarissa Christie, age 35 [she was actually 36]; height 5 feet 7 inches; hair, red, shingled part grey; complexion, fair, build slight; dressed in grey stockinette skirt, green jumper, grey and dark grey cardigan and small velour hat; wearing a platinum ring with one pearl;

no wedding ring; black handbag with purse containing perhaps £5 or £10. Left home by car at 9.45 p.m. Friday leaving note saying that she was going for a drive.

The failure of the police to locate Agatha, and the fact that they received no word from her by the end of the weekend, led to the forfeiting of her privacy. What might have remained a private incident in the life of an intensely private woman instead rapidly fell under the harsh glare of the media spotlight.

8

THE SEARCH WIDENS

NEWS EMERGES (handwritten)

WHERE AGATHA had gone after vanishing from Styles on Friday 3 December was the focus of the first newspaper reports to appear on Monday the 6th. News of her disappearance even reached the United States, where the *New York Times* ran a front-page headline: 'Mrs Agatha Christie, Novelist, Disappears in Strange Way from Her Home in England.' Closer to home, the weekend search had resulted in more questions than answers for the man in charge of the inquiry, Deputy Chief Constable Kenward of the Surrey Constabulary.

He wondered whether there was any significance in the fact that the car had been abandoned within six miles of Colonel Christie's rendezvous with Nancy Neele. Also, if Agatha had accidentally run off the road, why had she failed to apply the brakes on her way down the long decline? If she had decided to commit suicide, why had she driven fourteen miles from home to do so? The fact that Agatha had not taken her dog Peter with her as usual that night gave credence to the suicide theory. *(handwritten margin note: SH his rpr)*

What made suicide less likely was the fact that the writer's zip handbag and purse had been removed from the car, although Agatha's continued absence led the Surrey police to presume that the abandonment of her journey at Newlands Corner had been as unexpected to herself as to others. *BAG TAKEN* (handwritten)

The problem once again confronting the Surrey police on the Monday was to know where to take up the search. The undulating countryside around Newlands Corner included woods, streams, ponds, copses and fields in which the growth was often knee-high, so Deputy Chief Constable Kenward's task could not have been more difficult.

The search for Agatha was thorough and precise. Wilfrid Morton, who was based at Woking at the time, remembers it well: 'The first I knew was that I was ordered to be at the police station in the early hours of the morning for some unknown purpose. I was told to be there dressed in plain clothes and to bring a walking stick. I was a probationary constable and living in at the time. I couldn't find out what it was about until I paraded about in the yard outside and found that there were about thirty other people there. A charabanc pulled up outside and we were all put aboard and off we went. As we were driving along somebody who knew said: "It's Newlands Corner we're going to."' He had no idea why.

By the time they disembarked day was breaking. The men were lined up at six-foot intervals and told to link hands with the officer on either side of them and slowly move forward. They were not told what they were looking for and were instructed to report anything unusual they found.

Wilfrid Morton recalls: 'We were to go through bushes, not round them, and if we came to a tree we couldn't get through we had to go round it, but we were to look up in its branches and see that there was nothing unusual up there. And there was no rush. Just do it slowly and keep the line intact. Eventually, after an hour or so, we came out into open ground again. We were then reassembled and rested for a little while, then told that we were going to have another go and were taken to a fresh piece of ground to do the same thing again. Various things were found – old garments and so on – which meant an interruption to the whole line until a senior officer was bought along to examine whatever it was that was found. We pushed on and by the time we had got out into the open ground again it was midday and we were all hungry and tired and thirsty. We had refreshments. By that time, of course, we had an idea what it was all about. Somebody had got hold of a newspaper and read the headlines about the disappearance.'

Meanwhile, Archie drove to Scotland Yard that morning with his solicitor and his wife's secretary. He was told by senior police there that they could not intervene in the investigation unless the Surrey or Berkshire police requested their assistance. All Scotland Yard could do was place Agatha's description in *Confidential Information* and the *Police*

Gazette, effectively alerting every police station in England to her disappearance. Archie left London resigned to an unhappy wait for news. To encourage Charlotte's loyalty, and thus to minimize any disclosure of his personal life to the police or the press, he encouraged her to invite her sister, Mary Fisher, to visit Styles and was relieved when Mary stayed for the duration of the disappearance.

His anxiety was exacerbated by the fact that because Sunningdale was situated on the borders of Berkshire and Surrey he was attempting to deceive two different county police forces into believing that talk of marital problems between him and Agatha was merely unkind servants' gossip. However, his account of the state of his marriage was undermined on the Monday when the parlour-maid at Styles finally admitted to investigators that Colonel and Mrs Christie had had a major argument on the morning of the disappearance. Q: SHOT RUSS

Superintendent Charles Goddard, head of the Berkshire Constabulary's investigation, had been in charge of the Wokingham Division for over twenty years. He was assisted by Inspector Sidney Frank Butler of the Ascot police, a stalwart officer with a flair for dealing with members of the public.

Unlike their Surrey counterparts, the two police officers were inclined to believe that Agatha was still alive. They had quickly formed the impression that she was a somewhat immature person with a tendency to carry her stories over into real life. They found significance in the fact that she insisted on calling her secretary 'Carlotta', because she thought it sounded more exotic, although it was apparent that Charlotte did not much care for this. Archie appeared to them a no-nonsense, practical man, not an especially good match for his perhaps over-imaginative wife. It was their belief that in her unhappiness after the row the novelist had wanted to bring the situation to a head and had given the impression she was going away for a day or two to think things over but had intentionally not stated where she was going. When she failed to return or make contact, it was inevitable that some people would fear she had attempted suicide in a last-ditch attempt to gain sympathy. The Berkshire police were inclined to believe that Agatha may have used similarly dramatic tactics to get her own way – or

Archie's attention – on previous occasions. Although the Colonel had been obliged to report the disappearance to Inspector Butler at Ascot Police Station he had plainly been very angry at being forced to admit the situation.

After a telephone call shortly after midday on Monday from Campbell, Archie's hopes that Agatha was alive were boosted. The postmark on the envelope of the letter Campbell had received revealed that it had been franked at 9.45 a.m. on 4 December in London's SW1. Campbell was convinced that this meant the letter must have been posted in London on the day that Agatha's car had been found abandoned and that she was in all probability still alive.

The suggestion that Charlotte might have posted the letter while she was in London on the night of the disappearance was disregarded. 'It is true that I was in London on Friday evening, but I posted no letter there for Mrs Christie,' she stated. 'I had posted nothing for her for several days before her disappearance.' Subsequent inquiries revealed that the letter's postmark indicated it could only have been posted some time between 3 a.m. and 8 a.m. on Saturday the 4th – some four hours at least after the secretary had returned to Styles the previous night.

The crux of Agatha's letter to Campbell, which was undated and addressed from Styles, indicated she was going away for the weekend to an unnamed spa in Yorkshire. The letter had been addressed to him at the Royal Woolwich Military Academy, and on going there on the morning of Sunday the 5th Campbell had found it on his desk. There was nothing in the letter to indicate that his sister-in-law was suffering from any nervous strain or that she was contemplating any untoward action. After reading the letter he had set it aside and forgotten about it. He explained to Archie that he had only heard on the Monday morning that Agatha was missing and had immediately looked for the letter – but it, too, was missing, possibly either thrown away or torn up with other papers. Campbell considered it highly unlikely that anyone had posted the letter on her behalf, and he was convinced that when Agatha composed the note she was in a perfectly normal state of mind and that it had been written before she left Styles on the Friday night. The envelope with its postmark had been retained, and Campbell promptly forwarded it to Archie. The most intriguing question confronting the police was why the envelope had been addressed to her brother-in-law's workplace rather than to his home.

Meanwhile the press was having a field day. In an era of unsophisticated communication systems the story was taken up with amazing speed; it was as if someone had pressed a button and released an avalanche of publicity. Massive speculation ensued.

The press reporters did not always find time to distinguish conjecture from fact. They feverishly sought out witnesses, some reliable, others not, followed up potential leads and shadowed the police to try to glean snippets of information. The abandoned car was a case in point. Some newspapers failed to clarify the sequence in which it had been seen by various individuals on the Saturday morning, and this led to contradictory reports regarding whether the lights had been discovered on or off. Although it was stated by the police that the car had been found with its brakes off half-way down the long decline, Alfred Luland, who ran the refreshment kiosk at Newlands Corner, excitedly insisted to eager journalists that he was 'almost certain the brakes were on'.

Several newspapers reproduced maps of Newlands Corner, indicating where the car had been found. Some of the maps were so inaccurate as to give rise to the suspicion that they were reproduced from descriptions given by reporters over the telephone.

The response of the press to the disappearance was both unexpected and extraordinary. On Monday the 6th the *Daily Mail* was hot on the trail, regaling its readers with the car's discovery at Newlands Corner and a description of the authoress. The fact that Agatha was not yet a household name was evidenced by its headline: 'Woman Novelist Disappears.' In the absence of any knowledge of Agatha's whereabouts, the *Daily Sketch* blithely descended into fanciful speculation: 'Mrs Christie herself has made one of her heroines drown herself in the Silent Pool. In local tradition there is a feeling that the pool has an irresistible fascination on those who are brought into close touch with it, as Mrs Christie was. All the evidence available at the moment tends to suggest Mrs Christie's mind had given way.'

On Monday night, a gravel worker, Edward McAlister of Hallshurst,

Merrow, went to the police to report an alleged sighting on the morning of Saturday the 4th. He claimed that he had been cycling to work along the Merrow Downs when he had been stopped in Trodd's Lane at 6.20 a.m. by a hatless woman who asked him to start her car and that after he had cranked the engine she had driven off in the direction of Guildford. While this was in the opposite direction to where Agatha's car was later found, the press made much of the account, although not always with great accuracy. In one case he was named incorrectly as Ernest Cross of Gomshall; in another the encounter was relocated to the plateau of Newlands Corner; and yet another article claimed the stranded motorist's hair had been 'covered in hoar-frost', while the radiator of her car had been 'hot to touch'. More bizarrely it was variously maintained that the woman had driven off in such diverse directions as the forked road leading to Clandon and Merrow or towards Shere, the latter being a favoured suggestion since this was in the direction of the sinisterly named Silent Pool.

By Tuesday the 7th the media circus was in full swing. Fleet Street's best reporters, including Stanley Bishop of the *Daily Express* and Jim Barnes of the *Daily News*, were on the case, staking out Styles which they regarded as their main command post. Less experienced junior colleagues, such as Trevor Allen of the *Westminster Gazette* and Ritchie Calder of the *Daily News*, were based at Guildford in order to participate in the search of the Surrey Downs.

Theories were rife. One popular but unsubstantiated suggestion was that Agatha had stopped for a rest on the plateau of Newlands Corner and, misjudging her gears when she started the car, had accidentally careered off the plateau. Newlands Corner, according to the *Westminster Gazette*, was 'a dark, bleak, desolate place . . . the last place a normal woman would think of driving to unaccompanied'. This overwrought depiction of the landscape was given additional significance by the popular assertion, deliberately encouraged by Archie, that Agatha was suffering from a nervous breakdown owing to 'literary overwork'. In the absence of a corpse, 'loss of memory' was widely touted in all the newspapers in the early days as a reason for the writer's disappearance. The press wondered whether she might have planned to meet someone at

Newlands Corner and changed cars or whether she had been waylaid and her body successfully disposed of.

After the *Daily News'* offer on Tuesday the 7th of a £100 reward for 'first information leading to the discovery of the whereabouts, if alive, of Mrs Christie', the newspapers reported a plethora of suspected sightings from people who claimed to have recognized her from published pictures.

One, Ralph Browne of Battersea, insisted he had seen Agatha at 11.15 a.m. on Saturday the 4th as he drove past Albury Heath: 'She seemed to be in the kind of mood when she did not care what happened. I offered her a lift, but she said, "I am going nowhere in particular; thanks for the offer, but I would rather stay where I am."' His story had an added frisson of interest for the public since he had also seen a gypsy knife-grinder in the vicinity.

A Mrs Kitchings of Little London, a hamlet near Newlands Corner, came forward claiming to have seen a woman walking in a lane near her home around noon that same day. Mrs Kitchings had been struck by the vacant look in the woman's eyes.

The Mayor of Godalming's chauffeur, a Mr Lindsey, insisted that Agatha had called at his house around nine o'clock on Saturday night. The woman had had supper with Mr Lindsey and his wife, and they had last seen her going in the direction of Milford.

A railway porter called Mr Fuett insisted he had been approached on the morning of Sunday the 5th at Milford Station by a confused woman with a hat asking the way to Portsmouth and Petersfield, and his story was confirmed, in part, by a Milford carrier called Mr Warner. The woman had last been seen going in the direction of Hambledon.

Mr B. Daniels of Vicarage Road, Plumstead, said a 'dark-haired' woman resembling the writer had knocked on his front door at 10.50 on the night of Monday the 6th asking if he could give her change for a pound note. He was unable to help but insisted the stranger had looked exactly like a photograph of Agatha he had seen in the *Daily News*.

According to reporters, a Mr Clark of New Broad Street, London, stated that a woman bearing a resemblance to the missing authoress had travelled by the 5.08 train from Cannon Street on Monday evening. She appeared haggard, and he had formed the opinion that she was mentally disturbed because she had been making notes on a tear-off pad when she was not staring oddly out of the window.

While the reporters were unable to shed any light on the mystery, the police search on Tuesday the 7th saw men brought once again from the divisions of Woking, as well as from Chertsey and Dorking. At Albury Mill Pond huge nets were placed in position across the sluice and the gates were opened. A great torrent of water poured through and the river almost drained to the bed, but nothing was found in the net. The Postford Mill Pond was also dragged. It was thought that if Agatha had wandered along the adjacent lane she might have been attracted in the dark by the lights from the mill and slipped and fallen into the pond. Her cries for help would have been drowned out by the noise of the mill, which operated continuously night and day.

As press speculation on Agatha's fate grew increasingly doom-laden, the police retained a sense of proportion despite their difficult task. One of the young officers to arrive in a charabanc at Newlands Corner was Constable Eric Boshier, under orders from his father Superintendent Boshier who was in charge of the Woking Division. Eric Boshier, then aged nineteen, has told me that, unlike earlier search parties, his group was told in advance that they were searching for Mrs Agatha Christie. Their search went without incident, except for a light-hearted encounter with a tramp, who they jokingly suggested might be able to shed some light on Mrs Christie's fate. The tramp good-naturedly agreed to empty out the contents of his sack, and the officers had a good laugh at the extraordinary profusion of tin cans that fell out on to the grass.

On the evening of Tuesday the 7th the mood of the press was buoyant, since journalists had discovered the existence of the letter Agatha had written to her brother-in-law. It was suggested that the most likely place Agatha might visit in Yorkshire was Harrogate, but reporters from the *Daily Chronicle* and the *Daily Express* had visited all the hotels there and found no one registered under her name.

Despite the fizzling out of the Yorkshire lead the press continued to gather information at a remarkable pace. Although Archie declined to reveal to journalists where he had spent Friday night, the *Daily News* and *Daily Express* now revealed that his host had been a Mr James of Hurtmore Cottage, near Godalming. The *Daily News* disclosed the fact that Agatha's passport had been found at Styles, which rather scotched the rumour that she had left England for Switzerland in the company of an elderly man, supposed to be a peer. It was also revealed that Agatha had recently visited her chemist, Charles Gilling, to have a sleeping draught made up for her and that during their conversation methods of committing suicide had been mentioned. The authoress had allegedly said: 'I should never commit suicide by violent means when there is such a drug as hyoscine available.' ✳

On Wednesday the 8th there was no official search. Deputy Chief Constable Kenward was, however, aware that a large number of civilian searchers were out and was kept informed of their progress by constables stationed at Newlands Corner. Furthermore, at his request the Guildford and Shere Beagles, totalling fifteen couples and a large number of spectators, kept a look-out during their hunt. The major discovery of the day was made around 1.30 p.m. when two boys, Stanley Lane and Frederick Jones, came across a message in a tin discovered under a bush twenty yards from where the abandoned car had been found. The message, clearly a hoax, read: 'Ask Candle Lanche. He knows more about the Silent Pool than —'

The picture presented to the public in the early days of the search was of a beautiful and intelligent writer happily married to a dashing and handsome war hero. But it was a false image destined to crumble as the police and press competed to reunite the couple.

9

PERSISTENT SCRUTINY

AGATHA'S CONTINUING ABSENCE ensured that Archie's movements were monitored by the police inside Styles and the press outside. It was abhorrent to him that his friends should have been dragged into the matter: the staff of the James household had described the evening of Friday the 3rd as an 'unofficial engagement party' for Archie and Nancy. A more remarkable aspect of the gathering that emerged during police inquiries was that <u>Sam and Madge James</u> had presumed the Colonel was definitely estranged or living apart from his wife.

Nancy, whose liaison with Archie cast her in a less than respectable light, was viewed by the police as a naive young woman who had been misled by an older man. While she was loyal to Archie throughout, her parents, who were shielding her from the public gaze at their home at Croxley Green, Ricksmansworth, were an added complication. Charles and Mabel Neele had been horrified to learn of their daughter's affair and of the illicit weekend, and they applied intense pressure on Nancy to have nothing more to do with the Colonel.

Sam James, their host on the evening of the disappearance, did his utmost to defend Archie by insisting that the only car at Hurtmore Cottage that night had been shut in a garage and that the household would have been alerted to any departure by the barking of the family dog.

✱ Deputy Chief Constable Kenward was not so sure. <u>If Archie had murdered</u> his wife it was possible he might have arranged an assignation with her at Newlands Corner after the James household had retired for the night. While there was no direct evidence of a scuffle by husband and wife on the plateau, the possibility of murder could not be ruled out. The police officer found Archie 'vague and defensive' when questioned about his private life and his movements on the night of the disappearance, and this had the effect of drawing the policeman's suspicions to him like a magnet.

With the threat of public scandal Archie stood on the brink of losing everything: his business reputation, his social standing and the woman he loved. He was no longer under any illusion that Agatha was dead; after the discovery of the letter to his brother, Archie was convinced she was alive and well and playing games with him.

Campbell's disclosure of the letter his sister-in-law had posted to him did not diminish police and press scrutiny of Archie's private life, since it was deemed possible that someone might have posted the letter on Agatha's behalf or that she might have doubled back to Newlands Corner after posting it herself.

In a bid to curtail the inquisition into his affairs Archie urged the Berkshire police to issue a missing persons poster and, as an incentive, he said he was prepared to foot the bill.

Sebastian Earl, who worked in the office next to Archie's in the City, broke a lifetime's silence years later to recall how, while Agatha was missing, the two men had found themselves sharing a lift as they rode up to the sixth floor of the Rio Tinto Company building in London where the offices of Austral Ltd were situated.

'He was in a terribly nervous state and told me the police had followed him up Broad Street and all the way to the office and were now waiting outside. "They think I've murdered my wife," he said. He went into his office and though I saw him several times during the week when he looked progressively worse he never referred to it again – and of course I didn't either.'

By Wednesday the 8th the press was aware that Archie was suspected by the police of having murdered Agatha, and speculation was rife, in particular regarding the catalyst for Agatha's departure from Styles on the night of Friday the 3rd.

Jim Barnes of the *Daily News* was convinced that the first intimation that the authoress had of Archie's plans for the weekend with Nancy was when Charlotte had rung her employer at Styles shortly after six o'clock on the evening of the disappearance. What the journalist did not realize was that Agatha had learned of Archie's plans that morning. Barnes mistakenly believed that Charlotte had rung Archie at the Jameses' home near Godalming that evening to warn him that Agatha had been upset to discover where he was spending the weekend and was on her way there to confront him. This led Barnes's colleague Ritchie Calder to speculate whether Archie might not have muttered his excuses and left the Jameses' house to drive to Newlands Corner to way-lay and perhaps silence his wife. The fact that both Archie and the police denied this far-fetched scenario made the press all the more suspicious, not least because he was already the police's prime suspect; they still thought he might have left the house after the others had retired for the night.

Stanley Bishop, the *Daily Express*'s leading reporter, was so convinced that Archie was implicated in Agatha's disappearance that he repeatedly exhorted Deputy Chief Constable Kenward to call in Scotland Yard to assist in the combing of the Surrey Downs. The police officer was unable to consider such a move, despite his belief that Archie was a murderer, because his Chief Constable, Captain Sant, was vehemently opposed to the idea.

Although the police were permanently stationed at the front and back doors of Styles to prevent the press from mobbing Archie and the other inhabitants, they were unable to prevent him from being accosted away from his home. The Colonel began to crack and, in attempting to run the press gauntlet on the night of Wednesday the 8th, he made a series of ill-advised remarks which appeared in the London *Evening News* the following day:

ill-advised remarks.

I cannot account for her disappearance save that her nerves have completely gone, and that she went away for no real purpose whatever.

I left home on Friday to spend the week-end with friends. Where I stayed I am not prepared to state. I have told the police. I do not want my friends to be dragged into this. It is my business alone. I have been badgered and pestered like a criminal, and all I want is to be left alone. My telephone is constantly ringing. All manner of people are asking

This is bad. Very bad.

about my wife. Why, I even get clairvoyants ringing me up and telling me the only hope I have of finding her is by holding a seance.

I am worried to death. When I heard that she had disappeared I at once went to Newlands Corner, where I was told the car had been found. That was on Saturday, and I have been here ever since.

My wife was going to spend the week-end away. I usually spend the week-end away.

On Thursday the 9th the *Daily Express* was one of several newspapers to criticize the Berkshire and Surrey police forces for their failure to call in Scotland Yard. The reporters believed there was rivalry between the two constabularies, and their conviction was reinforced by the fact that the Berkshire police were not helping in the search of the Surrey Downs. What the journalists were not aware of was that Scotland Yard was already actively involved in investigating a large number of suspected sightings by people who thought they had seen Agatha.

The report of a suspected sighting of Agatha on an omnibus in London failed to take the heat off Archie. A Miss Bishop had contacted the Wokingham police in Berkshire to inform them that the woman in question had worn a curiously spotted sealskin coat. After hearing the details of the incident Superintendent Goddard said: 'I'm afraid that not much importance can be attached to her statement, but personally I think Mrs Christie is still alive.'

Two distinct avenues of investigation became evident on Thursday the 9th. The Berkshire police circulated a missing persons poster with a full-length photograph of Agatha, while Deputy Chief Constable Kenward instigated another search of the Surrey Downs. The press speculated that the reason for this was because a member of the public had found a shoe on the lower slopes of Albury the previous day, but as the officer explained in his report to the Home Office: 'The lady disappeared under circumstances which opened out all sorts of possibilities; she might have been wandering with loss of memory over that vast open country around Newlands Corner, or she might have fallen down one of the numerous gravel pits that abound there and are covered in most instances with undergrowth and lying in helpless agony, or she might have been, as was strongly suggested to the police, the victim of a serious crime.'

The intensified search, the largest yet, saw parties dispatched in a northerly direction from Newlands Corner, others to Albury and Chilworth and still another as far as Peaslake. That afternoon the chief suspect drove to Newlands Corner with his wife's dog and accompanied Deputy Chief Constable Kenward for three hours to no avail. Archie's agitation was growing hourly, for the one thing he had dreaded all along had finally become a reality: Nancy's name had found its way into the morning newspapers as 'a friend' of the Jameses.

On Thursday evening Archie lost his nerve completely. He gave an exclusive interview to his wife's favourite newspaper, which, contrary to his intention, made it obvious that his marriage had disintegrated and set tongues wagging more energetically than ever.

Christie refuses to say what is
in the letter, and is given up
on by H/R left to his
own devices.

"I know what it is like to be
in the public eye (unwantededly)

10

'The Suspense of the Uncertainty Is Terrible'

T HE INTERVIEW ARCHIE gave to the *Daily Mail* for its Friday the 10th edition had a profound effect on the public's perception of his marriage. His suggestion that he was clinging to the hope that his wife had stage-managed her disappearance, far from gaining him sympathy, made more apparent the rift between the couple.

The story ran at considerable length under the headlines 'Five Hundred Police Search for Mrs Christie, Husband's Statement to the *Daily Mail*, Belief in Voluntary Disappearance', during the course of which Archie unwisely elaborated his theory:

> It is quite true that my wife had discussed the possibility of disappearing at will. Some time ago she told her sister 'I could disappear if I wished and set about it properly.' They were discussing what appeared in the papers, I think. That shows that the possibility of engineering a disappearance had been running through her mind, probably for the purpose of her work. Personally, I feel that is what happened. At any rate, I am buoying myself up with that belief.

Archie, intent on avoiding any suggestion of murder, continued:

> You see, there are three possible explanations of her disappearance: voluntary, loss of memory, and suicide. I am inclined to the first, although, of course, it may be loss of memory as a result of her highly nervous state. I do not believe this is a case of suicide. She never threatened suicide, but if she did contemplate that, I am sure her mind would turn to poison, but that she used poison largely in her stories. I have remonstrated with her in regard to this form of death, but her

mind always turned to it. If she wanted to get poison, I am sure she could have done so. She was very clever at getting anything she wanted. But against the theory of suicide you have to remember this: if a person intends to end his life he does not take the trouble to go miles away and then remove a heavy coat and walk off into the blue before doing it. That is one reason why I do not think my wife has taken her life. She removed her fur coat and put it into the back of the car before she left it, and then I think she probably walked down the hill and off – God knows where. I suggest she walked downhill because she always hated walking uphill.

Archie spoke in veiled terms of the morning of the disappearance:

I left home at 9.15 a.m. in the ordinary way and that was the last time I saw my wife. I knew that she had arranged to go to Yorkshire for the week-end. I understand that in the morning she went motoring and then lunched alone. In the afternoon she went to see my mother at Dorking. She returned here in time for dinner, which she took alone. I do not know what happened after that; I only know what I have been told by the servants. I imagine, however, that she got into such a state that she could not sit down quietly to read or work. I have got into that state myself many a time and have gone out for a walk just aimlessly. That, I think, is what my wife did, but instead of walking she took the car, a four-seater, and drove off. She apparently packed a small suitcase before she went and took it with her. It was found in the car with all its contents complete, so far as we know.

When his unusual relationship with his wife was challenged in light of his sensational theory, Archie resorted to lies:

It is absolutely untrue to suggest there was anything in the nature of a row or tiff between my wife and myself on Friday morning. She was perfectly well – that is to say, as well as she had been for months past. She knew I was going away for the week-end; she knew who were going to be the members of the little party at the house at which I was going

to stay and neither then nor at any time did she raise the slightest
objection. I strongly deprecate introducing any tittle-tattle into this
matter. That will not help me to find my wife; that is what I want to do.
My wife has never made the slightest objection to any of my friends, all
of whom she knew.

Returning to his original theme of his wife having staged her
absence, Archie truthfully stated that he did not know how much
money Agatha had on her:

If she had planned this disappearance it is quite possible that she may
have accumulated a considerable sum of money secretly. I do know that
neither of her two banking accounts – one at Sunningdale for
household purposes, and the other at Dorking for private purposes –
has been drawn upon since she disappeared. Indeed, both of her cheque
books are in the house . . . That is all I know, and I need hardly tell you
that the suspense of the uncertainty is terrible.

Short of telling the truth and confiding the real reasons for Agatha's
recent anguish, Archie could not have made a more disastrous move in
his bid to disarm suspicion and gain public sympathy.

Meanwhile the *Daily Mail* had interviewed the proprietor of a West
End store in Albemarle Street who disclosed that Agatha had visited
the store on the Monday before her disappearance and had chosen an
elaborate white satin nightgown trimmed with lace, saying she particularly wanted it for the weekend.

On Friday the 10th Archie had another unpleasant surprise: he was
invited by both the Berkshire and Surrey police, who had finally learned
of his destruction of his wife's letter to him, to explain his reasons for
failing to report the matter. His insistence that the letter had referred to
a purely personal matter, which he refused to disclose and which he
maintained had no bearing on events, was regarded with the utmost
incredulity by the police officers. His admission that he burned it after
being recalled to Styles on the morning of Saturday the 4th, following
news of the discovery of Agatha's abandoned car, was not regarded as

consistent with a man who had nothing to hide and who was distraught to learn of her disappearance.

Subsequently a long police conference between the two investigating counties was held at Bagshot Police Station. Deputy Chief Constable Kenward and Inspector Butler were present. The meeting was not attended by Superintendent Goddard of the Berkshire police, whose opinion throughout the investigation was: 'When she has worked out her little problem she will return.'

The same day the *Daily News* scooped their competitors in a minor way when the detective novelist Dorothy L. Sayers gave her explanation for the disappearance:

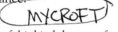

In any problem of this kind there are four possible solutions: loss of memory, foul play, suicide or voluntary disappearance. The first – loss of memory – is bound to present us with a baffling situation, because it implies an entire lack of motive, and it is an axiom of detection that where there is a motive there is a clue. But a voluntary disappearance, also, may be so cleverly staged as to be exceedingly puzzling – especially if, as here, we are concerned with a skilful writer of detective stories, whose mind has been trained in the study of ways and means to perplex.

She sounded a cautionary note when she pointed out that the newspaper reports, which were all the public had to go on, were necessarily 'very incomplete' and 'one cannot ask all the questions which one's own ideal detective would instantly put'. A number of unanswered questions suggested themselves to her: Were the car's lights good when Agatha left home or so dim that she might have accidentally run off the road? Had the brakes been applied when the car left the road at Newlands Corner? How long did the car stand in the bushes before it was first seen? Was Agatha an experienced or an erratic driver? Had her family known of the intended visit to Beverley? Was the writer known at the boarding-house?

Dorothy L. Sayers concluded: 'These are only a few of the things one wants to know about before one can even begin to "have a theory" . . . We can only hope that the explanation will turn out not to be a tragic one, and wish the real detectives a speedy success in their quest.'

On the night of Friday the 10th reporters found out that Agatha had left a letter for Archie at Styles, and the next day they were quick to tell their readers that he had destroyed it without revealing its contents. The public were in very little doubt by now that Agatha's communication to her secretary Charlotte on the night of the disappearance was more than a 'note saying she was going for a drive', as stated in the guarded police circular.

The Christie household was not the only one to come under increased press scrutiny. In an interview with the *Daily Mail*, Sam James, who had dismissed his servants for gossiping to the press about Archie's liaison with Nancy, tersely denied that his friend had any involvement in the authoress's disappearance: 'The party consisted of my wife, a Miss Neele, the Colonel and myself. Suggestions have been made that Colonel Christie was called up by his wife while he was here, or that he went out and met his wife, or that she came here to meet him. Nothing of that kind happened. I believe that Mrs Christie returned home and found that the Colonel was spending the week-end with us, and that she then drove off in a fit of pique.'

The scenario of Agatha being a scorned wife and Archie being a philandering, pleasure-seeking husband looked increasingly plausible. The fact that the *Liverpool Weekly Post,* on Saturday 4 December, had begun a three-month serialization of *The Murder of Roger Ackroyd,* under the novelist's original title, opened up the possibility to the public that she might have disappeared voluntarily as a publicity stunt. Her career was perhaps all she had left, as it was evident that her marriage was in tatters.

Edgar Wallace, whose play *The Ringer* was drawing audiences at Wyndham's Theatre, added to the flames of speculation in the *Daily Mail*. Although his reconstruction of the disappearance was flawed by his assumption that the chalk pit into which her car almost plunged was between Newlands Corner and Guildford instead of Newlands Corner and Albury, he was correct in his speculations as to Agatha's motive and why he thought the amnesia theory did not hold water:

The disappearance seems to be a typical case of 'mental reprisal' on somebody who has hurt her. To put it vulgarly, her first intention seems to have been to 'spite' an unknown person who would be distressed by her disappearance. That she did not contemplate suicide seems evident from the fact that she deliberately created an atmosphere of suicide by the picturesque abandonment of her car. Loss of memory, that is to say mental confusion, might easily have followed, but a person so afflicted could not possibly escape notice. We must exclude the possibility of her being in some institute or in the care of somebody who has found her. The wide publicity that has been given to her disappearance disposes of such a possibility.

It needed very little imagination to deduce that Archie was the person Agatha wished to spite. Edgar Wallace believed that she had been surprised by the excessive publicity and was finding it difficult to reappear. In summing up, he said: 'If Agatha Christie is not dead of shock and exposure within a limited radius of the place where her car was found she must be alive and in full possession of her faculties, probably in London. It is impossible to lose your memory and find your way to a determined destination.'

Undeterred by his inability to pinpoint Agatha, in December 1927 Edgar Wallace produced one of his more sensational tales, published in the *Pall Mall Magazine,* in which the discovery of bloodstains in and around a bungalow in Berkshire leads the police of that county to entertain the gravest concerns for its missing occupant, Mrs Gray, who is linked to a mysterious motoring ordeal on a hilltop in the neighbouring county of Sussex. The short story was entitled 'The Sunningdale Murder'.

Peg, distressed by Archie's ill-judged interview with the *Daily Mail,* came to her son's defence by allowing herself to be interviewed and informing the newspaper's readers that Archie and Agatha were 'a devoted couple' and that, in her opinion, her daughter-in-law had not recovered from her mother's death earlier that year. Peg suggested that after leaving the car Agatha had probably walked a considerable distance before meeting her end: 'It is my opinion that she will not be found in water, as she was a strong swimmer, and the suddenness of any immersion would, I believe, at once restore her to her senses. I note that Colonel Christie thinks she voluntarily disappeared, but I cannot agree with my son.'

Later on Saturday the 11th the evening press publicized the Surrey Constabulary's appeal for the public's voluntary assistance in searching the Surrey Downs the following day. It was a calculated move, involving the cooperation and pooling of resources of police and press, to determine once and for all if this was where the solution to the mystery lay.

11

GREAT EXPECTATIONS

suicide

THE GREAT SUNDAY Hunt, as it became known, began inauspiciously with rain falling until seven in the morning. Staff from the Duke of Northumberland's <u>Albury</u> estate were the best qualified of all to assist. Each day that Agatha had been missing the estate had sent out thirty of its men to search for her, including Fred Baker, Ben Merrit, Ern Tyso and Frank Tuilip. They knew Newlands Corner and the land for miles around like the backs of their hands and their intimate knowledge ensured that the police searches to date had been meticulously conducted. The opinion of the estate workers was that Agatha had committed suicide, and it had become a matter of pride for them to locate her before anyone else did. The competition, however, was considerably stiffer than on the previous weekend owing to the public response to the police appeal broadcast in the press.

The *Sunday Express* featured an article by ex-Chief Inspector Walter Dew (the man who had arrested the wife-murderer Crippen as he fled across the Atlantic on the *Montrose* with his lover Ethel Le Neve). The retired police officer asserted that Agatha's disappearance was altogether different from that of Crippen's wife, Belle Ellmore. Dew maintained that no clever writer of Agatha's standing would believe that to disgrace herself 'for publicity's sake' would be of service to her in her work. He was happy to accept loss of memory or hysteria as the likeliest reasons for Agatha's absence: 'If Mrs Christie's mind became hysterical she may have gone wandering over the country, on and on, with the false strength of the half-demented, until she dropped in some spot miles away from where she is being sought now.'

On the morning of Sunday the 12th the news coverage of the disappearance shows that the authoress was the country's most talked-about woman. People arriving at Newlands Corner were confronted by newspaper placards from *Reynolds's Illustrated News* advertising a three-month serialization of *The Murder on the Links*: 'Missing Novelist's Finest Serial Begins Today'. Two points of considerable interest for the public were the chalk pit into which Agatha's car had almost plunged and the Silent Pool some quarter of a mile away.

Of all the visitors to the Silent Pool the one who was to become the most famous was Dorothy L. Sayers. She looked around for a few moments, then announced in her robust, forthright manner: 'No, she isn't here.' She later incorporated aspects of her visit to the scene of the disappearance into her third detective novel, *Unnatural Death*, published the following year, in which not one but two women are found missing from an abandoned car on downland which she relocated to the South Coast. Ironically, the registration number of the abandoned car corresponded in real life to her own Ner-a-car and passages from the book are reminiscent of reports from Sunday the 12th: 'Reporters swarmed down upon Crow's Beach like locusts – the downs near Shelly Head were like a fair with motors, bicycles and parties on foot, rushing out to spend a happy week-end amid surroundings of mystery and bloodshed.'

The keenness of the public to find Agatha was demonstrated by the fact that a large contingent of helpers turned up at Newlands Corner before the official start of the search at 9.30 a.m. Under Deputy Chief Constable Kenward's direction fifty-three search parties, each under a police officer and averaging between thirty and forty people, were mustered at Newlands Corner. Before the parties moved off he appealed to them to carry out a thorough search, not merely a perfunctory one, since he was convinced that Agatha would be found somewhere in the district. After the early groups had started off, many more volunteers arrived by car, omnibus, motor cycle and bicycle. Members of the Automobile Association and the Royal Automobile Club were on hand to direct traffic, and responsible individuals were selected to guide new parties over the downs. Special omnibus services from Guildford and other neighbouring towns also brought their quota of people to swell the throng that gathered on the hilltop.

Among the early arrivals was a well-known breeder and exhibitor of bloodhounds who brought along three of her dogs. It was not expected that they would pick up the scent of the missing novelist after so long, but it was thought that if Agatha had wandered off and had fallen from exhaustion the hounds might locate her. At the suggestion of Deputy Chief Constable Kenward they were first taken along the old chalk road which runs towards Dorking and afterwards allowed to explore a track in the vicinity of the Silent Pool.

The public had its first thrill shortly before noon when rumour spread that a number of articles, including a black handbag and an attaché case, had been discovered at a lonely spot off the beaten track near Shere and were being brought by car to Newlands Corner. But it was soon established that the articles were of no assistance to the inquiry. Similar discoveries were made throughout the afternoon; this was hardly surprising since Newlands Corner had a notorious reputation for articles being stolen from parked cars. It was common practice for thieves to steal the contents of handbags and then dispose of them in the undergrowth.

An unfortunate aspect of the search was that by mid-afternoon many onlookers were drawn to the hilltop through idle curiosity, with no intention of taking part, and their presence hampered the genuine volunteers. There was an even greater carnival atmosphere than on the previous weekend: anticipation, excitement, high spirits and frivolity were as much in evidence as determination to find the missing woman. There was as much speculation over whether the missing novelist's body would be found as there was over whether her husband would join in the search. Although *Reynolds's Illustrated News* had reminded amateur sleuths that Agatha had dedicated *The Murder on the Links* 'To my husband, a fellow enthusiast for detective stories, and to whom I am indebted for much helpful advice and criticism', Archie was conspicuously absent that day.

Alfred Luland's refreshment kiosk, together with the Newlands Corner Hotel, did a roaring trade. How expansive the hunt for Agatha became is attested to by the use of horses to carry instructions to the outlying flanks. Albert Raven, a fourteen-year-old apprentice motor engineer who took part in the search on horseback, recalled: 'There was an enormous number of people around, the press was everywhere, and it was the number one topic of the day.'

During the search the public set out under police direction from three other major assembly points: Coal Kitchen Lane near Shere; Clandon Water Works on the Leatherhead to Guildford main road; and One Tree Hill on Pewley Downs on the eastern outskirts of Guildford. Innumerable special constables assisted with operations. Large numbers of the public, preferring to rely on their own intuition, set out independently. One party walked all the way along the summit of the downs from Dorking, a distance of nine miles, searching the woods and bushes that bordered the little-used track. Another party, who decided to beat the common and woods around St Martha's Chapel, found that in many places the bracken was taller than a man.

Meanwhile, having obtained a glove of Agatha's, Sherlock Holmes's creator Sir Arthur Conan Doyle gave it to a medium called Horace Leaf. 'I gave him no clue at all as to what I wanted or to whom the article belonged,' Conan Doyle later recalled. 'He never saw it until I laid it on the table at the moment of consultation, and there was nothing to connect either it or me with the Christie case . . . He at once got the name Agatha. "There is trouble connected with this article. The person who owns it is half dazed and half purposeful. She is not dead as many think. She is alive. You will hear of her, I think, next Wednesday."'

The hunt at Newlands Corner ended that evening as a mist fell, and a flare was lighted to guide those searchers who had lost their bearings. Police scouts were sent out to collect stragglers, while a deflated and exhausted Deputy Chief Constable Kenward issued a statement to the press asking journalists to thank the public for its cooperation. In an earlier statement that day he had made a point of saying that anyone who claimed Agatha had staged her disappearance was doing her a great injustice.

Around eleven o'clock that night in Harrogate, an exclusive northern spa town half-way between London and Edinburgh, two local bandsmen went to the local police to report that a woman resembling the missing novelist was staying at the hotel in which their band regularly played. They had, in fact, been suspicious of the hotel guest for some days, as a consequence of having their attention drawn to her by a keen-eyed chambermaid, but had done nothing about it until their wives had taken an interest in the matter.

Although the lateness of the hour precluded the Harrogate police from being able to investigate that night, since the woman suspected of being Agatha had already retired to her room, the two bandsmen had set in motion a chain of events which, over the next two days, would finally resolve the question to which the whole country was seeking an answer.

⟶ to find her

12

A Call for Divers

O N MONDAY THE 13th the news coverage revealed that the outcome of the Great Sunday Hunt had been failure. The estimates in the press over how many people had taken part ranged from 2,000 to 15,000.

Over the weekend the *Daily Mail* had followed up a suspected sighting which had taken place late on the night of the disappearance in a lane near Pyrford, seven miles north-east of Guildford. A Mr Richards had seen a car similar to Agatha's 'eventually driven away towards Newlands Corner', followed by a dark red four-seater. The following day the dark red car had been seen in the lane with a man and a woman inside. While the *Daily Mail*'s disclosures gave rise to speculation that Agatha might have gone off with a man and spent Saturday hiding in the lane, there was no reason any astute person should have considered this to be the case, because one of the witnesses, Mr Fauld of Warren Farm, had described the woman as having 'fairish bobbed hair' and wearing a 'smart blue coat'.

The *Daily Sketch* disclosed that a well-known medium in Guildford and her spirit guide Maisie, 'a 12-year-old African girl, tribe unknown', had asked to be given something belonging to Agatha in an attempt to locate her. The *Daily Sketch* told its readers that the request had been met when an unnamed 'London journalist' (in fact the *Daily Sketch*'s own reporter) had supplied the medium with a used powder-puff that he said belonged to Agatha:

The powder-puff worked like a charm. As soon as the medium went into a trance 'Maisie' took command . . . Sensational claims were made by the medium, who afterwards described Mrs Christie's fate as a tragedy almost too terrible to speak about, and suggested that the Black Pond should be dragged.

In recounting this story and emphasizing that the powder-puff had *never* belonged to or been seen by Mrs Christie, the *Daily Sketch* virtuously asserted that it was 'animated by the sole desire to prevent the public from being misled by a too-ready faith in the supernatural powers of mediums'.

In recent years former *Daily News* reporter Ritchie Calder has mistakenly recollected that the clairvoyant consulted by the *Daily Sketch* claimed that the body would be found in a log-house. None the less, he has told an entertaining story regarding the discovery of a summer retreat in Clandon Wood, involving himself and the *Westminster Gazette's* Trevor Allen, which gives insight into the journalists' rampaging imaginations:

We peered through the front windows and saw, silhouetted against the rear window, the shape of a body lying on a cot. It proved to be a bedroll. Nevertheless, the house, obviously closed up for the winter, had been recently occupied. Trevor Allen in great excitement discovered a 'bottle of opium'. Actually, it was ipecacuanha and opium, in discreet proportions, used in the treatment of chronic diarrhoea. Accepting our wild goose chase, we went back to Guildford and told our colleagues, as an amusing story about our adventure. They immediately swarmed off to the clearing. One picture-paper reporter took the barmaid of a Guildford hotel with him. He scattered face-powder on the doorstep, and got her to step in it. Next day the shoe-print appeared with the caption 'Is this Mrs Christie's?' Another used the 'oppii' without the 'ipec'.

On Monday the 13th many of the tabloids now indulged in their most fanciful theory to date: that Agatha might be living in London disguised as a man. While it seems extraordinary that the press could have advanced such a ludicrous suggestion, the public was not inclined to dismiss it. After all, had not Ethel Le Neve been dressed as a man when

Scotland Yard's Chief Inspector Walter Dew had arrested her and the murderer Crippen?

In apparent support of this outrageous theory, the afternoon edition of the *Westminster Gazette* revealed that Inspector Butler of the Berkshire Constabulary had left Ascot earlier in the day to make inquiries in London. While the police officer did indeed travel up to London that day, his purpose was to visit Scotland Yard in order to liaise with the police there and was in no way influenced by the melodramatic speculations in the press.

Meanwhile Stanley Bishop of the *Daily Express* (who had heckled Deputy Chief Constable Kenward for not searching all the pools on the Downs) had persuaded the London diving firm Siebe, Gorman and Company to participate on a voluntary basis in the search (in addition to supplying interviews and posing for photographs for the press). This led to the Surrey Police being erroneously blamed for the expense of hiring the divers. In conversation with the Home Office, Deputy Chief Constable Kenward later gave one of its officials, Arthur Dixon, to understand that 'all talk of divers, aeroplanes and other stunts were merely press invention', but this only told part of the story. When the press discovered that Stanley Bishop had engaged the divers, they laughed at him because many of the pools were so shallow that the divers would have had to crawl about on all fours.

The London *Evening News* was one of several newspapers to report Agatha's disappearance alongside that of a woman called Una Crowe, who had gone missing from her London home on Saturday the 11th and was found drowned on Sunday the 19th. While there was no connection between the two disappearances, such editorial juxtaposing undoubtedly gave the two cases full prominence – and led some readers to wonder if there was a link.

Unknown to the press and its readers, the West Riding police had spent Monday investigating the claims of the two Harrogate bandsmen, Bob Tappin and Bob Leeming, and interviewing the staff at the hotel in the town where the guest suspected of being the missing authoress was staying.

Bob Tappin's widow, Nora, has since explained how she was the

Mon. 13th

catalyst for the two Bobs going to the police on Sunday the 12th with their suspicions: 'Bob and I and Bob Leeming and his wife Beatrice were together later that night. The two men were on about this woman they thought was Mrs Christie, and I said a bit cheekily: "If you don't go to the police, I will."'

Rosie Asher, the chambermaid who originally alerted the two bandsmen to her suspicions, confided that she had first noticed the mysterious guest because of her unusual shoes with their large buckles and her distinctive black handbag which boasted the latest in fashion accessories, a zip. Until then, Rosie had only seen the handbags with zips in London magazines. Since her retirement from the Harrogate Hydro in the mid-1970s Rosie has explained why she did not go to the police herself:

> I didn't dare let on at the time. I suppose I was one of the first to know [it was Agatha Christie], but it was more than my job was worth to get involved. I just went about my normal business. She had only one small case but said her luggage was coming along later. I thought it all a bit odd. I was putting some papers on a table when I saw some pictures of this person. I noticed right away that she had unusual-looking shoes and handbag. I thought: I've seen those somewhere before. Then it dawned on me.

Her lasting impression of Agatha from all those years ago: 'I do remember she liked dancing. She was often in the ballroom and was a most attractive woman.'

After surreptitiously observing the mystery guest on Monday the 13th, the West Riding police concluded that this was the woman for whom the whole country was looking, and they got in touch with Deputy Chief Constable Kenward that night. He, not believing in the substance of their claims, failed to pass on the information to the Berkshire police or to the household at Styles. He instead drew up plans to extend the search around Newlands Corner to forty square miles, starting on the Wednesday. No less than eighty members of the Aldershot Motor Cycling Club offered their assistance.

On the morning of Tuesday the 14th the West Riding police once again contacted Deputy Chief Constable Kenward, requesting his help in establishing whether or not the hotel guest in question was the missing novelist. The result was that the policeman rang Styles around midday to ask Charlotte to travel north to identify the woman suspected of being her employer. The secretary declined on the grounds that she had to collect Rosalind from school and rang Archie at work in London. The information she passed on, while scant, convinced them both that his wife had almost certainly been located, and he caught the 1.40 p.m. train from King's Cross.

As a result of a tip-off, a large contingent of Fleet Street reporters had travelled by train to Harrogate late on the evening of Monday the 13th. Among them was Sidney Campion, late-night reporter for the *Daily News*. What was especially intriguing about this new lead was that the hotel guest suspected of being Agatha had registered as a Mrs Neele – the same surname as Archie's mistress Nancy.

It was the opinion of the press that the coincidence was too uncanny to ignore. But where exactly was the suspected woman? Contradictory sources suggested she was staying at either the Cairn Hydro or the Harrogate Hydro. A discreet police cordon erected on the afternoon of Tuesday the 14th suggested it was the latter, but the journalists could not be sure. The police were being unusually tight-lipped, declining to comment on the reason for the delay in telling reporters what was going on and why they had not already approached the woman in question. Something unusual was happening, and the press were quick to feel the tension.

Rather than wait for statements from the police, the London *Evening Standard* decided to blow the whistle. It gained the Fleet Street scoop of the week by supplying accurate information on Agatha's suspected whereabouts in its 2.30 p.m. edition, when it revealed that a woman staying at an unnamed hotel in Harrogate was awaiting identification by Colonel Christie, who was still some four hours away by train.

13

OFFICIAL PROTOCOL

SHORTLY AFTER 7.30 on the evening of Tuesday the 14th Archie ceased to be suspected of murdering his wife when he formally identified her at the Harrogate Hydro in Yorkshire. The West Riding police officer in charge of arranging the identification was Superintendent Gilbert McDowall of the Claro Division. The plan adopted by him was to tread delicately, given that the spa town depended on attracting distinguished and affluent visitors, whose stays often required the utmost discretion.

Beyond keeping the woman thought to be the authoress under observation with the help of Sergeant Baldwin of the Claro Division and Superintendent Hellewell of the Harrogate police, it was decided that nothing further should be done until her husband's arrival. The authorities had set the stage for what, if handled badly, could turn out an embarrassing fiasco or the happy resolution to a baffling mystery that had fascinated the nation for eleven days.

One of the most intriguing questions to arise – once suspicion had given way to certainty about the mysterious guest's identity – was how the most talked-about woman in the country could have escaped detection for so long when she was staying in one of the best hotels in the most prestigious spa town in England. Agatha had not only read the newspapers on a daily basis but had been observed doing so by other guests and staff. Why had no one noticed the likeness between the photographs emblazoned all over the front pages of the newspapers and the female guest sooner?

Within the rigid British class structure of the time, Harrogate's prosperity as a spa town depended on its assuring comfort, excellent service and total discretion to its wealthy and influential visitors. It was unheard of for locals to approach a famous person in public for an autograph or a photograph. Harrogate's status as the pre-eminent hydropathic centre of Europe arose from its eighty-seven mineral waters and the first-class service of its hotels and shops. The standard of discretion and service was such that Harrogate's shopkeepers would deliver goods on request to hotel guests, so it was not necessary to pay a visit to the stores unless one wished to do so. Queen Mary, however, who often visited her daughter Princess Mary and son-in-law Viscount Lascelles at nearby Goldsborough Hall, liked to browse around the Harrogate antiques shops with her ladies-in-waiting. The spa was equally popular with foreign dignitaries and aristocrats. Many guests, including members of the Russian Royal Family, often stayed there incognito, which is one of the reasons why Agatha's identity went unchallenged for so long.

Other reasons for her not being approached were that she had created a plausible new identity for herself and her reluctance to get involved in discussions about the celebrated missing crime writer with staff and other guests at the hotel. It became clear that many of Harrogate's residents had suspected that Agatha was staying there but did not do anything about it. 'Of course, we knew it was her,' recalled Mary Topham, daughter of one of the town's councillors, 'but we didn't say anything.' Harrogate's reputation for discretion was upheld. While the writer's discovery created a sensation throughout the rest of the country, there was barely a ripple in Harrogate society: when the town published its retrospective official account of the year's social events in the journal *Ackrill's News* the story did not warrant a mention.

The Harrogate Hydropathic Hotel, more usually known as the Harrogate Hydro, was one of the town's largest and most elegant establishments. It was set in five acres of ornamental gardens, with tennis courts, bowling green, putting green and a garage lock-up for twenty-six cars. There was hot and cold water in every bedroom, electric light throughout, baths on each floor, an American-style elevator, numerous public rooms, as well as a well-equipped suite of baths, including 'Turkish, Electric, Needle and Medicated', with massage treatment available from a physician in daily attendance.

It was in the Winter Garden Ballroom that the Harry Codd Dance Band, known to residents as the Happy Hydro Boys, had played at

DESCRIPTION of HYDRO

night, its members quietly speculating among themselves whether the attractive woman who often danced and sometimes sat on the sidelines in the shadows doing newspaper crosswords was the missing authoress. The band consisted of Harry Codd, its only professional member, on violin, Frank Brown on drums, Reg Schofield on piano, Albert Whiteley on banjo, in addition to the two bandsmen who had gone to the police, Bob Leeming on saxophone and Bob Tappin who played drums and banjo (and who wore a monocle, something of a gimmick at that time). A Miss Corbett regularly accompanied them as a singer.

It was 6.50 on the evening of Tuesday the 14th when Archie arrived at the Harrogate Hydro with Superintendent McDowall of the West Riding police. They were shown into the office of the anxious manageress, Mrs Taylor, and Archie was informed by her that the woman thought to be his wife was playing billiards. By now the authorities and Mrs Taylor had compiled a considerable dossier of information on the mystery guest, and Archie, impatient to see the woman calling herself Mrs Neele, was forced to hear them out.

The police had discovered that the woman thought to be the novelist had arrived in a taxi shortly before 7 p.m. on Saturday the 4th and was thought to have arrived by the 6.40 train from London. She had given staff and guests to understand that she was Mrs Teresa Neele of Cape Town, South Africa, visiting England for the first time. She said she had been in the country three weeks and had passed through Torquay. Staff had told the police they presumed she had left the bulk of her luggage either with friends or had stored it. When Mrs Neele had checked into the hotel her only baggage had been a handbag and a new attaché case. The West Riding authorities were aware that Agatha's attaché case had been left abandoned in her car. Where, then, had this new case come from? The police had ascertained from Miss Corbett, the band's singer, that on the night of her arrival Mrs Neele had entered the ballroom wearing a green knitted outfit similar to the one later described in all the newspaper accounts of the missing writer. The singer had assumed that the unaccompanied guest would not take to the dance floor since she was not wearing evening dress, but she had danced the Charleston when the band had struck up 'Yes, We Have No Bananas'.

The police had also found out that on Monday the 6th Mrs Neele had paid a visit to the Messrs W. H. Smith library in Parliament Street and borrowed a number of books: *Ways and Means*, a family saga by Noel Forrest; *The Perennial Bachelor*, a novel of contemporary American family life by Anne Parish; *Fly Leaves*, a volume of romantic poetry by Charles Caverley; *The Double Thumb*, the title story in a collection of fourteen mysteries by Francis G. Grierson; *The Phantom Train*, a mystery by Douglas Timins; and *The Third Messenger*, an adventure thriller by Patrick Wynton. Miss Cowie, the librarian, has since recalled: 'She appeared in every way just like an ordinary subscriber, but I gathered from her selections that she had a taste for novels of sensation and mystery. She showed no hesitation in the matter of terms, or of registering, or of choosing her books.'

The band's singer, Miss Corbett, had been privy to Mrs Neele's desire to place an advertisement in *The Times*, and the police had confirmed that Mrs Neele's advertisement had appeared on Saturday the 11th: 'Friends and relatives of Teresa Neele, late of South Africa, please communicate. Write Box R 702, The Times, E. C. 4.' The advertisement cost fifteen shillings and had initially suggested to the police that Mrs Neele might really be who she said she was.

The police also knew that on Sunday the 12th, the day of the Great Hunt, Mrs Neele had asked Miss Corbett if she could obtain a copy of the previous day's newspaper since she was anxious to see whether her advertisement had appeared. During the week, when Mrs Neele had noticed the other hotel guests leaving – there were only fifty during the time she stayed there owing to its proximity to Christmas – she made a half-laughing remark to Miss Corbett along the lines of: 'You won't leave me, will you?'

Archie was informed by the police that they had searched Mrs Neele's room while she was out the previous day and had found the pile of library books described by Miss Cowie. They had also found a bottle of laudanum, used in the treatment of neuritis, which bore the label of a Torquay chemist and the word 'poison'. The most interesting discovery was a small photograph of a girl on the bedside table, which turned out to be Agatha's daughter Rosalind.

The chambermaid Rosie Asher had spoken at length to the police. Since she had taken Mrs Neele's breakfast up to her nearly every morning she was able to provide her questioners with the following diary of the guest's movements during her stay.

— *COPY* —

Saturday the 4th – Arrived in taxicab in the evening; very little luggage. Nothing about the room except a comb, new hot-water bottle and a small photo of a little boy, across which was written 'Teddy'.

Sunday the 5th – Slept until 10 a.m., had breakfast in bed and then went out.

Monday the 6th – London newspaper taken up with breakfast in bed. New hat, coat, evening shoes, books and magazines, pencil and fruit and various toilet requisites ordered from, and sent in by, local tradesmen. *Holmes/R find her*,

Tuesday the 7th – Had breakfast in the dining-room; appeared to be very bright.

Wednesday the 8th – Breakfast in bed with a newspaper to read.

Thursday the 9th – Very cheerful and bright; had a newspaper as usual in the morning and went downstairs carrying a novel.

Friday the 10th – Seemed rather strange for a minute or so when breakfast was taken to bedroom, went downstairs early and then to Leeds for shopping and did not return until 10 p.m.

Saturday the 11th – Breakfast in bed, but seemed agitated when reading a newspaper.

Sunday the 12th – No newspaper taken up to bedroom with breakfast. Nothing unusual in demeanour. Had dinner in a dress very much resembling the one in her published photographs. Bottle marked poison in drawer; also paper bag from a London store.

Monday the 13th – Detective downstairs; told all I knew. Lady in question came to her room, and I noticed her face was red and that she appeared agitated.

Although Rosie Asher mistakenly thought the child in the photograph was a boy, she stated that three days after the guest's arrival a registered parcel had come from a London store, believed to contain a ring which Mrs Neele said she had lost in London while shopping. She had worn the diamond ring on several occasions subsequently – but never a wedding ring. Although Sally Potts, another chambermaid on the same floor, was not convinced the guest was the missing authoress, she recalled that Mrs Neele was no bother and 'spent a lot of her time writing'.

Before the Christies' reunion, the hotel's manageress described Mrs Neele's unusual handbag and the clothes she had been wearing to Archie, but all he could say for sure was that his wife was thought to have taken from her car her handbag and purse containing between five and ten pounds. Discreet questioning of the hotel's guests by Mrs Taylor had elicited further information about the woman. Mrs Neele had given some of the guests, including a Mrs Robson of Harrogate, the idea that she had recently suffered a traumatic bereavement with the death of her baby girl, and she also gave them the impression she knew she was suffering from loss of memory as a consequence of the death of her child.

Otherwise Mrs Neele had seemed perfectly ordinary in every other respect. She had furnished herself with a new wardrobe of clothes from shops in Harrogate and Leeds. One evening she had appeared in a new shawl and, on noticing a price tag still attached for seventy-five shillings, a guest jokingly had asked if that was all she was worth; Mrs Neele had smiled and observed she was worth a lot more than that. She had shown a preference for reading the *Daily Mirror*, and when another guest had suggested that she looked very like the missing novelist Mrs Neele's unequivocal and apparently uninterested reply had been: 'This Mrs Christie is a very elusive woman, but I don't want to bother with her.' She had a massage at 3.30 most afternoons in the hotel, in addition to taking the beneficial sulphur waters known as the Cure. While she never seemed short of money, Mrs Neele had lived quietly during her stay at the hydro.

The police and hotel management were edgy, because the information they had unearthed about the mystery guest suggested that she was a fashionable and affluent woman who would not be pleased to be mistakenly identified as the missing authoress. But there were two clues that clinched the matter for Archie: the guest's writing in the hotel register was just like his wife's; and when he learned that the photograph of the child in Mrs Neele's room had the word 'Teddy' written across the corner – the Christies' nickname for their daughter – he was convinced that Agatha had been found.

By the time Archie left the manageress's office he was impatient to see Mrs Neele, but the woman had left the billiard room and gone upstairs to her bedroom. Archie was asked to remain in the lobby, since neither Superintendent McDowall nor Mrs Taylor approved of him going up to confront the woman in her bedroom. It was their belief that she would shortly come down to dine, as was her habit every night.

Archie stationed himself in an armchair, concealed behind a newspaper, while Superintendent McDowall and his men were hidden out of sight from the stairs down which the guest was expected to come. Outside the hotel the press were growing impatient in the cold night air, anxious to know what was happening inside.

When Agatha at last appeared it seemed evident to witnesses that she was no more suffering from amnesia or mental breakdown than was Archie. And as she came downstairs, dressed in a stylish salmon-pink georgette evening dress, there was no doubt that she was the woman the country had been seeking.

Archie had last seen Agatha on the morning of Friday the 3rd when they had had a row after his refusal to accompany her to Yorkshire after admitting he would be spending the weekend with his mistress, Nancy Neele. Given the intense acrimony that had already passed between the scorned wife and the husband who had twice betrayed her, the scene about to unfold in the lounge of the Harrogate Hydro promised to be even more dramatic and poignant than any they had previously shared.

Nan
Watts

14

LAST-MINUTE CANCELLATION

ONCE AGATHA HAD been found, the real problems began. The subsequent cover-up, perpetrated by Archie, in which Agatha and certain other members of her family colluded, was undermined by his statement during her absence that Agatha had previously discussed the possibility of disappearing in order to experiment with a plot for a book. Any potential sympathy their dramatic reunion might have invited had been forfeited by Archie's ill-considered remarks.

In an atmosphere bristling with tension, the now famous authoress, who had answered to the name of Mrs Teresa Neele for a week and a half, walked into the hotel lounge and picked up from a table a newspaper containing an account of the search with a picture of herself. From behind his own newspaper Archie gave a prearranged signal to Superintendent McDowall to confirm that the woman was his wife.

There was instant recognition in Agatha's eyes, although she said nothing to betray herself. There was neither fuss nor melodrama. Archie was immensely relieved to find her at last. While he was unaware of the part Agatha's sister-in-law Nan Watts had played in helping deliberately stage the disappearance, he had suspected almost from the beginning that Agatha was alive and playing games with him.

After she returned his greeting with apparent nonchalance, Agatha agreed to sit down by the lounge fire and was spotted a few moments later by a fellow guest, Mr Pettleson, a wine merchant from London, who had just returned to the hotel. Agatha indicated Archie with a nod and quietly informed Mr Pettleson that her brother had arrived unexpectedly.

Archie, who was sitting opposite her, was too embarrassed to reply and gazed into the fire. Mr Pettleson joined them, unaware of the scene he had interrupted. Although he had read of the disappearance, he did not realize that the couple he was talking to were the famous Christies. There was an air of constraint over them, and he later admitted it had occurred to him that they might have quarrelled since they were sitting so far apart. But when Archie rather awkwardly suggested to Agatha that they both go in to dinner a few moments later, she accepted without fuss or demur.

Although she had previously arranged with another hotel guest, Mrs Robson, to attend a dance at the Prospect Hotel that night, Agatha cancelled the arrangement on the way into dinner, explaining to Mrs Robson that her brother had arrived. As the novelist and her husband proceeded towards the dining-room, Agatha, in the full hearing of the police and other onlookers, spoke to Archie about an experience that had befallen Mrs Robson's daughter: 'There is a lady here whose daughter had a baby just like I had, and her memory went. But you know, I shall get all right, because the lady staying in the hydro says her daughter was like this when she had a baby, but she became all right.'

When the police intervened to ask her if she knew who she was and what she was doing at the Harrogate Hydro, Agatha said she had left home in some confusion and had lost her memory, which had only just come back to her. Agatha and Archie then took a corner table in the restaurant. The authorities, sceptical of Agatha's claim, left them alone, and over dinner they were forced by the extraordinary circumstances in which they found themselves to face a number of unpleasant home truths. The exchanges they made over dinner, following their subdued reunion, were very low key, and Archie was left in no doubt over the miscalculated circumstances that had brought Agatha to Harrogate.

As dinner proceeded, a despondent Agatha made no attempt to conceal from her husband the fact that she had deliberately staged her disappearance because she had known that her marriage was irretrievably over and she had wished to spite him. She revealed she had spent the night of her disappearance with Nan. Archie was staggered, because Nan had given everyone to understand she was as upset over Agatha's inexplicable absence as the rest of her family.

There was no need for Agatha to remind Archie how their endless marital rows – resulting in tears and loss of sleep and appetite – had strained her nerves almost to breaking point. Unable to cope with the loss of her husband, she had sought to punish him in the only way she knew how: through intrigue, mystery and revenge. She also made it clear that her plot had exposed her to much greater anxiety than she had anticipated because she had failed to realize that the press would become obsessed with the disappearance and fan it into a sensation.

Agatha told him that after their row on the morning of the disappearance she had driven up to London to confide her problems to the one person who she knew would understand. Nan's parents, James Snr and Anne, had died, respectively, in June and November that year, and she empathized with Agatha over her loss of Clarissa. Also, because her first husband, Hugo Pollock, had walked out on her without explanation she had an intuitive understanding of the pain that Archie had caused Agatha.

Nan had moved to 78 Chelsea Park Gardens, and Agatha had been in a dreadful state when she had arrived there on Friday morning. Her failed reconciliation with Archie had left her feeling twice betrayed, and she now told him that she had confided to Nan that she was thinking of doing something desperate if he went ahead with his plans to leave her for Nancy. Agatha revealed that she had spoken to Nan of abandoning her car at Newlands Corner because it was only a few miles from Hurtmore Cottage, and she wanted the car's discovery to disrupt his weekend with Nancy and to lead to three or four days of very unpleasant questioning by the police, who she hoped would suspect him of murdering her.

Nan considered that Archie had behaved very badly and had agreed that if Agatha went ahead with her scheme she could spend the night with her, since her second husband, George Kon, was away. The two women had decided that Agatha should claim to be suffering from amnesia when she was found, because it would later release her from awkward explanations.

After returning to Sunningdale Agatha had lunched, then driven with Rosalind to Dorking to have afternoon tea with Archie's mother. When Agatha had returned to Styles with her daughter there had been no sign of her husband, and his failure to come home from work on the evening of Friday the 3rd had confirmed what Agatha had already guessed: that her marriage was over. Charlotte, who was aware of Agatha's fragile state but who had at no time been privy to the scheme to spite Archie, had rung early in the evening while she was in London to see if her employer was all right. Agatha had pretended that things were fine and had urged Charlotte to return to Sunningdale, as intended, by the last train, because she had wanted her secretary out of the way.

At 9.45 p.m. Agatha had left the letter for Charlotte asking her to cancel the trip to Beverley, as well as a letter of recrimination to Archie over his affair with Nancy. The writer had then driven directly to New-lands Corner, where she had let the car roll off the plateau with the hand brake off and the gears in neutral. She had intentionally left the head-lights on to draw attention to the car, and her fur coat, an attaché case of clothes and her driver's licence had been left inside so that it would look as if something untoward had happened.

Having removed her handbag from the car before it careered down the steep embankment and ended up by the edge of the chalk pit, she had walked to <u>West Clandon Station</u> and <u>travelled by train to London</u>. When Agatha had arrived at 78 Chelsea Park Gardens later that night Nan had been half expecting her and had not been at all surprised to learn that Archie had gone ahead with his plans to spend the weekend with Nancy. Nan's ten-year-old daughter Judith was away at boarding school, so the two women had spent the night discussing the details of Agatha's scheme. Neither had any reason to suppose that Agatha's plot to make Archie suffer for three or four days would lead to such disastrous consequences.

Agatha told her husband she had posted the letter to her brother-in-law Campbell early on the morning of Saturday the 4th, in which she stated her intention to visit a Yorkshire spa. She had deliberately sent it to his workplace, rather than his home address, knowing there would be a slight delay in his receiving it. Her decision to take a rest cure in Harro-gate had arisen from her and Nan's belief that the authorities would be bound to look there once Campbell was in receipt of the letter, because Harrogate was the most famous spa in Yorkshire. On Saturday morning, before Agatha left London, the two women had visited the Army and

Navy Department Store in Victoria, where Nan gave Agatha money to acquire some items of clothing and other articles and a small case to take to Harrogate with her, since the clothes she had packed in her attaché case the previous night had been left behind in the abandoned car. They had rung two or three of the best-known hotels in Harrogate to see which had vacancies and, after discovering that none were full owing to the Christmas lull, had decided that Agatha should just turn up at the Harrogate Hydro since this would later support her claim of having lost her memory.

Agatha also told Archie that she had left her diamond ring to be mended at Harrods that morning, as she had been meaning to have it repaired for some time. She had requested that the department store forward it to her in the name of 'Mrs Neele' at the Hydro in Harrogate.

After they had lunched together, Nan had given Agatha some more money, then Agatha had caught the 1.40 p.m. train from King's Cross, which arrived in Harrogate at 6.40 p.m. She had taken a taxi from Harrogate Station and, a little before seven o'clock, had booked into room 105 of the Harrogate Hydro as Mrs Teresa Neele of Cape Town, South Africa. Her choice of surname was quite deliberate, while the Christian name she adopted had been inspired by St Teresa of Avila.

Agatha revealed she had been surprised when her letter to Campbell had failed to lead to her immediate discovery and the press had taken up the story of her disappearance. She was sure the news coverage had come as just as much of a shock to Nan. Agatha had resolved to sit tight on the assumption that she would soon be tracked down. But the search had dragged on and on. What neither woman had predicted was that Archie would crack under the strain of the police investigation and tell the *Daily Mail* that Agatha had discussed with her sister the possibility of disappearing at will. Agatha had placed the advertisement in *The Times* because it had been the only thing she could think of doing that would support her claim to have developed amnesia. ✼

Horrified by events, she had lived very quietly as a guest in the hotel. Part of her had, of course, enjoyed knowing that her husband was suffering. She had occupied her time reading newspapers and books and had done a lot of writing to take her mind off the situation. She had also occupied herself by knitting, playing bridge and billiards in the public rooms, taking the waters in the hotel and spending her evenings in the ballroom dancing or sitting quietly at a table doing crosswords.

Agatha's and Archie's meal was a muted occasion, in which the full significance of the roles each had played bitterly came home to them both. Although he was forced to contain himself, Archie was furious at Nan's involvement. It was apparent to them both that their marriage was beyond repair. Given his anger over what had happened, his restraint in dealing with his wife, who was deeply distressed by it all, might have been touching – if his main concern had not been so evidently to protect his mistress's reputation, so that he might still marry her once the press had lost interest in the story.

Adversity had united Agatha and Archie in the past, and they were to present a united front once more over the next sixteen hours. Neither wanted their private lives splashed further across the newspapers' front pages.

After leaving Agatha in her hotel bedroom Archie rang Styles to tell Charlotte that his wife had been found suffering from amnesia. The secretary, who had already been informed of Agatha's discovery by the Surrey police, accepted Archie's lie in apparent good faith. She was immensely relieved and delighted that Agatha had been found, and at his suggestion she arranged with the local garage in Sunningdale for his Delage to be driven up to London the following day, so that after arriving on the King's Cross train Agatha and Archie could drive together back to Styles.

It was a trip, however, that was never to be made. Although Archie had hidden Agatha from the press in the nick of time, the reporters invaded the public rooms of the hotel. Owing to the many loose ends and discrepancies in the case, the news that Agatha had amnesia was received with the utmost incredulity.

The unrelenting journalists, well aware that Archie had attempted to deceive them about his affair with Nancy, asked themselves, not unreasonably, whether the Colonel's explanation might not also be a lie. It quickly dawned on Archie that if he were to effect a cover-up he was going to need additional help.

15

Public Charades and Frozen Stills

THE PRESS REPORTERS applied considerable pressure to Archie on the evening of Tuesday the 14th to make a statement about Agatha's reappearance. The *Yorkshire Post* had been the first to reveal the discovery of the crime writer in a late edition that evening under 'stop-press', with the tantalizing and not wholly reassuring headline 'Agatha Christie Found' and, on the recommendation of Superintendent McDowall of the West Riding police, Archie reluctantly arranged to speak to Archie Kenyon, the newspaper's reporter. He did not agree to an interview but, instead, gave a carefully worded statement, which Kenyon transmitted to his press colleagues:

> There is no question about her identity. She is my wife. She is suffering
> from complete loss of memory and identity. She does not know who
> she is. She does not know me, and she does not know why she is in
> Harrogate. I am hoping to take her to London tomorrow to see a doctor
> and a specialist, and I hope that rest and quiet will put her right. Great
> credit is due to the police for their untiring efforts in the matter, and for
> the inquiries which have led to her discovery.

It was a well-known fact among reporters that Agatha had told Campbell in the letter that she posted after her disappearance that she planned to visit a spa in Yorkshire and, since this was what she had done, the press suspected deliberate intention. Rather unwisely, Archie confided to Archie Kenyon that while he appreciated the publicity given in the press to the facts of his wife's disappearance he said he felt that certain newspapers had made a 'stunt' of it. While the journalists were naturally euphoric that their publicity had led to the authoress's discovery, her husband's tactless words fanned their suspicions, and as they delved more deeply into the circumstances of her arrival and stay at the hotel their questions multiplied.

To begin with, if the writer was suffering from amnesia, why had she not recognized pictures of herself in the newspapers? Also, how could she have ended up over two hundred miles from Newlands Corner, staying in a luxury hotel? Moreover, did the Colonel really expect them to believe that when his wife had signed the hotel registrar she had hit on the exact spelling of his mistress's surname by coincidence? Why had she called herself Teresa? An anagram for 'teaser'? Where had she spent the first night of her disappearance?

Why had her car, containing her fur coat and other items of property, been deliberately pushed over the edge of the plateau at Newlands Corner, and by what means had she contrived to reach Harrogate from there? Given her alleged mental confusion, if she had travelled by train, how had she managed to navigate her way across London from the southern terminus to the northern, obtaining the right tickets, catching the appropriate trains and alighting at the correct station?

Was there any significance in the fact that in one of her books, *The Secret Adversary*, the character Jane Finn had simulated amnesia as a means of extricating herself from a dangerous situation? The journalists also thought it seemed an extraordinary coincidence for Agatha to put an advertisement in *The Times*, because this was exactly what two of the characters in her novel had decided to do.

The press also thought it was strange that the names Mrs Agatha Christie, Colonel Archibald Christie, Rosalind, Miss Charlotte Fisher, Mrs Hemsley, Captain Campbell Christie, Styles, Sunningdale and so on, which had continually been splashed across the front pages of the newspapers for a week and a half, accompanied by photographs, had not triggered even a flicker of recollection in Agatha during her stay at the hotel.

Moreover, in the December issue of *Flynn's Weekly* magazine Agatha's latest Mr Quin story, 'The Voice in the Dark', told a brooding if improbable tale of an amnesiac whose memory returns after forty years to wreak a terrifying revenge on the woman who has usurped her home and possessions. The press were keen to know what sort of games the creator of the story was playing.

In an interview with a representative from the Press Association, Mr Taylor, the hotel manager (who was no longer publicity-shy now that the matter of his guest's identity had been established), described the reunion between the wife and husband as 'pathetic'. The *Daily Mail*, who had chartered a special train to take Agatha to London, offered Archie £500 if she would give them an exclusive story of her adventures. The specially chartered train was ready and waiting at Harrogate Station at 7.55 p.m. on Tuesday the 14th, but Archie flatly refused their offer and the *Daily Mail* was left with a large bill.

The press's doubts about the amnesia explanation deepened after interviewing several of the hydro's guests, who described Mrs Neele's behaviour during her stay as perfectly normal. Reporters from the *Daily Sketch* and *News of the World* photographed Agatha's signature in the hotel register. Many of the journalists checked into the hotel themselves, including the Northern Editor of the *Daily Mail*, who was determined to foil any attempt by the Christies to slip away quietly during the night.

Meanwhile Ackrill's printing presses belatedly rolled into action, printing the weekly Wednesday 15 December edition of the *Harrogate Herald and List of Visitors* in which the story of Agatha's dramatic discovery was headlined 'Mrs Christie Found at Harrogate, Identified by Husband'.

In the uncertainty leading up to the official identification, extreme discretion had been exercised by the printing firm for fear of the harm to the newspaper's reputation and its sales if information about Agatha's suspected whereabouts was not confirmed first by the police. While Ackrill's employees were aware that a major story was breaking in the town, none of them were permitted to discuss the matter. Even Albert Whiteley, who played in the Harry Codd Band at the hotel in the evenings, was not prepared to say anything before the West Riding Police confirmed Agatha's identity: 'We dared not. We weren't sure.' More recently, however, he has broken his silence to describe his recollections of the woman whose adventures captivated the entire country.

I wasn't a professional musician. By day I was a printer working in the machine room of the local newspapers. I'd rush home and just have time to change into my monkey suit before getting to the hotel for the evening dance in the ballroom. At first I didn't think there was anything remarkable about this 'Mrs Neele'. The newspapers had been making a sensation of Agatha Christie's mysterious disappearance for days with front-page photographs of her, but the reproduction wasn't good in those days. Then one paper offered £100 reward for information about her whereabouts and ran a picture which was a good likeness. That night, while we were playing in the band, the saxophone player and drummer asked me if I thought the lady dancing was Agatha Christie. I agreed it could be. The band leader didn't want to know because if it turned out we were wrong he'd lose his job. The hotel was a very exclusive place. I was earning four shillings an hour in the band there, which was top money in those days, and I needed it to run my motor bike. So finally it was just the other two members of the band, after discussion with their wives, who went to the police to say they'd found Agatha. They always kicked themselves afterwards because if they'd gone to the newspapers they would have got the £100 reward.

The evening of Tuesday the 14th saw the press compete to be the first to interview everyone connected with the writer. Peg was flabbergasted to learn of the circumstances of Agatha's discovery from her son but rallied quickly, saying that her daughter-in-law's mind must have given way like one of the characters in her books. Meanwhile Charlotte, who had rung round as many family members and friends as possible on first hearing the news from Deputy Chief Constable Kenward, fended off questions from reporters about her employers' private lives as best she could, while emphasizing that Agatha had been very upset over the death of her mother eight months earlier. Sir Godfrey Collins, who had had no idea of the whereabouts of his best-selling authoress, was relieved to hear she was alive and he happily anticipated even bigger sales for her current novel, *The Big Four*, then in production.

Archie's brief statement made it clear that he intended to return to Sunningdale via London with his wife. Later that evening he telephoned her sister Madge and brother-in-law Jimmy. The couple had moved to Abney Hall after the death of the latter's mother following a long illness the preceding month. After prolonged discussion the Wattses agreed to come to Harrogate to help Archie deal with the press. They were extremely glad that Agatha had been found and their anger at learning from Archie of Nan's involvement was outweighed by their concern to shield Agatha from the consequences of her misguided actions and remove her to Abney Hall. The Wattses were as good as their word, arriving at the Harrogate Hydro early the following day.

Meanwhile the Chief Constable of the Surrey Constabulary, Captain Sant, had issued orders that none of his subordinates were to grant interviews to journalists on the subject of the expense of the search around Newlands Corner and why the Surrey police had persisted in combing the downs after the Berkshire Constabulary had decided that Agatha was, in all probability, still alive. The reporters, who called repeatedly at the Woodbridge Road Headquarters in Guildford and at Deputy Chief Constable Kenward's home in the police station grounds, found he had become as elusive as the woman for whom he had searched in vain.

Superintendent Goddard and Inspector Butler of the Berkshire Constabulary remained highly sceptical, after liaising with the West Riding police, of the claims that Agatha was suffering from amnesia. Superintendent Goddard issued a statement to the press in which he made clear his reasons for believing almost from the beginning that Agatha was alive:

Frankly, I had nothing to go on save my own deduction on the facts before me. But I may admit this. I knew that when she left her house it was her intention to drive around for a little while until she had made up her mind what she was going to do. An important factor, to my mind, was the finding of a fur coat in the abandoned car. A woman who was going to commit suicide, I argued, would not get out of a car, take off her coat, and walk a considerable distance away. She would in all probability, having made up her mind, take her life where she sat.

Another factor in my deduction was the manner in which Mrs

Christie was dressed. She could have passed the night comfortably driving around in her car wearing a fur coat, and then when she had made up her mind to leave the car have discarded the coat, which was too heavy for walking in. Under the fur coat she wore warm clothing of the sort a woman wears for country walks.

I thought from all these facts that she had walked from her car and had taken a train for some very definite destination. Hence I got busy with posters, circulating them to all police stations. I never believed in the suicide theory. I never believed Mrs Christie had been the victim of foul play. I am delighted she has been found and that the search is at an end. It has been a worrying time for everyone.

What Superintendent Goddard failed to realize was that Agatha had decided on her course of action before she left home. Nevertheless, his remarks, which were uncomfortably perceptive, were widely reported in the *Daily Mail*, *Daily News* and *The Bulletin and Scots Pictorial*. The letter Agatha had addressed to her secretary, which had been kept by the Berkshire police while she was missing, was returned to Charlotte. The police officer who unwittingly came closest to perceiving the truth was Tom Roberts, the 21-year-old probationary constable. In his 1987 biography, *Friends and Villains*, Roberts recalled: 'It seems that Mrs Christie had chosen this site deliberately, as she could leave her car there and then walk to the Guildford–Waterloo main-line station at West Clandon and disappear.'

On Wednesday 15 December the morning newspapers had a field-day reporting the writer's discovery. Ex-Chief Inspector Walter Dew in the *Daily Express* bluntly contradicted Archie's explanation of the affair: 'It may be that when Mrs Christie vanished the tremendous publicity given to her case was rather more than she had bargained for. If this was so we can understand a little better why she remained silent for so long.'

Archie had taken a room near Agatha's and each breakfasted alone in preparation for their public ordeal. His wife welcomed the idea of going to Abney Hall, partly because Styles contained too many distressing memories for her. Archie was extremely agitated by the public furore that had erupted, while Agatha was so bewildered and apprehensive that she displayed an almost unnatural calm. On their arrival at the hotel Madge and Jimmy acted as intermediaries between husband and wife, since Agatha and Archie were no longer talking directly to one another.

A few moments before their departure, male and female decoys were seen to leave the front entrance of the Harrogate Hydro and get into a Laudellette. The press frenziedly flung themselves on to the wings of the car and photographed the couple they believed to be the departing authoress and her husband. Agatha and Archie descended the main stairs of the Harrogate Hydro at 9.15 a.m. for what was to become the most publicly scrutinized journey of their lives.

The *Daily Mail* had stationed a lone photographer by the side entrance of the hotel. As Archie and Agatha made their way along a corridor towards the door their departure was witnessed by the manageress, Mrs Taylor. The public charade they enacted was therefore for her benefit. When Agatha asked Archie why they were not leaving by the front entrance, he reassured her that she must not be alarmed because she had lost her memory and that everything would be all right. She was wearing a new two-piece pale pink outfit with a double collar, pale pink striped black cloche hat, a row of double stranded pearls, a coat trimmed with fur around the collar, cuffs and hem, black gloves, champagne-coloured stockings and elegant black shoes. The stylish ensemble hardly reinforced the public's perceptions of Agatha as someone who had lost her memory and was in a state of mental confusion, but the writer was determined that Archie should know what he was losing in divorcing her for Nancy.

As the novelist stepped outside, the *Daily Mail*'s photographer captured the only photograph of her leaving the Harrogate Hydro, her inscrutable expression caught in profile. A buttons boy was holding open the door of a waiting taxi cab, and when Agatha heard the click of a camera she darted inside. The Christies and Wattses were relentlessly pursued to the railway station. Word of their impending departure had leaked out, and there was pandemonium. The railway staff, in an attempt to keep the growing crowd at bay, had placed an 'Out of Order' sign on the ticket machine that sold penny tickets for access to the railway platform, but the more enterprising members of the press and public bought tickets to the next station and thus gained access to the platform in a bid to catch a glimpse of the Christies' departure.

Through a prior arrangement with the railway authorities, the two couples did not enter the station by either of the usual public entrances. Instead they used a goods entrance that led on to the up-line platform from the East Parade side. As the Glasgow–London train steamed into the station they made their way along the platform to a private compartment reserved for 'Mr Parker's Party'. Mr Parker was the name of the stationmaster, and the notice gave onlookers to understand that the party would be proceeding to King's Cross Station in London. The platform was so crowded that many of the journalists had difficulty identifying Agatha, since none had previously seen her in person. In a desperate bid to catch the train, many of the reporters, who had entered by the front entrances, ran across the tracks to the far platform. The *Daily Mirror* photographer Edward Dean triumphantly boasted that he had spotted her. The two sisters hid inside their compartment, while Archie and Jimmy remained briefly on guard on the platform outside until the train was ready to leave.

Agatha was deeply shocked by the mob of reporters and photographers, and she burst into tears after the train pulled out of Harrogate. But she was to discover that there was worse harassment to come when they arrived at Leeds Station. By then she had regained her composure. While they were expected to continue all the way to London, they caught the reporters off-guard by changing trains. As Agatha left the London train she had the misfortune to step straight into the path of the waiting *Daily Chronicle* photographer. The resulting picture, which was undoubtedly the most poignant of all those taken at the time, shows her faltering in her stride, her face a mask of dismay and revulsion at the situation. She is clutching her handbag in the crook of her arm, while in her other arm she is carrying two of the detective novels on loan from the Harrogate library, which would subsequently be posted back.

She did not falter for long. Raising her head and determinedly ignoring bystanders, Agatha walked through the battery of cameras trained on her by the *Westminster Gazette*, the *Daily News*, the *Daily Mail*, the *Leeds Mercury* and the *Daily Sketch*. Madge was appalled by the invasion of their privacy by the photographers. However, her cloche hat and large fur collar enabled her to keep her face partly shielded. She carried the by now notorious new attaché case and the shawl that Agatha had acquired in Harrogate. Archie and Jimmy followed with the rest of the writer's newly acquired luggage. Agatha, desperate to escape the attention of the press, briefly led the way and, in doing so, betrayed her familiarity with the station because, without instruction, she unhesitatingly turned on to the platform for the Manchester train. Agatha had used the station many times over the years on her visits to Abney Hall, and the press considered her knowledge of her whereabouts inconsistent for someone who was supposed to have no recollection of her past.

By the time her companions had caught up with her it was evident to Agatha that they were not going to be able to shake off the press, and she resigned herself to this fact. When her grim-faced sister chastened her for letting herself become distracted by bystanders, Agatha made a laughing remark and patted her on the shoulder, much to the astonishment of witnesses. Madge and Jimmy were tight-lipped, fearing that Agatha might get carried away, while Archie was appalled at all the attention they were getting.

Agatha's light-hearted banter to Madge surprised many of the reporters. After his wife and in-laws had ensconced themselves in a private compartment of the Leeds train, Archie, in the few minutes left before the train departed, braved the gauntlet of reporters and photographers to dispatch a telegram from Leeds Station informing Charlotte of their plans. He had not previously dared to tell the secretary where they were going, in a futile bid to maintain secrecy about their movements.

The Christies and the Wattses were not the only ones whose plans were foiled. The London *Evening Standard*, who had obtained a series of photographs of Agatha leaving Harrogate, was less lucky than its competitors. The pictures were driven immediately to Sherbourne, an aerodrome near Harrogate, where a specially chartered plane was waiting to fly the negatives to London in time for publication in the *Evening Standard*'s 2.30 p.m. edition. But because of heavy fog the pilot was forced to land the plane less than fifty miles away at Brough Aerodrome and the *Evening Standard*'s elaborately devised plan had to be aborted.

As soon as the pursuing journalists realized Agatha's true destination they telephoned their colleagues, who were thus waiting when the train drew into Manchester's Victoria Station. The Christies and Wattses now had an even bigger contingent of the press on their trail. As they neared the barrier of the platform, a bystander, demanding an explanation for the furore, tried to intercept Agatha, but Archie rushed forward. He blocked the man's way and insisted that his wife must not be addressed as she was very ill. Ignoring the man, the novelist and her companions hurried on.

The most damaging photographs that were taken of Agatha that day were those printed in the London *Evening News* and the *Daily Mirror*. The *Evening News* picture showed her grinning so broadly that it was apparent to all that she had been laughing. The *Daily Mirror* photographed her leaving the station in Manchester, smiling broadly, just before she climbed into her sister's waiting chauffeur-driven Wolseley.

In fact Agatha found the journey a thoroughly humiliating and degrading experience and her one consolation throughout it all was Archie's intense embarrassment at being pursued by the press – it was the one time in the disintegration of their marriage when his suffering appeared equal to her own.

The journey for Agatha and her companions ended with a ten-mile drive to Abney Hall. A frenzied chase ensued, with reporters and photographers commandeering every available taxi cab.

Meanwhile, in London, the extraordinary publicity given to the disappearance led to unprecedented scenes at King's Cross Station. A large crowd surged round Platform No. 1 in the hope of glimpsing the arrival of the country's most talked-about woman on the 1.55 train. Newspaper stands quickly sold out. Police were called in to control the mob, while press photographers perched on the bridge over the platform and even on top of taxi cabs. Some people had even brought along opera glasses. The crowd let out a roar of disappointment when it realized that Agatha had not travelled on the train after all and soon dispersed.

In the meantime, having unsuccessfully tried to shake off their pursuers, Agatha's party finally reached its destination. After the Wolseley swept past the lodge gates at the entrance to the grounds of Abney Hall the gardener swiftly padlocked the gates and put up a sign up saying 'Trespassers Will Be Prosecuted'. With Agatha safely removed from public view her co-conspirators were united in relief, believing the worst to be over. But, as events were to prove, the press were far from daunted.

Above: Abney Hall, Cheshire, home of the Watts family. Agatha used this setting as a basis for many of her mysteries including *After the Funeral* and *They Do It With Mirrors*

Judith and Graham Gardner Collection

Above: Agatha and Nan Watts in 1908 on the Princess Pier in Torquay

Judith and Graham Gardner Collection

Right: Archie's stepfather William Hemsley, a schoolmaster at Rugby School after the First World War

Rugby School Archive

Archie in the early 1920s after he had left the Royal Flying Corps and started working in the City of London

Above, left to right: Archie,
Major Belcher, Mrs Hyam
and Agatha during the
British Empire Tour, 1922

Jared Cade Collection

Right: Nan and George Kon
at Le Touquet golf course,
France, during their
engagement, 1925

Judith and Graham Gardner Collection

Left: Nan's husband George, Archie and Nancy Neele on Sandwich Golf Course, Kent, 1926, photographed by Nan

Judith and Graham Gardner Collection

Below: Judith aged ten at Brancaster, Norfolk, 1926

Judith and Graham Gardner Collection

NEWLANDS CORNER, WHERE AGATHA CHRISTIE'S CAR WAS FOUND

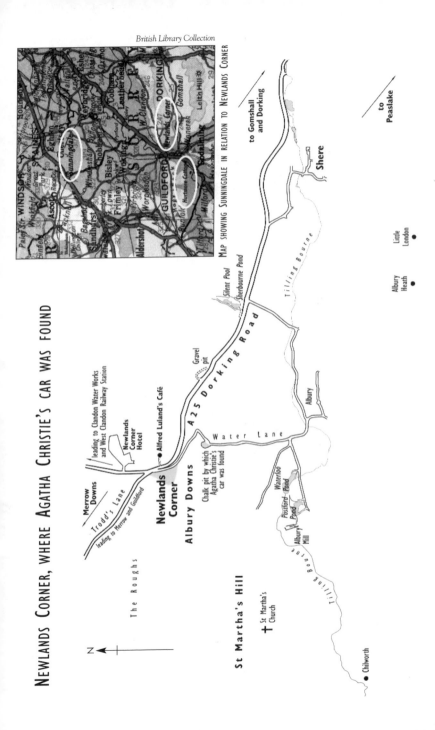

British Library Collection

MAP SHOWING SUNNINGDALE IN RELATION TO NEWLANDS CORNER

leading to Clandon Water Works and West Clandon Railway Station

Newlands Corner Hotel

Alfred Luland's Café

Merrow Downs

Trodd's Lane
leading to Merrow and Guildford

Newlands Corner

Albury Downs

Chalk pit by which Agatha Christie's car was found

The Roughs

A 25 Dorking Road

Gravel pit

Silent Pool

Sherbourne Pond

Water Lane

Albury

to Gomshall and Dorking

Tilling Bourne

Shere

St Martha's Hill

✝ St Martha's Church

Waterloo Pond

Postford Pond

Albury Mill

Tillingbourne

Chilworth

Albury Heath

Little London

to Peaslake

N

Berkshire Constabulary missing persons poster, 9 December 1926

Berkshire Record Office

Scenes from the 'Great Sunday Hunt', 12 December 1926, reproduced in the *Westminster Gazette*. Top right: Deputy Chief Constable Kenward of the Surrey Constabulary, who was convinced that Agatha had been murdered, directing the searches

Left: Front page of the *Daily Sketch*, 15 December 1926, after Agatha was found; pictures on the left show Agatha and Rosalind; on the right, Archie was no longer suspected of killing Agatha, diving operations for her body ceased, as did speculations regarding the hut in Clandon Wood

British Library Collection

Right: A smiling Agatha photographed during the journey to Abney Hall after her discovery; reproduced in the London *Evening News*, 16 December 1926

British Library Collection

Left: Front page of the *Daily Mirror*, 16 December 1926. Main picture shows Agatha with her sister Madge Watts in front; right shows Agatha entering her sister's car, people standing guard over the train at Leeds station in which Agatha travelled to Manchester, instead of continuing to King's Cross station, London, where crowds waited in vain

British Library Collection

Top: Albert Whiteley of the Harry Codd Dance Band who observed 'Mrs Neele' in the Harrogate Hydro ballroom

Christine Wilde Collection

Inset: Rosie Asher, the young hotel chambermaid; she was too afraid to go to the police with her suspicions

Patsy Robinson Collection

Left: Superintendent Goddard of the Berkshire Constabulary who always believed that Agatha was alive

Wokingham Times and Berkshire Record Office

Above: A flyleaf personally inscribed
by Agatha to Nan

Judith and Graham Gardner Collection

Above left: Nan's niece, Eleanor Watts, later Lady Campbell-Orde, who visited Agatha
at Abney Hall on 16 December 1926 after the writer was found

Mrs Jane Davies Collection

Above right: Nan, Agatha's sister-in-law and life-long friend, whose family closed ranks
and helped Archie hush up the scandal of her disappearance

Judith and Graham Gardner Collection

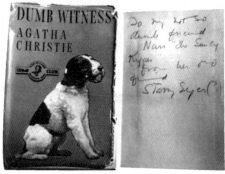

Above: Personal inscription from Agatha to Nan

Judith and Graham Gardner Collection

Top: On 24 January 1927 the *Daily Express* was just one of the many newspapers that reported Agatha's departure from England to the Canary Islands, five weeks after her disappearance

British Library Collection

Left: Agatha's 22-year-old nephew Jack with his father, Agatha's brother-in-law, Jimmy Watts, 1926

Mrs Jane Davies Collection

MURDER IS EASY

To my old friend
B. Huids

from
Agatha.

AGATHA
CHRISTIE

Left: Agatha with her brother-in-law Jimmy, one of two people who gave her the central idea for her novel *The Murder of Roger Ackroyd*, photographed outside Judith and Graham Gardner's house in Paignton, Devon, in the mid-1950s

Judith and Graham Gardner Collection

Below: Judith and Graham Gardner in the Middle East during the winter of 1962; Graham photographed the artefacts unearthed by Agatha's second husband Max Mallowan, the celebrated archaeologist

Judith and Graham Gardner Collection

Facing page (clockwise from top left): Charlotte Fisher, Agatha, Nan and Mary Fisher outside Greenway. Inset: Agatha and Judith, 1950

Judith and Graham Gardner Collection

Facing page (far left) and below: Two more inscriptions to Nan from Agatha

Judith and Graham Gardner Collection

Agatha Christie

Cat Among the Pigeons

CRIME CLUB CHOICE

Above: Max and Agatha photographed by the *Daily Sketch* on holiday in Toledo, Spain, 8 November 1967

Jared Cade Collection

Left: Lady Mallowan (Barbara Parker) after Max's death, c.1988

British School of Archaeology in Iraq and British Library Collection

16

HER HEELS DUG UP

THE REPORTS IN the daily papers on Wednesday the 15th should have provided a warning to the inhabitants of Abney Hall of the prolonged press siege they were to endure. During the night many reporters, refusing to admit defeat, slept outside the main entrances to the estate in chartered taxi cabs. The nation was agog to discover the reasons for Agatha's extraordinary conduct, and the press were determined to get to the bottom of the mystery.

After the Christies and Wattses had retreated behind doors the united front they had presented in public almost immediately dissolved into recriminations, and their agitation was not helped by mounting public pressure. Although the ground staff were instructed by Jimmy to keep a sharp eye out for trespassing journalists, Agatha was advised not to leave the house in case she was spotted. She had no desire to do so and retired to her room in an attempt to avoid the inevitable recriminations.

The *Daily News* sent her a bluntly worded telegram: 'In view of widespread criticisms of your disappearance strongly urge desirability of authentic explanation from yourself to thousands of the public who joined in costly search and shared anxiety and who cannot understand loss of memory theory in view of reports of your normal life at Harrogate and assumption of name of real person named Neele.'

Anxious to avoid further scandal, Archie telegraphed a response to the newspaper on her behalf: 'Wife suffering from loss of memory and probably concussion. She has no recollection of events on Friday or Saturday before arrival Harrogate. Has only recollected her true identity today. Remaining quietly under doctor's orders.'

The suggestion that Agatha had concussion failed to convince the press. Noise is anathema to someone who is concussed, and journalists knew that on the night of her arrival at the hotel in Harrogate she had energetically danced the Charleston to the accompaniment of a five-piece band. Reporters, reluctant to believe Archie's excuses of amnesia and concussion to explain his wife's strange behaviour, maintained falsely that she had regularly played the piano and sung in several languages during her stay.

It became apparent that something else had to be done to silence press doubts about the novelist's mental state. Madge and Jimmy persuaded Agatha to agree to a consultation with her family doctor. Her claim to Henry Wilson on the morning of Thursday the 16th to be unable to remember anything of her past was supported by her sister and brother-in-law, and Archie too played his part, emphasizing how upset his wife had been earlier in the year at her mother's death. Dr Wilson had signed Clarissa's death certificate, and what he was told about Agatha's grief was consistent with what he knew of her close relationship with her mother. The family impressed on him that newspaper reports of the 'normality' of her behaviour at the hotel could not be relied on and claimed that staff had told them that at times she had appeared distressed and disoriented.

Agatha was advised to rest by Dr Wilson in order to recover from her stressful ordeal. It was with some trepidation that her three co-conspirators fell in with the doctor's suggestion of calling in a second expert to confirm his diagnosis of amnesia.

Outside, the press refused to disperse from the main gates. Several ground staff on their way to work were forced to climb over the wall, and the baker was unable to deliver his order. Sidney Campion, the *Daily News*'s late-night reporter, has since recalled what prompted Archie to yield to journalists' demands for an interview:

> I came into the story quite fortuitously. I happened to be one of the late duty men at the *Daily News*, and I was rushed off to Harrogate because I happened to be a barrister in the making, the editor thinking that Agatha Christie would be amused to have a chap like me on her trail. Had it been Margery Allingham it might have been more appropriate for me to go, because her principal character was Inspector Campion [*sic*]. I

grant that I was in an exciting part of the story: I refer to the chase from Harrogate to Cheadle, Cheshire, where Colonel Christie blatantly demonstrated that the passport to success is the old school tie!

The journalists' waiting game outside Abney Hall finally paid off on the morning of Thursday 16 December, because by then Archie had realized they were determined to stay put. 'We shall stay here till we get news!' was their taunt, and at last Archie agreed to give an interview to one reporter to pass on to the rest. He scrutinized the fifty or sixty journalists and told John Young of the London *Evening News* he could have an interview – because the reporter was wearing the Colonel's old school tie.

Archie spent three-quarters of an hour on the terrace of Abney Hall unsuccessfully trying to convince him that Agatha could not remember the past three years nor recall details of her present life, including the fact she lived in Sunningdale in a house called Styles. John Young was asked to believe that Agatha had no recollection of leaving home or how she got to Harrogate. He was told that Agatha now recognized Archie and her sister but had been unable to remember their daughter when shown a picture of Rosalind. Archie confirmed that Agatha had been examined by a doctor and that a specialist in nervous disorders was coming to see her that afternoon.

Being an unimaginative man, he was ill-equipped to lie persuasively to an experienced journalist, and his responses to John Young's astute interrogation were defensive and unconvincing. Archie kept repeating it was a terrible tragedy and that all they wanted was to be left in peace.

However, medical specialists consulted by the *Evening News* had emphasized that loss of memory was a distressing condition and that Agatha could not have had amnesia as she would not have been able to talk calmly and dance with strangers, buy clothes and consistently maintain a false identity while staying in Harrogate. John Young emerged from the grounds of the mansion convinced that the writer had never lost her memory. He told his colleagues what Archie had said and expressed his doubts as to the veracity of the Colonel's statements.

Press speculation was far from ended. Archie's failure to account for the reason why Agatha had used the surname Neele resulted in reporters harassing the Neele family. Nancy's father, Charles, released a statement denying any relationship between his daughter and Archie. Reporters were given to believe that it had just been coincidence that Nancy had been at the home of the Jameses together with Colonel Christie on the night of his wife's disappearance and, in a particularly tactless remark, Nancy's father added that it might have been any other girl present. In fact Charles and Mabel Neele were appalled by their daughter's adulterous affair with Archie and were determined to put an end to it in order to salvage what was left of the family's reputation.

Sam James, Archie's host on the night of Agatha's disappearance, was having an equally hard time fending off the press. Sam stuck resolutely to his story, claiming that Archie and Nancy had previously been unacquainted with one another and that when he had heard Agatha was going to Beverley in Yorkshire he had invited Archie down for the weekend, unaware that his own wife, Madge, had invited Nancy. Disclosures in the newspapers that Nancy knew Agatha and had been a guest of the Christies at Styles could not have come at a worse time.

When Agatha was seen on Thursday afternoon by Donald Core, a Manchester specialist in nervous disorders, the consultation she had already had with Dr Wilson proved a satisfactory dress rehearsal. She maintained her story that she could not remember anything, and the two doctors were happy to accede to the family's request that they sign a brief statement to this effect; significantly this document did not endorse Archie's claim that Agatha had been suffering from concussion.

If the doctors had known what was really going on they would have been far from willing to back up the family's claim of amnesia. When Nan's eighteen-year-old niece Eleanor Watts (daughter of Nan's brother Humphrey and later to be Lady Campbell-Orde) came to tea that afternoon she was baffled to find Agatha reading one of her stories to Madge's 22-year-old son Jack: Agatha and her nephew had always been very close, and the normality of the scene could not have been at greater variance to the widespread reports of Agatha's distressed and confused mental state.

Although Archie could have had one of the servants deliver the signed medical bulletin to the journalists camped outside Abney Hall's gates on Thursday night, he preferred to do so himself, partly because he wished to project an image of someone who had nothing to hide and also because there was a danger that staff might say something indiscreet or allow themselves to be bribed by the press. He was accompanied by Dr Wilson, who had agreed to be present on the understanding that he would not be expected to speak to the press. The medical bulletin read as follows:

> December 16, 1926. – After careful examination of Mrs Agatha Christie this afternoon, we have formed the opinion that she is suffering from an unquestionably genuine loss of memory and that for her future welfare she should be spared all anxiety and excitement.
>
> (Signed) Donald Core, MD
> Henry Wilson, MRCS

Although Archie had no desire to say anything else to the pack of journalists, the medical statement left a number of questions unanswered, and he was heckled into further discussion. When asked to account for his wife's choice of name at Harrogate, he insisted, to the reporters' derision, that he and Agatha had a friend named Nancy Neele and that his wife had accidentally combined her surname with the Christian name of several of her relatives. Archie persisted in his claim that Agatha was suffering from probable concussion. When reporters asked Dr Wilson for confirmation of this, he said he was not prepared to comment.

In a stinging attack on the press Archie denied his intention of paying for the cost of the Surrey Constabulary's search, claiming that the police had felt the searches to be necessary to fend off newspaper accusations of negligence. Earlier that day he had been happy to read inaccurate reports in some of the newspapers that the only expense incurred by the Surrey police was the provision of tea and buns for the special

141

constables. He tactlessly berated the reporters for suggesting that his wife was faking amnesia and concussion and he categorically denied that her disappearance had been a stunt for increasing sales of her books or stage-managed in any way. He said he hoped that all publicity would cease so that 'my wife might be restored to normal health once more and be my companion throughout life'.

Shortly after he had performed his last public charade, nearly all pretence at family unity broke down, since Madge and Jimmy made it known that they thought that his disgraceful behaviour had been responsible for what had happened. Everyone at Abney Hall hoped that the press coverage on Friday the 17th would signal the end to an unfortunate drama that had dominated the front pages for nearly two weeks. Archie left Abney Hall early that morning to avoid further family recriminations.

Given that around 15,000 people went missing in Britain that year, why did Agatha's disappearance cause such a sensation? It was not just the fact that she was a mystery writer involved in her own real-life mystery. The answer perhaps lies in the fact that it was an unfolding drama whose resolution was both elusive and anxiously sought.

Despite the issuing of the medical bulletin, further embarrassing disclosures appeared in the newspapers on Friday the 17th. Although revelations concerning the diamond ring that had been posted to the novelist at the hotel were not wholly accurate, it coloured the public's perception of events. On the morning of Saturday the 4th Agatha had left the ring for repair at Harrods in London and had asked the store to send it on to her in the name of Mrs Teresa Neele at the Harrogate Hydro. The store had duly carried out these instructions, and Agatha had received it on Tuesday the 7th. Journalists were aware that the ring had been posted to Mrs Teresa Neele but wrongly stated it had been lost while she was shopping in a department store on the Saturday. At any rate it was obvious to readers that Agatha had been shopping in the West End on the morning after her disappearance and had evidently had a clear plan of her future movements.

The disclosure reinforced the public's perception of her as a shallow, publicity-seeking woman who had cleverly staged her disappearance as a stunt for increasing book sales. The public's belief that it had been a publicity stunt was reinforced over the next three months by the *Liverpool Weekly Post*'s and *Reynolds's Illustrated News*'s continuing serializations of *The Murder of Roger Ackroyd* and *The Murder on the Links*. But publicity for her books had been the last thing on Agatha's mind when she staged her disappearance; at the time she was bogged down half-way through *The Mystery of the Blue Train* and certainly not seeking the spotlight.

Vastly exaggerated estimates of the cost of the search appeared in the newspapers, ranging from £1,000 to £25,000. Letters from the public were published demanding to know whether Mrs Christie was prepared to reimburse the expenses incurred in the search. One indignant correspondent even suggested that no future book should be published under her name in order to discourage others from 'disappearing' as a publicity stunt. Agatha was also criticized for diverting attention from those who genuinely went missing.

A number of cartoons appeared, some more hurtful than others. 'Some People May Disappear For All We Care – And There Will Be No Search Parties,' declared the *Daily Express*'s cartoonist, depicting a rogues' gallery of characters lining up to catch the 'Disappearance Express'. *The Bulletin and Scots Pictorial* depicted 'a Jacket for the Book All About It', on which Agatha was caricatured, elegantly dressed, dancing in the arms of a shadowy male companion, while beneath their feet was pictured the Surrey Downs being extensively searched. The title on the cover of the book was 'My Pretty Dance by Agatha Christie'.

Trevor Allen of the *Westminster Gazette*, recalling how enthusiastically the public had responded to the *Daily News*'s offer of a £100 reward for the discovery of the novelist, suggested that if no one famous went missing why not challenge the public to unmask someone paid to disappear? A series of individuals were employed by the *Westminster Gazette* to play the part of Mr Lobby Ludd whose photograph, together with a general timetable of his movements around the country, was published in advance and the first person to rush up with a copy of his newspaper picture and announce: 'You are Mr Lobby Ludd, and I hereby claim my £10 pounds!' was rewarded on the spot. Those who missed out could read news reports on the chases, many of which led the latest Mr Lobby Ludd to be mobbed. When the *Westminster Gazette* amalgamated in 1931 with the *Daily News* to become the *News Chronicle*, this popular tradition continued for many years.

Although the story began to die down after Friday the 17th, it did not mean the worst was over for Agatha and her family, whose lives had been splashed across newspapers throughout the country. Now they had to assess the damage and begin to rebuild their lives, and these tasks would not be made easier by reminders of the past.

17

A Trip to the Canaries

SHORTLY AFTER ARCHIE'S departure from Abney Hall the Surrey Constabulary took the unprecedented step of approaching him to reimburse the cost of the search. He was shocked at the amount.

The Surrey Standing Joint Committee met on Saturday 18 December, two days after its hastily issued statement to the press about the only expense being refreshments for the special constables. The committee now decided that the overall cost of the Surrey search was £25.

Archie refused to pay and, indeed, was not legally obliged to do so, yet the fact he was asked to foot the bill indicated that the Surrey police, like their Berkshire counterparts, were sceptical of the family's claims that Agatha had lost her memory and that this accounted for her disappearance.

Christmas provided a brief respite for the writer's friends and relatives. Once reunited at Abney Hall with Agatha, a defiant Nan confronted her family, whose anger towards her was mitigated by their relief that Agatha had been discovered alive. Nan had been every bit as horrified as her sister-in-law when the press had got hold of the story and, despite the fact that they had both been taken unawares by the backlash, the two friends remained as loyal and devoted to each other as ever.

Family hostilities were temporarily suspended to allow Archie to bring Rosalind to Abney Hall on Wednesday 22 December to see her mother for the first time in three weeks. The poignant reunion with her seven-year-old reinforced in Agatha's mind her pledge of five months earlier to keep the marriage going for a year, so that Archie could be sure he was not making a mistake in divorcing her and becoming separated from his daughter.

Archie believed that Agatha was being vindictive in refusing to agree to an immediate divorce, but she felt it important to try to keep the family together for a full year, so she would later be able to tell Rosalind she had done everything she could to try to restore the marriage. Nor was Archie happy that Nancy's parents had sent their daughter on a ten-month voyage round the world in the hope that she would forget him.

After Christmas Archie returned to Styles to put it on the market, since neither Agatha nor he had any desire to live there again. The two bandsmen who had gone to the police each received – unbeknown to Agatha – a silver cigarette case from Archie with their initials engraved on the front and the inscription inside: 'With our very best thanks, Col. and Mrs Christie'. Archie sent a pencil to each of the other bandsmen. Ironically, none of the band members believed in the amnesia theory; Bob Leeming privately opined that she had gone to Harrogate to 'sort out a domestic problem'.

Charlotte remained loyal to Agatha, despite the notoriety that had befallen her employer, and Nan considered the secretary 'a pearl'. Other so-called friends and acquaintances did not remain so steadfast, and Agatha was to divide the people she knew into two categories: the 'FOD' (Faithful Order of Dogs) and the 'FOR' (Faithless Order of Rats).

Although the disappearance no longer occupied the front pages occasional references were made to it throughout the first half of 1927, which caused consternation and embarrassment for Agatha and those close to her. In one instance it was reported that a Willesden magistrate had told a deserted wife: 'You must supply your husband's address for service of summons. You are not Mrs Christie, and we cannot concentrate all police resources on your case.' The Surrey police received enough unsolicited donations from the public towards the cost of the search to pay for the building of a house. In order to stem the flow of contributions the Surrey police were forced to issue a statement to the press stating they were returning all the money they had been sent.

Five weeks after the disappearance Agatha left the country for the Canary Islands, accompanied by Rosalind and Charlotte. After preparing for their trip at Ashfield the trio travelled by train to Southampton, where they spent the night of Saturday 22 January 1927 at the South Western Hotel. The following day they boarded the liner *Geiria,* which was on its way from Amsterdam to the United States.

In Agatha's memoirs, which make no reference to the disappearance, she ambiguously states that 'in February of the following year' she took her secretary and daughter to the Canaries in order to finish her manuscript *The Mystery of the Blue Train.* This statement, immediately following Agatha's brief, veiled remark regarding Archie's request for a divorce – 'I held out for a year, hoping he would change' – has led many commentators to assume, wrongly, that the trip took place in February 1928. This was almost certainly Agatha's intention. But *The Mystery of the Blue Train* was serialized in *The Star* newspaper throughout February 1928 and published by Collins on 2 March that year.

An unpleasant incident occurred before their departure on the Sunday, when she was accosted by a *Daily Express* reporter. She had presumed that no one outside her circle of family and friends knew of her plans to visit the Canaries for a month and, after declining to say anything, she hurriedly joined her daughter and secretary on board the *Geiria.*

The Big Four was published four days after her departure by Collins on 27 January 1927, thus negating her claim in her autobiography that the book was worked on throughout that year instead of the preceding one. The *Daily News*'s reviewer, looking for parallels with her recent disappearance, was quick to quote the Scotland Yard inspector in the book: 'Either it's Apache work, and that's the end of it – or else it's voluntary disappearances – and that's a great deal the commoner of the two, I can tell you.' Incredibly, reviewers failed to comment on the most intriguing aspect of the plot: Hercule Poirot heroically fakes his own death in order to save mankind from a global conspiracy. Agatha loathed *The Big Four* for the rest of her life because it reinforced the fact that while her fictional characters responded to her wishes the same was not true of real people. The novel reminded her of the unhappy period in which she had unwisely attempted to exact a revenge on the husband who had betrayed her. She always referred to it as 'that rotten book'.

The novelist and her two companions stayed first at La Orotava on the island of Tenerife, but they left after a week as the morning mists and fogs obscured much of the mountainous beauty and reminded Agatha too much of England and the events she was trying to put behind her. The Metropole Hotel in Las Palmas, on another island, Gran Canaria, which Agatha later used as the setting in the Miss Marple short story 'The Companion', was much more to her liking.

Agatha devoted her days to finishing *The Mystery of the Blue Train*. The sheer will-power it took Agatha to complete this book resulted in her lifelong antipathy towards this book too. Her motive for denouncing it 'as easily the worst book I ever wrote' in her autobiography was deliberately to draw a veil over that period of her life preceding her divorce. Her disparagement of *The Big Four*, which is certainly not one of her best novels, and the much better *The Mystery of the Blue Train* was her attempt to distance herself and others from painful aspects of her past.

While in Las Palmas Agatha discovered that she was beset by the same worries and preoccupations that she had hoped to leave behind in England. She recognized that running away from difficulties solved nothing. Nevertheless, Las Palmas was the perfect place to recharge her batteries in the warmth of the sun and to indulge in the therapeutic pleasures of bathing. By removing herself physically from the immediate shadow of her past she was able to view the present with greater clarity.

The ending of *The Mystery of the Blue Train* (which was dedicated to 'Two Distinguished Members of the FOD, Carlotta and Peter'; that is, Charlotte, her secretary, and her dog) makes clear Agatha's determination to move on, despite her uncertainties over her future. A lovelorn American girl observes: 'Trains are relentless things, aren't they, Monsieur Poirot? People get murdered and die, but they go on all the same.' Poirot sympathetically replies: 'Trust the train, Mademoiselle, for it is *le bon Dieu* who drives it . . .' Although Agatha was still too shaken by her personal problems to re-evaluate her relationship with God, it would seem she was seeking to reassure herself that it is not the past that matters but the future.

18

Questions in Parliament

WHILE AGATHA WAS abroad Members of Parliament in the House of Commons were raising the issue of the cost of the search. When it was revealed on 10 February 1927 that expenses incurred by Scotland Yard had cost the Exchequer £12 10s., the Labour Party MP William Lunn swiftly denounced the disappearance as a 'cruel hoax'. On the 25th, however, there was surprise in the Commons when the Home Secretary did a complete volte-face and announced that the cost had been nothing.

So what happened to the £12 10s? After further review Scotland Yard had decided that the outstanding amount could be covered by one of its existing budgets for 'normal police duties'. As for the other legitimate costs, should the 'six to seven pounds' spent by Archie on the missing persons posters issued by the Berkshire Constabulary, along with the £25 spent by the Surrey Constabulary have been added to the £12 10s., then the combined cost of the search to the three major investigating police forces, if publicly acknowledged, would have amounted to either £44 10s. or £43 10s. By today's standards the amounts seem negligible, but they should be compared to the average weekly wage in 1926 for a police constable of £3 10s. Since Parliament had merely sought to clarify how much the search had cost Scotland Yard, this was now officially declared to have been nothing.

Ultimately, as far as the members of the public were concerned, the issue was not about cost; it was about class. The disappearance had come hard on the heels of the General Strike, and what the working class wanted to know was whether it could expect similarly intensive searches to be conducted for one of its own – and the conclusion reached had been a resounding no.

After she returned to England in late February 1927 Agatha looked around Chelsea for somewhere to live in order to be near Nan. The writer bought a small mews house at 22 Cresswell Place, a few streets from 78 Chelsea Park Gardens. Judith Gardner recalls that she and her mother Nan were among the first to be shown over Agatha's new home with its narrow stairs and tiny kitchen. Agatha enjoyed playing with Judith, finding in her company a welcome distraction from her problems. Moreover Judith and Rosalind were firm friends, and this pleased Agatha as she had been worried that her daughter would be lonely after being uprooted from Sunningdale.

Agatha's first priority after moving into Cresswell Place was to find a boarding school for Rosalind. Together they visited several and Rosalind finally settled on Caledonia School in Bexhill, Sussex. It proved a good choice. She was happy there and achieved good marks. Once, however, she wrote to her mother complaining that on Sunday nights the other pupils had just one letter to write to their parents, whereas she had two. Agatha was never to forget Rosalind's upset at the break-up of her marriage to Archie.

The writer next spent some time renovating and decorating the house. Unlike Nan, whose home was decorated quite conventionally with mahogany and chintz, Agatha went in for exotic wallpapers, a good deal of bric-à-brac and papier mâché and inlaid mother-of-pearl *objets*. Even the doorknobs were decorated with attractive floral patterns. Judith was very taken with it all and always enjoyed visiting Agatha's house.

Judith's mother Nan, meanwhile, was finding life complicated. There was friction in the Kon household – and not simply because she had been forced to tell her husband, George, that Agatha had spent the night of the disappearance in the house in Chelsea Park Gardens. For a short time he made a habit of bringing Archie back to the house after playing golf with him at weekends. Nan was horrified when she first discovered this, insisting that Agatha would be very upset if she knew of Archie's visits. George, however, was not prepared to let the Colonel down: Archie had been through hell over the disappearance, and George was determined to stand by his friend.

Archie was lonely and despondent as Nancy was on her enforced voyage around the world, and Nan lived in dread of Agatha finding out about his visits. Nan felt as if she was betraying her friend, and she gave her daughter strict instructions not to say a word about the matter to Agatha. Judith obeyed, and they successfully managed to prevent Archie and Agatha from bumping into each other in their house or Agatha from finding out about his visits.

Agatha believed she had become better equipped to deal with life's vicissitudes after surviving the breakdown of her marriage. She was, however, wary of men and especially the possibility of romantic entanglements. She could not imagine ever trusting a man again or allowing a lover to get close enough to hurt her, although she toyed momentarily with the idea of having brief affairs [SUSSEX-last ch.]

'The Edge' was one of Agatha's most compelling stories, but too many people guessed it was about her and Nancy when it was published in February 1927 in *Pearson's Magazine* and, despite repeated requests, Agatha did not allow it to be republished in her lifetime. But there were still bills to be paid, and work provided distraction from her continuing unhappiness. The May edition of *The Story-Teller* saw the publication of 'Harlequin's Lane', and this time the Archie–Agatha–Nancy triangle was more cleverly concealed.

'Harlequin's Lane' is a mystical story full of symbolism that gives an intriguing insight into Agatha's emotional state. John Denman, plainly based on Archie, is described as a respected business man, clever in his work but lacking in imagination outside it. His wife Anna is full of turbulent emotion owing to the discovery of her husband's infidelity. John Denman tells Molly Stanwell, a local village girl with whom he has fallen in love, that he cannot live without her.

After secretly witnessing the exchange between the two lovers, Anna proceeds to the home of Lady Roscheimer who is staging a Harlequinade concert that night. One of the female dancers has been injured, and Anna finds herself dancing opposite her former lover, Prince Sergius Oranoff. This character is obviously based on Reggie Lucy, the man Agatha was engaged to before Archie came into her life. Anna has jilted Prince Sergius Oranoff in favour of John Denman, but dancing with her former lover reawakens their ardour for each other. Ironically it also revitalizes John Denman's interest in his wife. But Anna recognizes that it is impossible to turn the clock back. She is no longer able to put up with her intolerable situation. She announces that for ten years she has lived with the man she loved and that now she is going to the man who for ten years has loved her.

Prince Oranoff waits in anticipation for Anna in Harlequin's Lane, but tragically the two former lovers are not reunited. At the end of the 'lovers' lane' is a rubbish heap overlooked by 'a house of dreams'. The guests at the house-party find Anna's body; she has been killed by some supernatural force. No explanation is given for her death, although her words earlier that evening perhaps offer a clue. She said there could be no third way out of her predicament; that one always looks for one thing, the perfect, eternal lover, and that it was the music of Harlequin, the protector of lovers, that one longed to hear. She maintained that no one lover could ever prove satisfactory, for all lovers were mortal. And Harlequin was only a myth, an invisible presence – unless, she added, his name was death. 'Harlequin's Lane' perfectly expresses Agatha's incurable romanticism.

Having jilted Reggie – he had since married – there was not the slightest possibility of rekindling their romance. She had taken a risk when she married Archie and, understandably, she had regrets over her broken engagement to Reggie. She realized she could have been happy with him, although she knew she would not have loved him as ardently as she had loved Archie. Archie had been her great love and passion; the marriage had failed, and what followed was a form of emotional death, symbolized by the fate of Anna.

A significant development in Agatha's work was her creation of the shrewd and intuitive Miss Marple. Most commentators of Agatha's literary output mistake the date the sleuth made her first appearance because they assume it to be her manifestation in the 1930 novel *The Murder at the Vicarage*. In fact her début came in a series of six stories appearing over as many months in the *Royal Magazine* from December 1927.

Miss Marple was the complete opposite of the young and impulsive heroines that had previously dominated Agatha's fiction. Based partly on her creator's Ealing grandmother, Miss Marple suspected the worst of everyone and everything often with uncanny accuracy and was firmly of the opinion that charming men were not to be trusted around young, naive girls. Given Agatha's emotional turmoil, it is poignant that she should have created the persona of the wise and belligerent old lady she herself was so far from being.

The effect of the authoress's disappearance on the sales of her books was to prove highly beneficial in the next three years: *The Big Four*'s sales reached 8,500 copies (topping its predecessor by 3,000 copies); nearly 7,000 copies of *The Mystery of Blue Train* were sold; while sales of *The Seven Dials Mystery* were in excess of 8,000.

The year 1927 was a period of emotional recovery for Agatha and happier times lay ahead. But the professional acclaim that awaited her was to be eclipsed by press gossip in the newspapers arising from a resurgence of public interest in her disappearance, leading to her only statement on the incident and the one thing she dreaded most: divorce.

19

Sequel to the Ripley Road Hold-up

DIVORCE WAS THE last thing Agatha wanted, but Archie was determined to end the marriage in the eyes of the law. Rosalind was far from happy about it and repeatedly told her mother: 'It's you he doesn't like. Not me.' These were not easy words for Agatha to hear, and she entreated her estranged husband to reconsider for their daughter's sake. She promised not to discuss his infidelities if he returned to her. But there was to be no turning back.

The love Archie and Nancy had for one another was undiminished; her reputation was of paramount concern to him and they lived apart on her return from her enforced trip – Nancy at her parents' home and Archie at 9 Upper Grosvenor Street, London. The couple had snatched, clandestine meetings; Nancy's parents did not want the relationship to be resumed, as they did not believe that Archie would behave honourably and marry their daughter.

Archie regarded Agatha as an obstacle to his happiness and was determined to marry Nancy. Since she could not bear to be hated by the man she loved, Agatha finally agreed to divorce him. The arrangement with Archie was that Agatha should not cite Nancy as the third party in the divorce in return for custody of Rosalind. Despite her deep repugnance at Archie's hypocrisy, Agatha was forced to comply with his wishes. He made it clear that if she did not he would tell the court that she had disappeared as a publicity stunt; he was prepared for a battle if Agatha made things difficult. She was terrified of further notoriety and agreed not to contest the evidence he would supply pertaining to his declaration of adultery with an unknown woman.

Meanwhile, Agatha had to obtain legal advice in February 1928 owing to the fact that her disappearance had become linked in the newspapers to what was known as the Ripley Road hold-up. The incident had taken place in Surrey on the night of 14 January 1927 after a Liberal Party club dinner in London, where the guest speaker, the well-known explorer Frederick Mitchell-Hedges, had denounced contemporary youth as 'knock-kneed Charlestoning men with no spirit of adventure'. Mitchell-Hedges falsely claimed to have been 'attacked' that night on the Ripley Road by indignant youths who had sought to teach him a lesson and who had stolen his Monomarks stamped briefcase. When the *Daily Express* accused Mitchell-Hedges of instigating a publicity stunt for Monomarks, he had unwisely stuck to his fabricated story and tried unsuccessfully to sue the newspaper for libel.

The libel trial, which occurred in February 1928, exposed a number of glaring discrepancies in Mitchell-Hedges's account of events: instead of immediately reporting the ambush to the nearest police station Mitchell-Hedges and his party had driven several miles to Guildford Police Station to report the matter to Superintendent Boshier – the same officer who had investigated Agatha's disappearance. One of Mitchell-Hedges's companions in the car had fainted under police interrogation and had later given a contradictory account; it was also demonstrated in court that the rope the bandits were alleged to have tied up Mitchell-Hedges's chauffeur with was in fact string; it was proved in court that the so-called bandits were actually friends of Mitchell-Hedges and that their chauffeur was the brother of his chauffeur. In a heated exchange, the prosecution compared the Ripley Road hold-up to Agatha's disappearance by citing the novelist as 'a woman who played a foolish hoax on the police'.

Although the Mitchell-Hedges trial was not the first time Agatha's disappearance had been alluded to as a hoax, the renewed publicity could not have come at a worse time, since her divorce was just two months away. Agatha knew that if proceedings became acrimonious her failure to defend herself against this slur on her reputation could be used against her by Archie. She therefore instructed her lawyer, Stuart Bevan, to make a statement during the Mitchell-Hedges case on her behalf, as well as to present to the judge the statement issued by the two doctors. Her lawyer's appeal for the judge's indulgence in the matter was denied, and Agatha had no alternative other than to defend herself publicly, since she was advised that it was possible for a husband to gain custody of a child if good reason was demonstrated in court.

Encouraged by Nan, Agatha broke what would otherwise have amounted to a lifetime's silence on her disappearance to give an interview to the *Daily Mail* on Wednesday 15 February 1928 which was published the following day. Her fictionalized account of her movements on the night of the disappearance naturally excluded all references to Nan. Agatha claimed to have developed amnesia after unsuccessfully trying to kill herself, and she confused things further by inaccurately stating she had called herself Tessa Neele. She gave the impression that she had developed a case of secondary personality as well as amnesia. Her claim that she had pointed out to several people at the Harrogate Hydro that she looked like Mrs Christie was false and was intended to transfer to others the blame for having failed to recognize her sooner. Contrary to what she told the *Daily Mail*, Agatha had not left home at ten o'clock on the night of the disappearance, and the *Daily Mail* was quick to point this out. It also commented on the fact that she was living in Chelsea with her daughter and was 'once again looking in excellent health'.

What Agatha's explanation did not take into account is that one cannot suffer from loss of memory and secondary personality at the same time. Medical experts are united on this. Agatha's disingenuous explanation, reproduced here in full after seventy years of obscurity, is all the more revealing because she unwittingly confused the symptoms of the two very different psychological conditions.

I thought everybody had forgotten about the affair, but the reference in the libel suit shows that many people still think I deliberately disappeared. Of course I know that at the time a large number of people thought I had gone away to seek publicity, to carry out a stupid hoax, or to have a subtle revenge on somebody.

What actually happened was this. I left home that night in a state of high nervous strain with the intention of doing something desperate. I drove in my car over the crest of the Downs in the direction of a quarry. The car struck something, and I was flung against the steering wheel and injured my chest and my head. I was dazed by the blow and lost my memory. For 24 hours I wandered in a dream and then found myself at Harrogate a well-contented and perfectly happy woman who believed she had just come from South Africa.

The trouble really began with the death of my mother in the spring of 1926. That affected me very deeply, and on top of this shock there came a number of private troubles, into which I would rather not enter. Instead of sleeping well, as I had done previously, I began to suffer from insomnia, and slept on the average only two hours a night.

On the day of my disappearance I drove over in the afternoon to Dorking with my daughter to see a relative. I was at this time in a very despondent state of mind. I just wanted my life to end. As I passed by Newlands Corner that afternoon I saw a quarry and there came into my mind the thought of driving into it. However, as my daughter was with me in the car, I dismissed the idea at once.

That night I felt terribly miserable. I felt that I could go on no longer. I left home at 10 o'clock in my car with a few articles of clothing in a suitcase and about £60 in my bag. I had drawn some money from the bank shortly before as I had decided to go that winter to South Africa with my daughter, and I wanted to make preparations.

All that night I drove aimlessly about. In my mind there was the vague idea of ending everything. I drove automatically down roads I knew, but without thinking where I was going. As far as I remember I went to London and drove to Euston Station. Why I went there I do not know. I believe I then drove out to Maidenhead, where I looked at the river. I thought about jumping in, but realised that I could swim too well to drown. I then drove back to London again, and then on to Sunningdale. From there I went to Newlands Corner.

When I reached a point on the road which I thought was near the quarry I had seen in the afternoon, I turned the car off the road down the hill towards it. I left the wheel and let the car run. The car struck something with a jerk and pulled up suddenly. I was flung against the steering wheel, and my head hit something.

Up to this moment I was Mrs Christie. I was certainly in an abnormal state of mind, and scarcely knew what I was doing or where I was going. All the same I knew I was Mrs Christie. After the accident in the car, however, I lost my memory. For 24 hours after the accident my mind was an almost complete blank. Since I recovered my health I have managed to recall a little of what happened in those 24 hours.

I remember arriving at a big railway station and asking what it was and being surprised to learn it was Waterloo. It is strange that the railway authorities there did not recall me, as I was covered with mud and I had smeared blood on my face from a cut on my hand. I could never make out how this cut had been caused. I believe I wandered about London and I then remember arriving at the hotel in Harrogate. I was still muddy and showed signs of my accident when I arrived there. I had now become in my mind Mrs Tessa Neele of South Africa.

I can quite understand why I went to Harrogate. The motor-car accident brought on neuritis, and once before in my life I had thought of going to Harrogate to have treatment for this complaint. While I was in Harrogate I had treatment regularly. The only thing which really puzzled me was the fact that I had scarcely any luggage with me. I could not quite make this out. I had not even a toothbrush in my case, and I wondered why I had come there without one.

I realised, of course, that I had been in some kind of accident. I had a severe bruise on my chest, and my head was also bruised. As Mrs Neele I was very happy and contented. I had become, as it were, a new woman, and all the worries and anxieties of Mrs Christie had left me. When I was brought back to my life as Mrs Christie once again many of my worries and anxieties returned, and although I am now quite well and cheerful and have lost my old morbid tendencies completely I have not quite that utter happiness of Mrs Neele.

At Harrogate I read every day about Mrs Christie's disappearance and came to the conclusion that she was dead. I regarded her as having acted stupidly. I was greatly struck by my resemblance to her and pointed it out to other people in the hotel. It never occurred to me that I might be her, as I was quite satisfied in my mind as to who I was. I thought I was a widow, and that I had had a son who had died, for I had in my bag a photograph of my little girl when young with the name 'Teddy' upon it. I even tried to obtain a book by this Mrs Christie to read.

When I was finally discovered it was not for some time that doctors and relatives restored to my mind memories of my life as Mrs Christie. These memories were drawn from my subconscious mind slowly. First I recalled my childhood days and thought of relatives and friends as they were when children. By gradual steps I recalled later and later episodes in my life until I could remember what happened just before the motor accident. The doctors even made me try to recall the events in the blank 24 hours afterwards, as they said that for the health of my mind there should be no hiatus of any kind in my recollections. That is why I can now recall at the same time my existence as Mrs Christie and Mrs Neele.

Of course a person with amnesia would have no difficulty in recognizing her true identity on seeing herself in the newspapers. A distinguished London psychiatrist consulted in the research for this book has confirmed that if Agatha had incurred a blow to her head her memory loss would have been most unlikely to last more than three or four days. The fact that she signed herself into the hotel register as Mrs Teresa Neele from Cape Town on 4 December 1926, borrowed library books under the same name on Monday the 6th, then later that week placed an advertisement in *The Times* using the name and answered to the same name throughout her hotel stay is not consistent with amnesia. The actions are the hallmarks of someone who has assumed a secondary personality or, alternatively, fashioned a new identity for an ulterior motive. Another eminent psychiatrist commented: 'An amnesiac wouldn't invent another name for themselves because they would be too busy trying to remember their own.'

Agatha's story also fails to account for the fact that it is impossible to see the chalk pit, into which her car almost crashed, when driving past Newlands Corner, because the brow of the hill obscures the pit, which is some three hundred yards further down the hill. Furthermore, if her car had been deliberately driven off the road at high speed the gearstick would not have been in neutral.

Fortunately for Agatha most readers of her explanation were not medical experts, nor were they familiar with Newlands Corner or the circumstances in which the car was found, so her version of events had the effect of reaffirming the official explanation by her family and the two doctors.

On Friday 20 April 1928, dressed in a brown tweed jacket and skirt, cloche hat and marten fur stole, Agatha faced a further ordeal when she testified in court that she wanted to divorce Archie. She abhorred the intensely personal questions put to her in the witness stand. Worst of all, she hated colluding with Archie, whose lawyers had presented evidence fabricated on his behalf, claiming that he had committed adultery in London's Grosvenor Hotel with an unnamed woman. The judge, Lord Merrivale, was not deceived by Archie's evidence, and in granting a provisional divorce and giving custody of nine-year-old Rosalind to Agatha his concluding statement implied sympathy for her: 'When a gallant gentleman frequents hotels with a woman in order to secure release from a marriage he dislikes I have no course but to grant a decree.'

Agatha had to wait six months before the divorce was finalized. Owing to the furore over her disappearance, film producers were drawn to her crime stories, and that year saw the release of a German-made film, *Die Abenteuer GmbH*, which was based on *The Secret Adversary*, and *The Passing of Mr Quin*, a British film that was a grotesque travesty of Agatha's original story. There was, however, a successful stage adaptation of *The Murder of Roger Ackroyd*, which opened under the title *Alibi* on 15 May at the Prince of Wales Theatre in London. Reviews of the opening-night performance mentioned that when the time had come for Agatha to take a bow with the rest of the cast she had remained hidden at the back of her box, denying the audience the opportunity of seeing the woman who had become so famous.

Agatha was understandably at a low ebb as she waited for her divorce papers, and she spent much of her time writing her first non-crime novel. *Giant's Bread*, which was the first of her books to be published under the secret pseudonym of Mary Westmacott, contained a number of autobiographical touches. The childhood of the protagonist, Vernon Deyre, has much in common with Agatha's own. He plays with the same imaginary characters as she did and develops a fanatical love for his childhood home. He also has disturbing dreams of 'the Beast', reminiscent of those Agatha had of the Gun Man.

When Vernon reaches adulthood, he discovers a latent artistic talent for musical composition. His wife Nell experiences poverty in the early stages of their marriage, just as Agatha did with Archie. Nell's experiences as a nurse during the First World War are also based on Agatha's. The other woman in Vernon's life is his unacknowledged mistress, Jane, who strains her voice and is forced to give up her career as an opera singer. After becoming a prisoner of war Vernon is presumed dead. He escapes and discovers through a magazine article that his wife has remarried. The shock results in him stepping in front of a lorry, being knocked down and developing amnesia for nearly four years.

Many have assumed that Agatha was imbuing Vernon with aspects of her own experience of memory loss, but nothing could be further from the truth: in a wholly unrealistic scenario he simultaneously assumes the 'secondary personality' of an ex-deserter, Corporal George Green of the London Fusiliers. Agatha had the valuable knack of perceiving life as did 99 per cent of her reading public, and her lack of specialist knowledge about amnesia was not radically different from the overblown imaginings of her fellow writers; nor was it challenged.

After 'recovering' his true identity Vernon finds himself travelling on a ship when it collides with an iceberg. When the boat lists dangerously and the two women he loves most slide down the deck towards him on their way to an icy death, he has only one free hand with which to reach out to save one of them. Vernon instinctively saves his former wife, because he has known her longer than his mistress. In her way Agatha was reconciling herself with the belief that it would take a similar melodramatic scenario for Archie to choose her over Nancy.

While *Giant's Bread* has an undeniably unrealistic and melodramatic story-line, it is none the less very readable. The novel explores the inequality of love between the sexes, and what remains striking about the book is that love and happiness elude all the main characters. The book ends, like a reflected image of Agatha's circumstances in 1928 when it was written, with the anti-hero Vernon, who has suffered most in love, deciding not to risk future heartbreak by avoiding relationships, immersing himself instead in his art.

Agatha's divorce was finalized on 29 October 1928, and less than three weeks later Archie married Nancy on 16 November in a private ceremony at St George's church in Hanover Square, London. Although their marriage went a long way to pacify Nancy's parents it was always a matter of regret for them that their daughter had married a divorced man.

Agatha's immediate reaction to the divorce was to tell her publishers that she wished to publish her detective novels and stories under another name. Sir Godfrey Collins, however, dissuaded her from this because he knew that such a change would confuse her readership. Nevertheless Agatha was so upset by the break-up of her marriage that she never saw Archie again.

She was always to regret that he had not cited Nancy as the third party in the divorce case. If he had done so Agatha could have told her daughter that she had had no other choice than to divorce him. By agreeing to the deception she felt she had participated in a lie and irrationally believed she had betrayed her daughter for the man she still loved.

Although the worst of Agatha's misery was over and she could now move on to a new life, the future was not made easier by constant reminders of the past. She was never to forget the man she loved nor the notoriety caused by her disastrous scheme for revenge.

Part 3

WHILE THE LIGHT LASTS

20

PARTNERS IN CRIME

AFTER HER DIVORCE Agatha had to accept the fact that her love for Archie had been no safeguard against his defection. Nor was his passion for Nancy a short-lived affair, as the couple were to live together happily for many years. Agatha soon came to realize that Archie would for ever remain the grand passion of her life – 'the Man from the Sea' for whom she had left safe shores and swum into uncharted waters. Although a number of changes she made in her life were to enrich her creatively, culturally, socially and financially, she was unable to put the past behind her completely, no matter how hard she tried. 'Agatha never got over Archie,' recalls Nan's daughter Judith.

Agatha's plans to have a holiday in the West Indies underwent a radical alteration in the autumn of 1928 when she met a married couple at a dinner party just two days before her anticipated departure. They had recently returned from Baghdad and spoke so glowingly about their stay that Agatha, on learning that it was possible to travel there on the fabled Orient Express, cancelled her trip to the West Indies and booked herself a ticket to the Middle East.

Rosalind was at school and Agatha decided to travel alone. Her secretary wondered if it was prudent for Agatha to do this, but she found 'safety at all costs' a repulsive creed. It was an important decision. She could cling to a life that was familiar and predictable or she could develop her independence.

The journey began badly. On the train Agatha met an experienced and overbearing woman traveller who attempted to take her under her wing. Unfortunately the woman was going all the way to Baghdad and promised to introduce Agatha to the social life of the English community. Agatha was anxious to avoid this. The two parted company, to

Agatha's relief, when the woman left the train at Trieste to continue her journey by boat.

Agatha remained on the train, which passed through Yugoslavia and the Balkans. She found the mountains and gorges awesome and took little interest in her fellow passengers. After the train entered Asia the frantic pace of modern civilization seemed to recede and time became less significant. The train stopped briefly and the passengers disembarked to admire the sight of the Cilician Gates by sunset. In her memoirs Agatha recorded that she was glad she had come, as a feeling of 'thankfulness and joy' overcame her.

Her journey continued through Turkey and into Syria. She became feverish after being bitten by bedbugs on the train but soon recovered, and was well enough to be shown around Damascus by a Thomas Cook guide and enjoyed visiting the bazaars at Baalbek in the Lebanon.

She then travelled across the desert to Baghdad accompanied once again by the well-intentioned but suffocating female companion from whom she had earlier parted at Trieste. She survived the two-day journey across the desert, however, which she found both fascinating and sinister. She recounted that the desert gave her a curious feeling of 'being enclosed rather than surrounded by a void'. She was invigorated by the sharp air, the feel of the sand running through her fingers, the beauty of the rising sun and the taste of simple food cooked on a Primus stove. She felt at peace with life and herself.

Once in Baghdad she was introduced to the husband of her travelling companion and was taken off to their home. She had intended to book into a hotel, but it was impossible to fend off their goodwill. Despite being caught up in the social whirl of the English colony in the city, she was still able to enjoy its sights, sounds and smells. She was entranced by the rickety buildings, the beautiful mosques and the gardens full of flowers.

She finally made her escape from her host and hostess. A highlight of her trip was a visit to the famous death pits at Ur, which were being excavated by Professor Leonard Woolley and a team of experts. Visitors to the dig were a constant source of annoyance since they interrupted the work, and Agatha initially owed her favourable reception to the fact that Leonard Woolley's wife had greatly enjoyed *The Murder of Roger Ackroyd*.

The relationship Agatha forged with the Woolleys was to alter the course of her life. Leonard was a quiet, rather snobbish scholar who tended to defer to his temperamental wife Katherine, whose first husband had shot himself in front of the Great Pyramid. Her friendship with Agatha came about partly because the two women had suffered in love; each recognized the pain through which the other had gone. Although Katherine loved Leonard and craved affection, she was terrified of allowing him, or anyone else, to get too close to her in case she was rejected. This resulted in a tendency in her to lead men on only to reject and humiliate them when they got serious about her. She was to become the basis for the character of the victim in *Murder in Mesopotamia*.

The writer's readiness to act as a sidekick to the flamboyant and wilful Katherine ensured that their friendship grew; also Katherine had enormous respect for Agatha's literary achievements.

Agatha was never to forget a meeting in Baghdad with a rather solitary man called Maurice Vickers, who lent her a copy of J.W. Dunne's *Experiment with Time*. The book gave her a sense of her place in the universe, and this trip to the Middle East marked the beginning of Agatha's lifelong fascination with time.

The novelist returned to England in time for Christmas at Abney Hall, having extended an invitation to the Woolleys to stay at her mews house in Cresswell Place if they came to England in 1929.

After the publication of *Partners in Crime* that year, Agatha felt able to make light of the disappearance when she added a message to the flyleaf of Nan's copy of the book in gratitude to her for sheltering her on the night of 3 December 1926: 'To Sweet Nan, of Old Chelsea, from Agatha.' The book was bequeathed subsequently to Nan's daughter Judith. Two of the stories from the collection were 'A Pot of Tea' and 'The Case of the Missing Lady', and the inscription was an in-joke between Agatha and Nan. 'A Pot of Tea' had originally been called 'Publicity', and in this story the character of Tuppence had arranged for a friend who was engaged to the heir of an earldom to disappear so that her new detective agency could gain kudos in the 'highest places' for apparently solving the baffling mystery.

These two stories, along with ten others, had first appeared in *The Sketch* between September and December 1924 under the title *Tommy and Tuppence: A Series of Adventures*. Agatha often edited her stories before they were issued in collections, and a previous mention of events of 'four' years ago was updated by her to 'six' before *Partners in Crime* was published in 1929, leading many people, including Agatha's authorized biographer, to assume that all fourteen stories were written after the disappearance (this was true only of 'The Unbreakable Alibi' which appeared in the December 1928 edition of *Holly Leaves Magazine*, while the origin of the remaining story, 'The Clergyman's Daughter', remains a mystery).

The most overt reminder of the disappearance that year came when Sir Godfrey Collins released *The Sunningdale Mystery*. The cover blurb emphasized that it was by the authoress of *The Murder of Roger Ackroyd*, and fans anticipating a new detective novel from Agatha found it was merely Chapters 11 to 22 of *Partners in Crime*.

On 20 September 1929 Monty died of a cerebral haemorrhage, and Agatha was forced to confront her feelings about her estranged older brother. He was buried in France, and his elder sister Madge cried at the funeral. Her patient and long-suffering husband Jimmy, who had footed Monty's bills and had provided him with a succession of minders for the last few years of his life, greeted the news of his death with a mixture of private relief and concern for Madge. Nan's daughter and son-in-law, Judith and Graham Gardner, recall that it was Jimmy's financial intervention that ensured that Monty's drug problem was hushed up, thus preventing family scandal. According to Judith, by the end of his life Monty was less difficult to deal with because his drug abuse had caused him 'to get to the stage where he was a bit blank'.

Nan was saddened to learn of Monty's death, for she had loved him as she might a recalcitrant child. The special affinity they had had for one another had arisen from their mutual recognition that they were, in their different ways, both rebels. Nan always cherished a ring Monty had bought back for her from South Africa.

Nan's affection for Monty helped Agatha to reconcile her ambiguous feelings towards him. He had never figured greatly in her life and, although she was aware that he had had great charm, she had often found his lack of consideration towards others maddening and frustrating. She had also been shocked by his indulgent and reckless use of illicit drugs.

Agatha's autobiography makes no mention of Monty's drug problem. She is understandably guarded in the few remarks she makes about him, stating only that his various schemes, such as starting a boat-running business in East Africa after the war, had never come to anything because he lacked the ability to apply himself.

Not long after his death, she met a Colonel Dwyer of the King's African Rifles at the Tigris Hotel in Baghdad. The Colonel had known Monty well and spoke at great length of the heroism of 'Puffing Billy' and the respect his men had for him. Agatha was forced to reconsider her brother in the light of this conversation. She came to realize that despite his selfishness, his considerable debts and his reckless lifestyle he had done what he wanted to in life because he had seldom cared what others thought of him. He expected people to take him as he was and had never attempted to impose his own lifestyle or morality on others.

The closest Agatha came to depicting her brother in her writings was in the unflattering role of Richard Warwick in her 1958 play *The Unexpected Guest*. Richard, like Monty, was a former safari hunter and invalid, who out of boredom would fire random gunshots out the window at visitors to the house in order to frighten them.

Archie continued to occupy Agatha's thoughts, and the October 1929 edition of *Britannia and Eve* saw the publication of an intriguing Mr Quin story, 'The Man from the Sea', which reveals the authoress's guilt and feelings of inadequacy after the divorce. When the main character, Mr Satterthwaite, wanders into the garden of a neglected villa on a cliff top, he challenges a man he finds there, realizing that he is intending to jump off the cliff into the sea.

The man, Anthony Cosden, confesses that he is terminally ill and that he came to the garden the night before to kill himself, only the presence of a stranger, who, it transpires, is Mr Satterthwaite's fellow sleuth Mr Quin, deterred him. Anthony Cosden has no idea who owns the villa. He says that his one regret in life is that he has never fathered a son. When Mr Satterthwaite refuses to leave the garden, the younger man reluctantly departs.

The owner of the villa appears and Mr Satterthwaite learns from her that twenty-three years earlier she had watched from the cliff top as her cruel and sadistic husband had drowned in the sea. The marriage had begun passionately but, because of their conflicting personalities, things had soon gone drastically wrong and she had been glad to be rid of him. A year had passed, then a chance night of passion with a stranger had left her pregnant. The offspring of that union, a boy, turned out so like his father that she had learned to love the stranger through his child and she confides that she would instantly know him if she met him again.

The widow is contemplating ending her life because her son is demanding to know about his father to convince his fiancée's parents that he is a suitable match for their daughter. The widow says that unless she kills herself the truth of her son's illegitimacy will emerge and wreck his chance of happiness with the girl.

Mr Satterthwaite averts a tragedy when he realizes, through parallels in their stories, that the father of the widow's son must be Anthony Cosden. He arranges a meeting and the happily reunited couple resolve to marry that very day. When their son comes home they will tell him there was some misunderstanding in the past. The overjoyed widow is confident that her son will marry his fiancée without his being any the wiser about the past. She is also determined to do everything in her power to prevent the man she loves, Anthony Cosden, from dying.

The story concludes when Mr Satterthwaite meets his enigmatic friend, Mr Quin, in the garden. Mr Quin states that he is 'an advocate for the dead' and that on instructions from 'the other side' he had come to prevent Anthony Cosden from taking his life. He tells Mr Satterthwaite that he is here on behalf of the widow's cruel, but now repentant husband who wishes to make sure his widow finally gets the happiness she deserves. Mr Quin points out that love can make men into devils as well as angels. She had had a girlish adoration for her husband, but he could never reach the woman in her and it drove him mad, he says. The husband tortured her because he loved her. The story ends with Mr Quin – the woman's husband reincarnated – walking towards the cliff to return to the sea, from whence he came.

Although aspects of Archie's character would appear several times in Agatha's writings, along with allusions to their ill-fated love, Mr Quin's final remarks are the closest she ever came to admitting that she had contributed to the breakdown of her marriage. She never shook off the feeling that she had failed her daughter, and 'The Man from the Sea' gave expression to her belief that a child needed to be raised by both parents to feel properly loved and that for a child to be denied his or her parents is to be denied potential happiness.

The Woolleys extended an invitation to Agatha to stay with them during 1930 at Ur, and her decision to take them up on the offer would alter the course of her life and lead to her becoming Mrs Max Mallowan. The decade that followed was to be one of the happiest of her life.

21

THE GOLDEN DECADE

IN A LETTER Agatha wrote in 1930 to her friend Allen Lane, the nephew of her former publisher, she stated that it had been a marvellous year. She was very happy because in March she had been introduced to her future husband at the archaeological site at Ur.

Max Mallowan had been ill with appendicitis when Agatha had met the Woolleys the previous season. But when Katherine Woolley asked her husband's quiet 25-year-old assistant to take the 39-year-old novelist sightseeing the stage was set for romance.

Max was dark-haired with a fashionable pencil moustache. His outward placidity and even temperament belied an inner idealism and determination. He had been raised in England by a tyrannical agnostic Austrian father and a French mother with a passion for romantic novels and painting. His parents' stormy relationship had cultivated in him a deep desire for peace and calm. The bullying regime of his public school had left deep scars on his psyche, and later, at Oxford, he had delighted in the feeling of camaraderie that he felt from being treated as a gentleman.

When Agatha met him he was a budding scholar and, as she had inherited Clarissa's enormous appetite for learning and history, they connected intellectually, aesthetically and artistically in a way that Agatha had never managed with Archie. She was still a very attractive woman, and her growing fame and prosperity meant she was not uninteresting to men.

After their return to England Max asked Agatha to marry him. She found that she was taken with the idea. She was not without qualms, after the experience of her first marriage, and she admitted to Max that she was afraid of being hurt. He refused to be put off and finally persuaded her to accept his proposal. Determined to heed the lessons of the past she accepted him on two conditions.

First, she insisted that they must divide all their money and possessions down the middle: what was hers was his. Given that Agatha was much better off than Max this desire to learn from her mistakes with Archie spoke volumes. Secondly, she extracted a promise from Max never to play golf. Although he was somewhat taken aback by this stipulation he had no difficulty in agreeing to it – cricket was the sport he most enjoyed.

Nan's daughter Judith recalls that Madge, who was considered within family circles 'a funny, crafty devil', was passionately against the idea of the couple marrying, since she suspected Max would hurt her sister and did her utmost to prevent the alliance. Meanwhile Katherine, a shrewd judge of character despite her temperamental nature, told Agatha she should make Max wait two years before they married because she thought it would be bad for his character if he assumed he could have anything he wanted while he was still so young. Unwisely, Agatha did not heed their advice.

Her own doubts about the marriage arose only when she was apart from him. With Max around, she said, she felt safe and happy. She begged him to be patient with her because she had become secure in her distrust of life and people and needed time to adjust to the idea of marrying again.

There were further problems: Clarissa had raised Agatha as an Anglican and Max was a practising Roman Catholic. She offered to be converted to Roman Catholicism, but because Max's religion would not sanctify his marriage to a divorcee, he left the Catholic Church. Meanwhile the person with the greatest influence on Agatha gave her blessing: Rosalind, who treated the idea of her mother marrying again as a huge joke, approved of Max.

After the publicity over the disappearance Agatha was fearful the press would hear of her wedding plans and spoil her happiness. In her autobiography she asserts that she married Max in 'the small chapel' of St Columba's, Edinburgh (St Columba's is, in fact, a cathedral). The couple actually took their vows, seven months after they met, on

11 September at the Edinburgh church of St Cuthbert's. By travelling to Scotland they successfully eluded journalists. In order to minimize their fourteen-year age gap Agatha gave her age on their marriage certificate as thirty-seven, while Max gave his as thirty-one. In fact Agatha was four days off her fortieth birthday and Max was twenty-six.

Before their departure to the Continent, Agatha excitedly wrote to Allen Lane that she was off to Venice and Greece with her husband. She said she did not quite know how it had happened as she had been determined not to be so foolish as to marry again. Still, she felt that safety at all costs was a 'repulsive creed'.

Their honeymoon ended in Athens in mid October when Max was obliged to return to the dig at Ur. He was reluctant to leave Agatha because she was ill with food poisoning at the time, but she urged him to prioritize his work. The Woolleys had made it clear to him that there was only room for one wife at the dig – and that was Katherine. Max's employers felt that women were an encumbrance to their activities at the site. In fact, the Woolleys returned a week late from their summer break, and Max, furious at being parted unnecessarily early from Agatha, took his revenge by erecting a new wing to the house on the site of the dig, in which he intentionally made Katherine's bathroom so cramped that it later had to be pulled down and rebuilt.

After the honeymoon Agatha found that the usual dread occasioned in her by memories of the disappearance was absent when she returned to England. She wrote to Max that for the first time in several years she had felt London, even in the rain, was a pleasant place after all. She added that he had lifted a great weight from her shoulders and that the wounds were slowly healing. She admitted that it would take little to open them up again, but she was convinced they would heal once and for all.

By 1930 the sales of her latest mystery, *The Murder at the Vicarage*, were a mere 5,500; as far as her books were concerned the publicity bonanza from the disappearance had ended. *Giant's Bread* appeared that same year under the pseudonym of Mary Westmacott. Nan immediately realized the novel was by Agatha. The two friends were sitting down to lunch one day at Abney Hall when Nan remarked that she had been sent on loan an interesting book by *The Times* Book Club: 'Now what was it called? Dwarf's Blood, I think.' Agatha knew that her secret was out, and the two women laughed. Knowing Agatha as well as she did, the style of writing, together with a poem and a childhood incident in the book, convinced Nan of the certainty that Agatha had written the novel. Agatha later gave her friend her own copy of the book, inscribed on the flyleaf: 'Nan from Mary Westmacott with love. Dwarf's Blood ha ha!'

Although Agatha was happy in her new marriage, one aspect of her life with Max caused problems in the early stages: this was the amount of time Max spent with Rosalind. No child could have asked for a more considerate and thoughtful stepfather, and Agatha's envy was both irrational and unjustified. Despite this, when Rosalind was away at boarding-school Agatha found herself missing her daughter. Judith recalls that because of Agatha's possessiveness the first few years of the marriage were rife with undercurrents of jealousy.

None the less Max's quiet devotion to Agatha and their shared mutual interests went a long way to healing the wounds of her previous marriage. So much so that she began to reassess her faith in God, badly shaken by the collapse of her first marriage.

The reawakening of religious beliefs stemmed from her fascination with time. Sir John Jean's book *The Mysterious World* made her consider the evidence for a divine plan, and she began to contemplate a future that included God once again. 'How queer it would be if God were in the future,' she told Max in a letter, 'something we never created or imagined but who is not yet – supposing him to be not Cause but Effect. The creation of God is what we are moving to – is one goal – the aim and purpose of all evolution.'

A residual effect of the publicity from the disappearance saw the release in 1931 of cinematic versions of her plays *Alibi* and *Black Coffee* starring Austin Trevor as Hercule Poirot. The actor reprised the role for a third film, *Lord Edgware Dies*, three years later.

Despite her newfound contentment there were moments of despair. In 1931 she had a miscarriage and she and Max decided not to try for another child. Then when Peter developed a growth on his shoulder

Agatha, fearing the worst, pointed out to Max that, unlike her, he had never been through a really bad time with nothing but a dog to hold on to. Fortunately Peter recovered.

Unlike Archie, Max always encouraged Agatha in her writing, especially when she became bogged down half-way through a book and felt she could not finish it. She outlined to him in advance the plot of her 1931 novel *The Sittaford Mystery*, in which the heroine cynically uses the romantic interest a journalist has for her to help save her fiancé from the gallows. It became a custom for Agatha to outline each new book to Max and write the opening chapter and the last chapter before completing the rest of the book. In this way she managed to keep a firm grasp on the plot. The 1930s saw the publication of twenty-five books.

Agatha dedicated her 1932 story collection, *The Thirteen Problems*, to Max's employers, the Woolleys. The peace of desert life in the Middle East led her to write her 1933 novel, *Lord Edgware Dies*, in Nineveh. In addition to the classic *Murder on the Orient Express*, 1934 also saw the publication of the collection *Parker Pyne Investigates*. Suggestions in Janet Morgan's authorized biography that Agatha incorporated from first-hand experience 'the glorious freedom loss of memory affords' in 'The Case of the Rich Woman' cannot be substantiated. The story concerns a rich woman abducted by captors who try, unsuccessfully, to brainwash her into thinking she is someone else. In her introduction to *Parker Pyne Investigates* in 'Penguin's Millions' series, Agatha revealed that the inspiration for the story came from a woman she saw peering into a hat shop window one day who complained she had too much money.

Despite being happy with Max, Agatha still missed Archie and this led her to re-examine the past in her second Mary Westmacott novel. *Unfinished Portrait* is in many ways an autobiographical novel, tracing Agatha's life from early childhood through to her marriage to Archie and its painful dissolution. The characters of Celia and Dermot are based on the Christies, and there is a raw emotional quality to it that reflects how close it was to her own experience.

Although the early part of Celia's marriage to Dermot is marred by poverty, she loves him passionately. Dermot is obsessed by Celia's looks and asks her to promise him that she will always be beautiful. When she falls pregnant with Judy (this is the one time Rosalind makes an appearance in Agatha's writing), Dermot worries about Celia losing her figure. As Judy grows older and becomes more like her father, Celia feels neither of them give her the love she requires. She is deeply upset when her mother dies and feels constrained by family, home and possessions. She longs to travel to exotic, far-off places such as 'the wilds of Baluchistan'.

Up to this point the novel is very much a reflection of Agatha's life until April 1926, then the image is distorted. Rather than delve deeply into the cause of her husband's eighteen-month-long affair with Nancy, Agatha ties everything up in a neat package: the death of Celia's mother instead becomes the catalyst for Dermot's affair. Although Celia has been unconsciously hoping for release from her marriage, when the time comes she reacts with horror and she refuses to divorce him.

While *Unfinished Portrait* avoids examining the reasons behind the breakdown of their marriage, it reveals Agatha's reaction to Archie's bombshell request for a divorce. Celia's pain and disbelief after eleven apparently happy years of marriage are genuine. At first it seems to Celia, still reeling from the shock of her mother's death, as though she has always loved Dermot and done everything he wanted, and then when she had really needed him he had stabbed her in the back. There is no mention of the rows over money that beset Archie and Agatha, nor how her success as a writer had driven them apart.

Agatha tries to persuade her readers that Dermot's mistress, Marjorie, based on Nancy, means little to Celia. *Unfinished Portrait*, unlike the short story 'The Edge', does not acknowledge the intense feelings of jealousy Agatha felt towards Nancy. Some experiences were simply too painful to explore in her writings again.

Celia is horrified when Dermot suggests a put-up job for a divorce in which his mistress's name is not to be mentioned. The loss of her religious faith is apparent when Celia tells Dermot that she had believed in him as she had believed in God and, she opines, 'that was stupid'. An unpleasant contest of wills ensues. Dermot becomes the 'Gun Man'.

In her grief and unhappiness Celia becomes afraid of her husband

and locks away the weed killer in the potting shed. At night she fanta-sizes that Dermot is trying to poison her, although during the daytime she recognizes her delusions as wild 'night fancies'. As her living night-mare worsens, she decides to take a photograph of her mother to the police in the hope that they will find her. Some commentators have wondered if either of these two aspects of the plot were a fictional depic-tion of Agatha's actions on the night of the disappearance. In fact these incidents simply serve to illustrate Celia's intense loneliness and lack of self-esteem.

There is an uneasy period of reconciliation for husband and wife, in which Celia battles to keep her marriage together by using their daugh-ter Judy as a pawn. But Dermot is unable to keep his promise not to see Marjorie again.

Unfinished Portrait recreates certain events from the day of Agatha's disappearance. After Miss Hood (based on Charlotte Fisher) goes to London for the day, Dermot has it out with Celia and admits he has not been able to stop seeing Marjorie. Although he does not reveal he is spending the weekend with Marjorie he says he is going away for two days, and Celia tells him that when he returns he won't find her there. She interprets a 'momentary flicker – of hope' in Dermot's eyes as a sus-picion in his mind that she might have committed suicide by the time he returns. She toys with the idea that he will be sorry and suffer remorse if she takes her life, but she knows this is not so, because he will be sure to deceive himself into believing he was not responsible. She will simply have made it easier for him to marry Marjorie. Later that night, after visiting Judy's room, Celia comes downstairs and pats her dog goodbye before leaving the house.

The tone of the novel changes at this point: it loses its emotional intensity. Celia jumps off a bridge but is saved from drowning by a passer-by, is restrained and forced to appear in court on a charge of attempted suicide. Creatively, Agatha always reworked and used left-over ideas from her fiction; in a similar manner, a remnant of her disin-genuous official explanation of the disappearance to the *Daily Mail* found its way into her novel.

She expresses the depth of her love for Archie when she observes of

Celia that Dermot was 'in her blood' and that she loved him for life. Sadly, however, when Celia had finally stood up to Dermot it was too late.

Writing *Unfinished Portrait* was a painful exorcism for Agatha of her first marriage, and the calm, stabilizing influence of her second marriage enabled her to reflect more calmly on her past. It is indicative of the hurt Agatha still felt that she cast her fictional counterpart as the innocent victim in the marriage, rather than reveal how she had contributed to its breakdown by being inflexible and difficult about money and trying to force Archie to do things against his will.

The sequence of events in the novel is sometimes distorted to omit certain unhappy details, yet Agatha once told Judith: 'If you want to know what I'm like read *Unfinished Portrait*.'

In order to protect Mary Westmacott's true identity, the contract Collins drew up for *Unfinished Portrait* was in the name of Nathaniel Miller (Agatha's late grandfather) and amended when she signed it to Daniel Miller. This time Nan received her copy directly from Agatha, inscribed on the flyleaf: 'To Dear Mrs Kon 1934 from M.W.' When presenting Nan with this and other Mary Westmacott books, Agatha always disguised her handwriting and never used her real name.

That same year Nan's second marriage floundered. George discovered she was having an affair and left her. She moved with her daughter to a block of flats, Cheyne Court in Chelsea, where Agatha regularly visited her to support her through this period of upheaval. George had never liked children, and Judith was pleased to see the back of her stepfather. Sadly, Nan's relationship with the man with whom she had the affair did not work out, and she decided against marrying him.

Agatha's financial commitments were considerable in the first decade of her second marriage, and it was fortunate that she and Max had her royalties to support them. In addition to paying for her daughter's maintenance and education and subsidizing Max's archaeological expeditions, Agatha initiated a yearly repair-and-redecoration programme for Ashfield and acquired Winterbrook House for Max in Wallingford, so that he could visit Oxford in connection with his work.

Christmas at Abney Hall created tensions. Although Max had been welcomed into Madge's and Jimmy's circle of friends after he married

Agatha, the one member of the Watts family he did not get on with was their son Jack. The two men had been at Oxford together and did not like each other. It was a matter of class. Jack despised what he regarded as Max's pretence at being a gentleman. For this reason it became impossible for Max to accompany Agatha and Rosalind to Abney Hall to spend Christmases there with Nan, Judith and the rest of the family. Agatha adored the festivities there and refused to forgo them on Max's account.

The sibling jealousy Agatha had felt towards her older sister's literary accomplishments was forgotten as her own stature as a writer grew. It was sometimes necessary, however, for her to stand up to her loquacious sister, who, like an ocean liner, tended to swamp smaller vessels in her wake. One evening Madge entered Ashfield's candlelit dining-room and turned on the main lights. Agatha, who had gone to a lot of trouble over the meal, was not pleased. 'Turn those lights off!' she snapped. 'This is my house.' As Madge grew older she became more egocentric, seldom allowing Jimmy to get a word in edgeways. In order to save on trips to the hairdresser she shaved her head and wore a wig. Ultimately Agatha came to regard Madge as 'really rather funny and sweet'.

Like all mothers, Agatha and Nan sometimes felt inept in attempting to relate to their daughters, and this led Agatha to inscribe Nan's copy of her 1935 novel *Three Act Tragedy* with the heartfelt words: 'From one mother to another with deep sympathy!' Rosalind had developed into a beautiful, direct and terrifyingly honest teenager. Agatha feared that the divorce had put a certain distance between them, and she concluded that the best she could do was to give her daughter a certain amount of freedom and independence, rather than attempt to impose a rigid set of rules on her.

Judith had become bored with school and left at the age of fifteen. She spent six months at a finishing school in Paris, then returned to London where she attended a school to train as a dance teacher. A broken ankle, however, put paid to her ambitions, and she went to Austria where she fell in love with an unsuitable boy. After two years she returned home. She had turned into an attractive, outgoing, vivacious young woman with a love of fashion. Her mother was shocked by her daughter's 'freakishly plucked' eyebrows and scarlet painted nails. Judith loved going to London nightclubs; her favourite was the notorious Shim-Sham, and Nan was dismayed that Judith often stayed out till two or three in the morning. Judith was more sensible than her overwrought mother gave her credit for; an anxious Nan told Agatha: 'She's going off the rails.' Agatha, commiserating with her friend, based her only Mary Westmacott play, A *Daughter's a Daughter*, on Nan's relationship with Judith. Despite the latter's enthusiasm for nightclubs, she was an affectionate daughter, and Agatha often took her on holiday with her and Max, including trips to the châteaux of the Loire valley.

Meanwhile, Rosalind, the younger of the two girls, had completed her school certificate and spent a short period abroad before returning home for her London season. She was a success as a débutante, but to Agatha's regret her divorced status prevented her from being able to present her daughter at Buckingham Palace. Rosalind instead went with friends. She announced that she wished to take up photography, but Agatha told her it was out of the question once she discovered that Rosalind actually wanted to take up a career in advertising as a bathing-suit model.

Despite her increasing fame, Agatha remained elusive as far as her readers were concerned. The wall of silence she built between herself and her public merely increased the mystique that had surrounded her since the disappearance. Her literary advisers found that one way of curbing speculation over the incident was to stipulate to the numerous magazines and newspapers that competed to serialize her work that no publicity for her writings should refer to the events of 1926.

Yet it is the view of those who knew her and appreciate how much of herself she put into her writing that 'nothing comes from nothing'. Agatha included minor incidents from her life in her detective fiction, and her creation of Mrs Ariadne Oliver, the detective novelist with a pretended scattiness, became a useful smokescreen to put off her reading public. The character became a spokeswoman for Agatha's literary views, and, in the absence of any intimate knowledge of Agatha's life, many of her fans mistakenly came to believe they knew her well through the character of Mrs Oliver.

The one fleeting reference to Harrogate in Agatha's fiction comes in her 1936 novel, *Cards on the Table,* when Mrs Oliver remarks chattily that she had a Welsh nurse who took her to Harrogate one day and went home having forgotten all about her.

For the initiated, like Nan, there was the occasional parallel in Agatha's detective fiction to other aspects of the disappearance: for example, the detailed description she gives in her 1936 novel of the newspaper coverage surrounding *The ABC Murders* was directly drawn from her own experience of the press in 1926.

In 1936 Nan was diagnosed as having cancer of the rectum. She was successfully operated on, and Agatha inscribed her other novel from that year, *Murder in Mesopotamia:* 'To Nan, the perfect mother because she has been very ill!' *Dumb Witness*, published in 1937, was officially dedicated to Agatha's beloved dog Peter. Nan's copy of *Dumb Witness* was inscribed by Agatha: 'To my not so Dumb Friend, Nan, the Smelly Kipper – from her old friend Starry-Eyes(?).' This was a reference to the occasion when as young girls they had nailed two kippers underneath the dining-room chairs at Abney Hall before the adults sat down to lunch. To their great delight the pungent odour had baffled their elders.

The work Agatha produced during the 1930s has come to epitomize what is now known as the Golden Age of detective fiction: the absence of reference to contemporary religious, political and socio-economic problems has ensured that her books remain timeless, fresh for each successive generation, unlike many other crime writers of the time.

While keeping her public at a distance after 1926, she allowed her attitude to marital infidelity to come through in her books. Her 1937 mystery, *Death on the Nile,* involves a romantic triangle, and here, as in most of her other novels, she treats the character of the 'other woman' sympathetically. This even applies when the 'other woman' is guilty of murder. The same cannot be said of the male home-wreckers in Agatha's fiction. She regarded men as the custodians of society and marriage and did not hesitate to denounce those who steal other men's wives as lounge lizards or even gigolos.

By 1938 Agatha had begun to tire of her public's insatiable demand for Hercule Poirot. When she had written her first book about him, she had not realized that he would become a millstone around her neck. She alternated between affection and irritation and went so far as to admit to her feelings of ambivalence in her introduction that year to the *Daily Mail*'s serialization of *Appointment With Death*.

By September 1938 Agatha had completed her latest Poirot tale, *Sad Cypress*, in which characters were drawn from herself, Archie and Max. Beneath her poised and aloofly attractive exterior Elinor Carlyle is unable to tell her fiancé Roddy Welman how much she loves him, because he has an intense aversion to talking about feelings and is acutely uneasy when others are unhappy or ill. She loses out to him in love but ultimately finds greater peace of mind with her doctor. Agatha sums up her feelings for Archie and Max, when she says of Elinor that she loved Roddy unhappily, even desperately, but with Peter she could be happy.

Judith's birthday fell on 16 September, the day after Agatha's, and it was a custom for them to enjoy their birthdays together with family and close friends. The last birthday they celebrated at Ashfield was in 1938: Judith was twenty-one and Agatha forty-eight. Agatha decorated the dining-room chairs with flowers and on the appropriate day the one whose birthday it was took her place at the head of the table. 'Agatha always made our birthdays such special occasions,' recalls Judith.

Encroaching suburbia was spoiling the tranquillity of Ashfield and, encouraged by Max, Agatha sold the house in 1938 to raise £6,000 to acquire Greenway, a white Georgian house set in thirty-three acres of grounds overlooking the River Dart in Devon. Not long after Agatha and Max moved in Peter died and was buried in the grounds behind the house. She was greatly saddened, because her beloved long-term companion had sustained her through many difficult periods in her life, most notably the weeks before and after her disappearance. Although she was offered another dog, she could not bear to get another for the time being.

Nan's friendship sustained her. She made light of her sister-in-law's recent illness when she inscribed her 1939 novel, *Murder Is Easy*: 'To my old friend B. Hinds from Agatha.'

The start of the Second World War in 1939 heralded the end of a decade that had brought both personal and professional happiness to the writer. It also led indirectly to the disappearance returning to haunt her once more.

22

DARKENED SKIES

As the war escalated and the skies over England darkened with enemy planes, Agatha came to rely on Max to provide love and consolation, despite their lengthy separations from one another. The fact that he wrote such loving and tender letters to her reassured her that she had not been a failure in life and that she had succeeded as a wife. She marvelled how she had changed from the forlorn, unhappy person he had met in the Middle East. She told him in a letter that he had done everything for her.

For much of the war Max served abroad as an adviser on Arab affairs. Agatha longed to join her husband, but official hurdles prevented her from acquiring a position as a wartime correspondent. Unlike some of her compatriots who took flight from England for the duration, she moved to London to dispense medicine at University College Hospital, denying herself the financial advantages she would have gained from living in a foreign tax haven.

Her main concern was for the safety of her daughter Rosalind and of Max. She was also worried that if anything happened to them she would be in a similar position to that in which she had found herself before her disappearance when she had wanted to write in order to consolidate her finances but had been prevented from doing so by her worsening marital problems. In the early 1940s she produced *Curtain: Poirot's Last Case* and *Sleeping Murder: Miss Marple's Last Case*. Both manuscripts were secured in a bank vault and made over as deeds of gift to Rosalind and Max. Her intention was that the books were to be published only in the event of her death so that her bereaved daughter and husband would at least have some kind of financial nest-egg. Other books Agatha wrote during the war years were quickly published in order to alleviate her cash-flow problems.

Shortly before the outbreak of war the US tax office had begun making inquiries about her financial affairs. Her literary advisers had hired a prominent tax lawyer to sort out the complicated tangle resulting from her prolific literary output. Wartime legislation meant that during this period she was prevented from receiving most of the large US royalties due to her, despite being forced to pay massive taxes on them in advance in England. What money she received after tax on her British income was not always sufficient to cover the deficit, and there were periods when she lived very much hand to mouth.

The thriller *N or M?*, in which the intrepid sleuths Tommy and Tuppence Beresford foil an attempted invasion of England by Hitler's fifth column, was serialized by the American magazine *Redbook* in March 1941. Its patriotic message struck just the right note of optimism for Americans eager to combat Nazism. For the most part Agatha avoided specific references in her stories to the war and other current events, partly because she did not wish to dwell on them and partly because she realized her stories would date quickly once the war ended.

Whenever trouble had loomed in the past work had been Agatha's best distraction, but as her financial situation became more parlous she felt as if she had been deprived of this crutch. What was the point of writing if she got no royalties, she wrote to her literary agent Edmund Cork. He consoled her with the news that Milestone, an American film company, had made an offer for the film rights to *N or M?* that were 'world-wide in their scope', which meant the money she earned could be paid directly to her in England. Crippling taxation nearly forced Agatha into bankruptcy twice during the war, and in a desperate bid to prevent this she tried unsuccessfully on two occasions to sell Greenway, which at the outbreak of war had become a home for evacuee children before being taken over by the Admiralty for the US navy. She was terrified of drying up creatively and desperate to keep afloat financially.

She confided to Edmund Cork that it was nerve-racking to feel unable to write when one needed to do so to keep the money coming in. She bitterly recalled how during the breakdown of her first marriage she could have done with a manuscript up her sleeve instead of having to produce 'that rotten book' *The Big Four* and having to force herself to complete *The Mystery of the Blue Train*.

After the outbreak of the war Nan and Judith became locked in conflict. Nan had been anxious to move from London to the country in the hope it would be safer there. Judith had refused to go, saying she would be bored. She knew she would miss London's night life, and Nan had reluctantly agreed that she could live for a year with her Uncle Lionel and Aunt Joan in Victoria Road, off Kensington High Street. The young woman had no fear of bombs, her one thought being to have a good time. 'When you're young, you never think it will be you.' Judith recalls that in her determination to enjoy London's nightclubs there had been many an occasion when she used the sounding of the air-raid sirens as an excuse not to return to Victoria Road until the early hours of the morning.

A major cause of conflict between mother and daughter was that Nan wanted Judith to train to become a nurse. It worried Nan that her daughter had no career. Judith confided her problems to Agatha and ended up weeping uncontrollably, since nursing did not appeal to her in the least. Agatha, who regarded Judith as a second daughter, knew that she loved children and found her a position near Greenway as a voluntary assistant at a crèche in Paignton for evacuee children. This solution satisfied everyone and enabled Judith to live first with Nan at Tor Close in Churston and later at Penhill in Brixham, both villages near Greenway.

Nan had no desire to return to London at that time; she preferred the quiet of country life. When the warehouse where she had stored her furniture from Cheyne Court was bombed in London Nan felt justified in her decision to move to Devon. It worried her that Agatha had moved to blitz-ravaged London to work in the hospital, but, as Judith put it, 'Agatha was a woman of enormous courage and loved England too much to ever leave.'

There were happier, more relaxed times for Agatha when the bombing abated. Nan would occasionally come up to London. She found running Penhill difficult and would stay at London's exclusive Hyde Park Hotel, where most of the guests preferred to sleep in the passageways, believing themselves to be safer from bombs that might fall during the night. When she met up with Nan, Agatha invariably asked: 'For half a pound tell me who's your latest?'

Being cut off at Penhill, Nan did not have as many admirers as before the war, although beneath her demure, lady-like appearance she had a challenging, risqué sense of humour that men adored. Agatha loved listening to news of her friend's latest conquests, and Nan became the prototype in Agatha's novels for the rich, attractive often divorced femmes fatales, most noticeably Ruth Van Rydock in They Do It With Mirrors, and Lady Sedgwick in At Bertram's Hotel.

In recognition of their friendship Agatha officially dedicated her 1942 novel The Body in the Library 'To My Friend Nan'. The second body in the story is found in a burnt-out car in 'Venn's Quarry', and the disused cart-track that leads to it was Water Lane and Newlands Corner thinly disguised. The hotel in the novel is not based on the Harrogate Hydro, as some might suppose, but Torquay's Imperial Hotel.

Ironically, the publication the following year of Five Little Pigs has led some readers mistakenly to read veiled references to the disappearance in it. This is because the victim, Amyas Crale, shares Archie's initials and was murdered, apparently by his wife, sixteen years earlier for having an affair with a young woman. Despite the coincidence of the victim's initials, Agatha in fact based the dead husband loosely on Amyas Boston with whom she had a teenage flirtation during the amateur production of The Blue Beard of Unhappiness.

Despite her financial worries, Agatha maintained her literary output, publishing twelve books during the war years. She found comfort in her strengthening religious convictions. Although the war seemed endless, her belief in the transitory nature of things sustained her. She found an additional source of income throughout the war by adapting for the stage three of her books, Ten Little Niggers, Appointment With Death, and Death on the Nile, with varying degrees of success.

Meanwhile, Rosalind had married Captain Hubert Prichard of the Royal Welsh Fusiliers in 1940 and was living in Wales. In September 1943 Agatha was delighted when a son, Mathew, was born. Agatha's pleasure at becoming a grandmother was diminished only by Max's absence. She missed Max terribly, telling him she was afraid that they would grow apart instead of maintaining a parallel track. Agatha longed to be with Max, partly because she was haunted by the spectre of the First World War and its detrimental effects on her first marriage. Would prolonged separation change her relationship with Max? she asked herself.

Her Mary Westmacott novel, *Absent in the Spring,* which was written in just three days in 1943, was both an exorcism of some of the more painful aspects of the writer's first marriage and a projection of her fears about the durability of the second. In her autobiography she admitted that the book had been gestating for six or seven years before she wrote it.

Absent in the Spring tells the story of Joan Scudamore who experiences a crisis when she comes face to face with herself after being stranded at a railway rest-house in the desert. The book is about emotional insecurities and religious faith. Agatha's journey towards spiritual peace of mind had been hindered by the fact she had never considered herself a sinner, so when she had needed religion to sustain her during the breakdown of her marriage to Archie she had felt forsaken by God. Likewise one of the characters tells Joan that her trouble is that she is not a sinner, which effectively cuts her off from prayer.

Joan recalls coming across a letter her father had written to her mother before he died, telling her that her love had been the crowning blessing of his life. Joan reflects that her husband Rodney has never written to her like this and wonders why. She intuits that Rodney has had an unconsummated affair in the past.

Joan recalls how Rodney successfully prevented their eldest daughter, Averil, from going off with a married man by pointing out to her that the scandal would undermine her lover's promising career in medical research. Rodney had claimed that no woman's love could compensate a man for losing his ability to do the work he was intended to do.

Joan belatedly realizes that Rodney would have been happier if he had pursued his ambition to become a farmer instead of training to be a solicitor to please her. She is forced to confront the fact that she has not always been the considerate wife she imagined herself to be. It also dawns on her that their three children do not love her, because she has been a rigid, inflexible mother who smothered them with her love and her desire to organize their lives.

As she comes face to face with these unpleasant realities she discovers she has wandered too far and is lost in the desert. She believes that God has forsaken her, and it is only when she sees the rest-house on the horizon that she realizes that this is not the case.

Unlike Agatha's childhood nightmare of the Gun Man, *Absent in the Spring* recognizes people's need to look within themselves to recognize their frailties so that that they never need fear censure by anyone else. The story makes the point that the best one can do for one's loved ones is to let them get on with their lives and simply be there when one is needed. Since the personal themes in *Absent in the Spring* were so close to her heart, Agatha was never able to articulate clearly why the book was so important to her. The conclusion she reaches in the novel is that one is never alone if one has established a relationship with God.

Significantly, the novel was written at a time when Agatha was deeply worried about whether Max would be able to resume his archaeological excavations at the end of the war. Max admitted that archaeology was an uncertain profession and he was worried about Agatha's financial situation and her ability to help finance his digs. Agatha feared he would be destroyed if he was separated from the work he loved, and the thought of how this might affect their relationship filled her with trepidation.

In his absence she kept in touch with the archaeological world through a mutual friend of theirs, Professor Stephen Glanville. Theirs was an unusual friendship, for Stephen had a tangled private life, and Agatha, in becoming his mother-confessor, learned much about the complexity of human relations. Stephen's problems led her to ponder in a letter to her husband whether she and Max had a tendency to idealize one another while they were apart. If so, she said, she would be heartbroken.

Agatha's newfound religious convictions were reinforced when the war came to an end. Being reunited safely with Max made Agatha feel closer to God than she had ever been before. They were immensely saddened, however, by the fact that Rosalind's husband had been killed in enemy action, and although her daughter's stoicism and disinclination to discuss the matter left Agatha feeling helpless and anxious she let Rosalind know she was there if she needed her.

Agatha had always been self-conscious about being older than Max, and it pleased her that he had turned forty, as she considered that it closed the gap a little. They were so happy that they failed to realize that they had both changed during their years of separation. By this time Agatha was more mature and philosophical in outlook than before. But the most obvious change in her was her appearance: she was now in her mid-fifties and no longer radiantly beautiful; her hair had turned grey and her figure was stouter.

Max's friends now joked that he behaved more like an English gentleman than the genuine article, and this secretly pleased him. He was no longer the untried young man Agatha had married. His war experiences had toughened him, and he was now able to look back on his unhappy public school days philosophically. His passion for archaeology had been strengthened by his lengthy separation from it, and he was fiercely ambitious to prove himself in his chosen field.

The unstable political situation in the Middle East meant that archaeological exploration of the region was out of the question. Agatha raised her spirits by writing a nostalgic and light-hearted domestic account of the excavations on which she and Max had worked in the 1930s, *Come, Tell Me How You Live*, while Max worked on *Nimrud and Its Remains*.

Agatha returned to her writing alias, Mary Westmacott, to express her new religious convictions. Had Max not betrayed her after the publication in 1947 of *The Rose and the Yew Tree* she would have been able, once and for all, to leave all the painful memories of her disappearance behind her for good.

23

MEMORIES SHADOWED

DESPITE THE PERSONAL troubles that befell her after *The Rose and the Yew Tree* was finished, it was Agatha's favourite Mary Westmacott book. The idea behind the book had been with her since around 1929, she revealed in her memoirs.

That the idea for *The Rose and the Yew Tree* came to Agatha so soon after her divorce from Archie shows how desperately she wanted to believe it could be possible for pure, unselfish love to redeem someone apparently beyond redemption. Max's safe return and apparent undying loyalty meant it was written at a time when, in her own words, she felt 'nearest to God'.

The Rose and the Yew Tree is the idealistic story of a self-centred and amoral former war hero, John Gabriel, who redeems himself by becoming a 'messiah' after the heroine, Isabella Charteris – whom he has seduced and mistreated – dies after throwing herself into the path of a bullet intended for him by a political fanatic.

When John Gabriel stands as a Tory candidate in the 1945 election, he is ruthless and ambitious. He privately admits that he is really a Labour supporter but that it is a matter of expediency. He needs a job, the war is almost over and 'the plums' will soon be snatched up. Agatha, a lifelong Tory, has one of the Conservative characters observe that nobody can help making a mess of things after a war and it is better that it not be one's own side.

Agatha supported the Conservatives because of their connections with the aristocracy and not because she believed they always served their country well. In *The Rose and the Yew Tree* a character denounces politics as little more than booths at a fair offering their own cure-alls for the world's ills. Meanwhile an aristocratic Tory supporter expresses the idealistic view of her creator that legislators should be drawn from the class that does not need to work for a living, the class that can be indifferent to gain – that is, the ruling class.

After an unconsummated liaison with a local vet's wife John Gabriel seduces the aristocratic and sheltered Isabella Charteris from St Loo Castle. They live together unmarried, and she copes with the squalid existence to which he subjects her through her 'art of repose'. She has the ability to recognize the important things in life and to live for the moment. She accepts people's different natures and never tries to manipulate anyone. Despite gaining Isabella's love, John Gabriel complains that he never really knows what she is thinking. Archie once said much the same thing about Agatha.

John Gabriel covets Isabella partly because of his sense of being inferior, admitting that he is class-conscious and hates arrogant upper-class women who make him feel like dirt. He also shares his creator's views on the aristocracy. It is not the title that matters but the sense of feeling sure of yourself and not having to wonder what people are thinking of you; merely being concerned with what you think of them. It had been a disappointment to him not to have been born into the aristocracy, just as it had been for Agatha.

When Isabella sacrifices her life to save John Gabriel, the choice is hers. Teresa, another character in the novel, tells the grieving narrator Hugh Norreys, who has always loved Isabella from afar, that time does not mean anything, that five minutes and a thousand years are of equal significance. No one's life is wasted, because the life of the Rose and the life of the Yew Tree are of equal duration. Few people recognize their true selves, their own 'design', but Isabella was one of them. She was difficult to understand not because she was complex but because she was extraordinarily simple and able to recognize life's essentials. A mature Agatha was in fact describing herself.

John Gabriel is devastated by Isabella's death, and his subsequent path to redemption is made plausible because Agatha imbues him with her own religious feelings. He says that he has never been able to believe in God the father, God of creation and of love, but that sometimes he does believe in Christ who descended into hell. He promised the repentant thief paradise but went to hell with the one who cursed and reviled Him.

The Rose and the Yew Tree gives the greatest insight of all Agatha's novels into her renewed religious faith. The book's main weakness lies in its use of fairy-tale motifs. These, however, make clear the enduring romanticism that lay beneath the authoress's apparently pragmatic exterior.

Agatha's idealistic belief that individuals have choice and that destiny is not entirely predetermined comes across strongly. Her more serene outlook was enhanced by her rediscovered faith and her happiness with Max, and she was dumbstruck by her publishers' response to the book.

Billy Collins, who had succeeded his late uncle, Sir Godfrey, as the head of her publishing house, missed the point of the book when he asked if it was wise to have a story based around the General Election, since John Gabriel was such an undesirable person as a candidate. From then on Agatha ensured that the Mary Westmacott novels were published by Heinemann, since she felt that Collins 'hated' Mary Westmacott and anything that distracted her from writing detective stories.

Judith and Graham Gardner recall that far greater personal upset for Agatha was to come following Max's appointment to the archaeological chair of London University in 1947. Max, an articulate, dedicated scholar, was in his element teaching the subject he loved. His students found him witty and stimulating, and he loved being in the spotlight. The adulation he received from his young female students, in particular, led to a number of deepening friendships.

It was Nan who broke the news to Agatha. Max's apparent attempt to recapture his lost youth greatly upset her. Nevertheless she was better equipped to cope with Max's occasional liaisons with his female students than with Archie's affair with Nancy because she never loved him as much as she had loved her first husband.

Max's generous nature was to blame for this blow to Agatha's happiness. Nan had approached Max for advice after a friend's daughter was uncertain how to pursue an interest in archaeology. Max had offered to help by giving the girl a place in his class and, although he formed no relationship with her, reports of his friendships with other female students got back to the girl's mother, who in turn told Nan.

When challenged by Agatha, Max insisted he was the victim of malicious gossip. Agatha was unsure whether or not to believe him, and her unease increased when she heard that Max had driven one of his female students home. He was shrewd enough to know that if he played his cards close to his chest Agatha would not divorce him. However, his wife's feelings of being betrayed ran deep and reopened the wounds left by Archie. Max's instincts were right. Agatha could not bear the thought of the publicity that would ensue if she divorced a second time.

She remembered her mother's advice on maintaining a marriage and whenever possible accompanied Max on trips and social occasions. His intermittent liaisons with young women were made easier for her to endure because he was always the perfect gentleman to her in private and looked out for her interests. Nan had moved back to London after the war, and Agatha got into a routine of visiting her while Max was teaching. Shortly before his class was due to end Agatha would often say to her friend: 'Look at the time. I must go and fetch Max on the dot.'

As her fame increased – she made history in 1948 when Allen Lane of Penguin Books published a million of her paperbacks in one day – Agatha did everything possible to guard her private life. The public's perception of her was of a happily married woman who had made 'more money out of murder than any other woman since Lucrezia Borgia', and Agatha was determined to keep it that way.

She had never sought fame. Judith Gardner recalls that when Max's mother remarked to Agatha one day how much she must enjoy her fame and wealth, Agatha turned to Nan saying: 'Tell her, Nan. Tell her it's not true. I never wanted it!' It was one of the few occasions Judith saw Agatha really angry. Both Nan and Judith were aware that the one thing Agatha had wanted more than anything was a happy family life with Archie and Rosalind.

By the end of the decade a lessening of political and financial tensions enabled Agatha and Max to embark once more on archaeological expeditions to the Middle East. Agatha received a distressing blow, however, when it was reported in the *Sunday Times* on 13 and 20 February 1949 that Mary Westmacott was Agatha Christie. (Her secret had almost become known two years earlier when the American Copyright Registry had written to inquire whether Agatha wanted the books copyrighted as Mary Westmacott or Agatha Christie; hence her authorized biographer's apparent confusion over the actual year in which the authoress's identity was publicly disclosed.) Deeply unhappy about Max's indiscretions, this uncovering of her literary *alter ego* could not have come at a worse time.

An angry Agatha wrote to her literary agent Edmund Cork in March from the British Consul in Baghdad criticizing his 'intelligence service' for not being the first to inform her that her identity had been discovered. Reluctantly she gave her consent for her publishers to acknowledge Mary Westmacott's true identity on the cover of the books. Her decision to capitalize commercially on the disclosure arose from the fact that the war had left her complicated finances in an even worse mess than ever.

Meanwhile, Rosalind had fallen in love with a barrister called Anthony Hicks. Although they wrote to tell Agatha of their impending London registry office wedding in late 1949, they intimated they did not expect her to attend because they were obliged to return to Wales immediately after the ceremony to 'feed the dogs'. Agatha surprised them on the day by attending the wedding anyway. Anthony was an entertaining scholar, interested in people and travel and lacking in ruthless ambition, and his marriage to Rosalind was to prove extremely happy.

In the decade that followed cracks were to appear in Agatha's own marriage. Max's flirtations, as well as their money worries, were contributing factors as to why the 1950s proved a difficult period for Agatha and why memories of the disappearance were to surface once more.

24

No Fields of Amaranth

Throughout the 1950s one woman threatened Agatha's marriage more than anyone else. Barbara Parker, a smiling 42-year-old spinster, was a former archaeological student of Max's who organized their Nimrud expeditions with such skill and good cheer that she made herself indispensable to the couple.

It was Agatha's habit to compose odes about the members of the expedition, and in the early, carefree days out in Nimrud she unsuspectingly penned one about her husband's future mistress. Agatha began her humorous ode 'In Blessed Nimrud did there live Saint Barbara the Martyr' and paid tribute to a woman who, she said, would willingly share her trousers or her scrambled eggs and was happy to do accounts from morn to night. Max is described as 'the stern director' who gave Barbara hell. Agatha's ode was a tribute to Barbara's capacity to shoulder responsibility with indomitable good cheer.

Her devotion to her employers afforded both admiration and amusement to others at the dig. Moreover her willingness and good humour in taking responsibility for whatever went wrong on the dig led her to assume something of the role of court jester. But Barbara's compliant nature and dog-like devotion masked unfulfilled sexual needs, and it was not long before Max reached out to satisfy them.

In the early years of his relationship with Barbara, Agatha lived in constant fear of him leaving her. The fact that he never asked her for a divorce meant she never had to face a recurrence of the press attention of the late 1920s, yet her intense dread of having her private life exposed once more to the world remained at the back of her mind. Judith and Graham Gardner recall that 'Max put Agatha through hell over Barbara.'

The writer's anguish was heightened because she still loved Max and she wanted to believe that he still loved her. In fact he had no desire to abandon his marriage, since he enjoyed a more affluent lifestyle with Agatha than he could have experienced through his archaeological pursuits alone and his wife did everything in her power to ensure that he wanted for nothing.

Given her intense fear of publicity, Agatha had no alternative but to ignore Max's relationship with Barbara. The writer sought consolation in religious faith. Judith recalls that Barbara's love of archaeology strengthened her relationship with Max. It was their common passion. Agatha's anxiety about her marriage led to her developing recurring outbreaks of psoriasis, a condition often exacerbated by stress. However, the marriage survived to the end of her life because she and Max had similar intellectual and aesthetic tastes as well as a shared self-deprecatory and humorous outlook on life.

In September 1950 the story of her disappearance came back to haunt her. A number of her readers wrote to her expressing indignation over a serial broadcast by the South African Broadcasting Corporation that contained detailed references in one of its episodes to an unnamed female novelist who had disappeared some years ago and obtained 'worldwide publicity of advertising value'. It was the opinion of Agatha's fans that the identity of the authoress in question could not be missed and that the interpretation of the incident was injurious to her reputation.

That same year Agatha began working intermittently on her autobiography, which was to take her almost sixteen years to complete. It was intended as a collection of happy memories, rather than a chronological examination of her past and its more painful aspects. She assumed a cheerful, self-effacing tone, which served her well as she skimmed over more sensitive or unpleasant events in her life. The book recalled in considerable detail her happy childhood and the first three-quarters of her life. Yet at no time does she state that her marriage to Max had brought her enduring happiness.

Although Agatha mentions Archie more often than Max, when she came to recount the break-up of her first marriage into a tape recorder she found herself so distressed that her voice was almost inaudible. She does not mention that Archie's affair with Nancy lasted a year and a half and implies that her grief over her mother's death was the reason for Archie's defection to Nancy and his subsequent request for a divorce. Agatha suggests that he left her because he had missed his usual cheerful companion in the preceding few months owing to her grief over her mother's death.

There is no mention of her disappearance at all, which is the one area of her life her fans would have wanted to read about. All she says is that after illness came sorrow, despair and heartbreak and that there was no need to dwell on it. She gives a fictitious account of having been unable to remember her name when she went to sign a cheque shortly after Clarissa's death. In a preface that was added as a tribute to the authoress after her death, Agatha's unsuspecting publishers seized on this incident, suggesting that it gave the clue to the course of events at the time of the disappearance. Yet the closest she comes to talking about the incident in her autobiography is when she comments on her dislike of the press and of crowds which developed after the breakdown of her marriage. She said that she had felt like a hunted fox. She had always hated notoriety and had had such a dose of it that she felt she could hardly bear to go on living.

Since she makes no reference to the disappearance, the context in which these remarks appear is ambiguous. There is no mention of Agatha's misleading explanation to the *Daily Mail,* because she had no desire to cause Archie further embarrassment, since she felt they had both suffered enough. It is interesting to note that, in the autobiography, she portrays herself as an inexperienced and nervous driver at the time of the General Strike in May 1926 (when, in fact, she was a competent motorist who had been driving for two years). A few paragraphs later Agatha gives herself away when she states that one of the great joys of having the Morris Cowley was driving down to Ashfield and taking Clarissa off to all the places they had never been able to visit before. As her mother had died a month before the General Strike, this negates Agatha's claim to have been a nervous driver at that time. It was obviously Agatha's hope that her fans would attribute her disappearance to some sort of accident combined with mental breakdown. This was the belief of many when her autobiography was released after her death.

Despite the wall of silence Agatha constructed between herself and outsiders, her increasing fame ensured that the disappearance was never forgotten. One person who was very conscious of it was Hubert Gregg, who directed several of her plays for the London stage, beginning with *The Hollow* in 1951. Before meeting the authoress he and the cast were given strict instructions by management not to mention the disappearance to her.

Meanwhile, there was a new addition to Agatha's circle of friends in 1951 when Nan's daughter Judith, then thirty-four, married a handsome 24-year-old photographer called Graham Gardner, whom she had met at a tennis club in Torquay three years earlier. Nan and Agatha approved of the match from the start, although Graham's mother was initially inclined to suspect Judith of cradle-snatching.

Judith and Graham enjoyed their visits to Greenway as much as Agatha liked being surrounded by her family and friends. Graham was very shy, and Agatha took him under her wing. She used to place him to her right at the huge oval dining-table. Agatha liked listening quietly to other people's conversations, which often gave her ideas for her stories. She herself was not shy; she was simply wary of confiding in people she did not know intimately. Yet Agatha could approach strangers and engage them in conversation with consummate ease, as a former beau of Judith's, Peter Korda (son of the film maker Alexander Korda), had discovered one day at a public library when Agatha had gone straight up to him and introduced herself.

Nan was also a frequent visitor to Greenway, where there was a pleasant absence of formality. It became a ritual for Nan and Agatha to retreat to the library after lunch to indulge in their passion for newspaper crosswords, leading members of the household to dub them the 'Crossword Queens'. They had not given up travelling either – Nan still went on a cruise every year, while Agatha always accompanied Max to the Middle East and took him on at least one annual holiday – and the two friends would regale each other with their adventures. Agatha nicknamed Nan the 'Cruise Queen'; she was 'Nomadic Agatha'. While Agatha still guarded her privacy, she agreed to invite a party of Swedish fans Nan had met in Oslo to Greenway in July 1951 on condition that Nan act as chaperone, and it was one of the few times in her life when Agatha enjoyed herself among her admirers.

Although she never forgave Nancy Neele for taking Archie away from her, Agatha could never really dislike Barbara, and she endured her rival's visits to Greenway 'on archaeological matters'. There was something so dog-like about Barbara's devotion to Max that Agatha could not find it in herself to hate her openly. Knowing that Barbara was attracted to Max for the same reasons she herself had fallen in love with him caused Agatha to pity and slightly despise her rival. Agatha was never able to forget the fact that her relationship with Barbara had begun as a friendship, and ambivalence in her attitude towards Barbara remained.

In 1952 Agatha published a new Mary Westmacott book, *A Daughter's a Daughter,* which was based on an unperformed play she had written in the late 1930s inspired by Nan and Judith. Basil Dean had intended directing a production of it in 1939, and Gertrude Lawrence's agents had expressed interest in the role based on Nan. The book benefits from Basil Dean's recommended alterations to the play, and the tempestuous but loving relationship between mother and daughter is finely drawn.

Meanwhile, *The Mousetrap,* based on a radio play Agatha wrote for Queen Mary's eightieth birthday, opened in the West End in November 1952. Agatha presumed it would only run for six months and rashly made over the royalties to her grandson Mathew. It has since earned millions and outstripped all records for the longest continuous run in the English theatre. Had she known that the US tax revenue's protracted investigation of her financial affairs would drag on endlessly until the early 1960s she would never have handed the royalties over in trust to the schoolboy at a time when her financial worries were compounded by her fear of possible abandonment by Max. She never ceased to regret the hardship she had imposed on herself.

Of all the mysteries Agatha wrote one of the most personally revealing is *Witness for the Prosecution*, which opened on the London stage in 1953 and a year later appeared on Broadway, where it achieved the rare distinction for a thriller of winning the New York Drama Critics' Circle award for best foreign play of 1954. The 1925 short story on which it was based, 'Traitor Hands', was written when Agatha was young, romantic and inclined to idolize Archie, and in this story she had, unusually, allowed a ruthless killer to escape justice owing to the duplicity of a besotted female. Agatha was under pressure from the play's producer, Peter Saunders, and the cast to adhere to the original ending, but she resolutely refused to allow the play to go on unless the killer experienced full retribution. Archie's betrayal and Max's furtive affair had brought home to her the belief that the innocent ought never to suffer at the hands of the guilty. Her conviction became more evident in her detective fiction as she got older, and after hanging was abolished in the late 1960s her killers almost invariably received punishment and retribution from the gods.

There were echoes of personal experience in Agatha's 1954 novel *Destination Unknown*. The heroine Hilary Craven's marriage has failed. Moreover the death of her daughter, Brenda, after a long illness has left Hilary without religious hope or optimism for the future. After her husband has defected into the arms of another woman, Hilary escapes cold, misty England in search of blue skies and sunshine. But on arriving in Casablanca she discovers she has not left her problems behind. She has resolved to commit suicide with sleeping tablets when a secret agent asks her to put her life in danger by impersonating the wife of a scientist who has mysteriously vanished; she is advised that the best way of impersonating someone is to feign concussion, because this excuses apparent memory lapses and unpredictable behaviour. Although a conventional thriller in many respects, the book deals with the causes and consequences of defection and assumed identity and makes the point that in the face of major problems there can be no easy escape.

Agatha sublimated her ambivalent feelings for Barbara in her last and most insubstantial Mary Westmacott book, *The Burden*, published in 1956. Its sketchiness arises from its uneven style and the cramming of too many ideas into a slim novel. *The Burden* is essentially a reworking of the Cinderella theme: the noble, long-suffering sister ultimately finds love while the self-indulgent, immature sister perishes.

Laura Franklin is a repressed child who yearns to be loved by her parents. She is unable to bear the thought of her younger sister Shirley getting more love from their parents, and so she lights a candle of Intention in the hope that her sister will die. When the house catches fire that night Laura is horrified by God's apparently brutal response. After her courageous rescue of Shirley, Laura vows always to care for her.

Seventeen years have elapsed and the sisters' parents have died in a plane crash. Laura has long acted as a mother to Shirley and has no personal life of her own. One of Shirley's admirers is a ruthless, care-free young man called Henry who turns up unexpectedly on a motor cycle. Romance blossoms. By marrying Barbara's fictional counterpart, Shirley, off to Henry, plainly based on Archie, Agatha was reinforcing her conviction that if Barbara had ever known the true joys and agonies of being in love she would never have dreamed of usurping Max's affections.

Shirley soon discovers what it is like to be married to an unfaithful husband who is constantly in debt. After Henry is crippled by polio, he takes his frustrations out on his wife. In a moment of selflessness Laura gives him an overdose of sleeping tablets in order to free Shirley from the marriage. His grief-stricken widow subsequently discovers that her much-longed-for escape with the attractive and considerate Sir Richard Wilding had been a mistake.

She becomes an alcoholic. After being married for three years to the doting Sir Richard and living in luxury with him on an island, Shirley discovers this is not what she wants from life. She confides to Llewellyn Knox, a former American evangelist, that while she was never very happy with Henry their marriage had been, in a way, all right; it had been a life she had chosen.

She mourns Henry's premature death, and her sentiments come straight from Agatha's heart in describing the man she still loves as selfish and ruthless in a gay and charming kind of way. She says she loves him still and would rather be unhappy with him than 'smug and comfortable' without him. Shirley says she hates God for letting Henry die, and Llewellyn reassures her that it is better to hate God than our fellow man because God has always been our scapegoat, shouldering the burden of our joy and our pain.

In the final part of the book, where the action becomes absurdly compressed, Laura learns from Llewellyn that Shirley has been killed after drunkenly stepping in front of a passing vehicle. Laura is devastated by her sister's death and questions whether it was suicide, but Llewellyn insists it was an accident. Laura confesses to her hand in Henry's death and explains how she has attempted to absolve her guilt by running an institution for 'subnormal' children. Llewellyn tells her that he has fallen in love with her, and Laura accepts his proposal of marriage within less than twenty-four hours of having met him. Although Agatha had a dislike of commercialized religion, the retired evangelist is cast as the perfect husband for Laura because he has retained his humility and belief in God. The story ends happily with Laura feeling loved for the first time.

This Cinderella-like ending represented a wish fulfilment on Agatha's part. The extraordinary courtesy Max always displayed towards her helped to sustain the marriage, despite his continuing affair with Barbara. Her pet dogs, those most faithful of companions, and cats were a constant source of comfort to Agatha during her bouts of agitation and depression and recurring outbreaks of psoriasis.

There was cause for celebration in 1956, when Agatha was awarded a CBE in the New Year's Honours List for her contribution to detective fiction and the stage. 'One up to the Low-Brows!' she triumphantly wrote to Edmund Cork from Baghdad, where she was helping Max in his work. Despite her elation fame never went to her head, and by now she was an extraordinarily famous woman.

Inevitably, there were allusions to her disappearance from time to time. She was very upset about an article on the elusive best-selling novelist Rowena Farre that appeared in the *Daily Mail* on 19 February 1957, in which Kenneth Althorp passed the comment: 'I'm sure she's not doing an Agatha Christie on me.' Although Agatha's secret remained safe with Nan, Edmund Cork was dispatched to have lunch with one of the *Daily Mail's* top executives to point out the newspaper's bad taste in bringing up the subject of his client's disappearance.

While the innocuous article did not warrant such a response, constant reminders of the incident made Agatha more anxious to avoid the limelight than ever. She also remained exceptionally modest. In 1957 the novel *4.50 from Paddington* was published. This absorbing mystery involves the ingenious disposal of a body from a passing train down a railway embankment into the grounds of a family mansion and was inspired by the railway line that abutted the corner of Abney Hall's grounds. Critics hailed the book as containing one of Miss Marple's finest deductions.

Agatha was at Paddington Station one day, looking for something to read at the W.H. Smith Bookstall, when she was accosted by a bookseller who recommended the book to her. He said all his regular customers had bought a copy and spoke highly of it, but Agatha's response was non-committal. Finally he asked incredulously: 'Don't you want to read it?' Agatha informed him she was not really interested. She was amused by the incident, because, as she later told her family and friends, if the man had looked at the back of the book he would have immediately spotted her picture.

During summers at Greenway Agatha went to Churston Church every Sunday. The east window was considered rather plain, and she gave some money towards a new one of stained glass. She asked if the design could include pastures and sheep; she felt children would relate to this idea as it harked back to her own childhood vision of Heaven. After the window, depicting the life of Christ, was installed in July 1957 Graham photographed it at her request.

By October that year Agatha had begun work on her new detective novel *Ordeal by Innocence*. Normally she liked to finish a project as quickly as possible, but she temporarily set it aside to write a supernatural story called 'The Dressmaker's Doll', in which she vented her feelings about Barbara. The life-sized velvet and silk doll is a puppet, a decadent product of the twentieth century that lolls in a dressmaker's studio, limp yet strangely alive, next to the telephone or among the divan cushions, looking sad but at the same time rather sly, determined and knowing. The women who work in the studio are never able to work out how she got there, and they feel a sense of menace when the doll assumes a macabre life of its own. Believing it to be evil, one of the women throws it out the window. An overwrought colleague insists that she has 'killed' the doll, when to their horror an urchin in the street makes off with it. The frightened women follow, but the child refuses to give up her find, exclaiming that she loves it and that being loved is all the doll ever wanted. Pitiful yet menacing, the creature was an expression of Agatha's deeply ambivalent feelings towards Barbara.

Judith Gardner has stated that Barbara made herself such an indispensable factotum to Max and Agatha that she regularly came to Greenway. She was very obviously more than just a secretary. Max and Barbara's passion for one another led them to become indiscreet. Once Graham encountered them embracing down by the boat-house and, on another occasion, on the Greenway ferry around dusk. It became a habit of Max's to rise from the table after lunch and announce that he was 'just going upstairs to get on with a paper'. While Max and Barbara were upstairs together Agatha and Nan did crosswords together in the library.

'The Night of a Thousand Stars', the lavish party theatrical producer Peter Saunders threw at the Savoy on 13 April 1958 to celebrate *The Mousetrap*'s achievement in becoming the longest-running play in the history of the British theatre, was a fraught occasion for Agatha and not just because the press turned out in force. As the most important star of the party Agatha agreed, with some reluctance, to arrive early to pose for some publicity pictures, only to be told by an officious doorman that no one would be admitted to the ballroom for half an hour.

Agatha's response to the rebuff was extraordinary. She went away, although she need only have said who she was and why she was there to have been let in. She was eventually admitted, however, and the pictures of her cutting the cake were taken and the party proceeded. The story that the crime writer was so self-effacing and shy that she allowed herself to be turned away appeared in the newspapers the following day, and it had the effect of helping to keep at a distance journalists and admirers who might have wished to get close.

Agatha was reluctant to appear in the publicity pictures because she knew she was no longer beautiful and she disliked seeing photographs of herself. Yet she loyally stood next to Peter Saunders and greeted the guests on their arrival. Later she agreed to make a short speech in which her still girlish, fluting voice shook with genuine emotion when she admitted: 'I'd rather write ten plays than make one speech.'

Although she was proud of her theatrical achievements, especially *The Mousetrap*, she regretted her rashness in giving away the royalties to her beloved grandson. 'Oh, why did I give the royalties to Mathew?' Agatha lamented to Nan on one occasion. 'It's the only play I've ever written that's ever made any money.'

By now, Agatha's marriage had survived almost a decade of infidelity, and she had persuaded herself that she had less reason to be anxious that Max might leave her than she originally thought. She had entered into a phase she liked to think of as her 'second spring' and she convinced herself that physical passion between a man and his wife was not necessary to the overall well-being of a marriage. She rejoiced in the fresh sap of creative ideas that rose up in her, stimulated by her travels with Max, visits to the theatre and opera and reading. Nevertheless she still grieved over the loss of Max's love for her.

By way of affirming what her marriage to Max meant she wrote the play, *Verdict*. She had wanted to call it *No Fields of Amaranth*, after the lines from Walter Savage Landor's *Imaginary Conversations* quoted in the play – 'There are no fields of amaranth this side of the grave' – but the title had already been used by another playwright. Although a murder is committed in full view of the audience at the end of Act One, *Verdict* is essentially a love story with the message that the cost of living with an idealist can often be high.

Max provided the inspiration for the central character of Karl Hendryk, a university professor who sacrifices the women he loves for his ideals and his work. His physically disabled wife Anya criticizes Karl for neglecting her for his work. When Anya dies after one of her husband's besotted female students, Helen, administers a drug overdose to her, an unsuspecting Karl is devastated by her apparent suicide. He turns to his secretary, Lisa, for sympathy; the two have always loved each other but never openly acknowledged the fact while Anya was alive. In a desperate bid to secure Karl's affections, Helen confesses that she killed his wife. Karl is shocked and stunned, but he decides not to go to the police because he pities Helen and recognizes that revenge will not bring Anya back.

His decision leads to Lisa being wrongly arrested for the murder and afterwards, when he tells the police of Helen's confession, they do not believe him, because Helen has been killed in a road accident and they think he is trying to save Lisa from the gallows. After Lisa is acquitted, she has to choose whether to start life afresh or to spend the rest of her life with an idealist who causes pain to those who love him. There is never any real contest in her heart. Her reason for staying with the man she loves comes straight from her creator's heart: 'Because I'm a fool.'

Rather than face the fact that Max no longer loved her, Agatha reveals her philosophy about relationships when one of her characters says that the young are mistaken in thinking love is just about glamour, desire and sex appeal: 'That's nature's start of the whole business. It's the showy flower, if you like. But love's the root. Underground, out of sight, nothing much to look at, but it's where the life is.'

Verdict failed at the box office because the title and the writer's name led her many mystery fans to expect a tense courtroom thriller that would have them on the edge of their seats. Although she rebounded from this setback within a month by writing the successful stage thriller *The Unexpected Guest*, Agatha was deeply upset over *Verdict's* reception. She later claimed that, with the exception of *Witness for the Prosecution*, it was the best play she had ever written. Albeit underrated, *Verdict* remains Agatha's most elegiac play about human relationships. It might have been hailed a success if it had been staged under a pseudonym.

The past came back to haunt her when Abney Hall was sold in 1958 and when Nancy died from cancer in August the same year. Although Agatha had not seen Archie once in all the years they had been divorced, she wrote to him expressing her condolences. He, too, was able to put the bitterness of the past behind him when he wrote back to say how deeply touched he was that she had not begrudged him his three decades of happiness with Nancy.

After they had married Archie and Nancy had lived together in Hampstead, north London. A son, Archibald, was born in 1930, and the Christies later moved to Juniper Hill in Surrey to be closer to Madge and Sam James, their hosts on the night of Agatha's disappearance. Their love survived the unwelcome publicity of 1926 intact, and golf remained an obsession for the couple, their back porch constantly littered with clubs. They were a sociable and loving family.

After Sam James's death Archie had looked after Madge's annual financial accounts and continued to do extremely well in the city as a company director. As a token of the enduring friendship that had sustained them through an exceedingly difficult time Nancy bequeathed an aquamarine gold brooch to Madge in her will.

Agatha was shocked when her lifelong friend Nan was diagnosed with lung cancer in mid-1959 and told she only had six months to live. Nan had been a heavy smoker all her life. She had left London for good and was living near Agatha in the same street as her daughter Judith and son-in-law Graham in Paignton, Devon. Nan was then aged seventy and Agatha sixty-eight. Nan's reaction to her illness was to continue to lead as vigorous a life as possible, driving around in her car as energetically as ever.

Despite her indomitable spirit, she grew thinner and her condition rapidly deteriorated. She was finally moved to Torquay's Mount Stuart Nursing Home where she would watch the seagulls soaring over the bay. Agatha visited her twice in the last week of her life. They talked of the old days and of the fun they had had. Before the end there was one last time-honoured ritual. Agatha's latest book, *Cat Among the Pigeons,* was inscribed in the flyleaf: 'To Nan, who once went hunting schools with me.' Nan's death on 2 December at the age of seventy-one left Agatha devastated; she had lost her best and closest friend.

25

ACCOLADES AND REMINDERS

AGATHA WROTE A moving letter of condolence to Judith after Nan's death telling her that if she or Graham ever needed help they had only to ask. The couple cherished the letter. Nan's fortune and the first editions of Agatha's personally inscribed books were, of course, bequeathed to Judith.

Dealing with Nan's death and other painful aspects of her past was made easier for Agatha when Graham, who shared her fascination with time, gave her a copy of James Coleman's *Relativity for the Layman*, which he bought for her from the bookshop in Dartmouth. The book, with its exposition on the relativity of time, helped Agatha come to terms with her loss, and she was further sustained by religion.

When the detective novelist Christianna Brand told Agatha that the former cub reporter of the *Daily News*, Ritchie Calder, intended to write an article about the disappearance to coincide with her seventieth birthday in September 1960, Agatha maintained a philosophical tone when communicating the news to her literary agent Edmund Cork. She told him not to worry about her hearing the news; it was just one of those reminders of the past that cropped up every few years and, after all, what did it matter after so long? Now she was seventy, she said, she did not care about what people said about her. She said the reminder was 'just slightly annoying' and that the less notice she took of it the better.

By now Agatha's finances were beginning to look much healthier. Her decision to sell the film rights to her work to Metro-Goldwyn-Mayer had come about after discussions with Graham and her son-in-law Anthony Hicks. She respected the two men's grasp of business matters and she had taken each of them aside separately to ask whether they thought she should form a company to handle her literary affairs. She took their advice and discovered that the advantages of being Agatha Christie Ltd were that she received a fixed income in return for producing a manuscript annually and the company became responsible for sorting out her business headaches. Other advisers and accountants had worked hard since the end of the Second World War to sort out her tangled finances, and during the 1960s her money worries eased considerably.

In July 1961 Agatha's nephew Jack Watts broke his leg while dancing. He died four days later from a blood clot. Agatha, Rosalind, Mathew and Judith were the beneficiaries of Jack's will, and Agatha inherited his Chester Street home in London. At the wake Agatha asked Graham if he would like to travel to the Middle East the following year to take some archaeological photographs for Max. Although Max's excavations had ceased, there was much work to be done to bring to fruition his book *Nimrud and Its Remains*. Graham expressed interest, and this led to talks between him and Max.

Meanwhile Agatha found the process of extracting herself from her tangled financial affairs was not without its pitfalls. Metro-Goldwyn-Mayer released four Miss Marple Films between 1962 and 1964, starring Margaret Rutherford, and the writer disliked them all, considering the actress good but badly miscast. She nevertheless dedicated her 1962 novel *The Mirror Crack'd from Side to Side* 'To Margaret Rutherford in Admiration'. This is the only book in which Agatha makes light-hearted reference to amnesia, when Miss Knight remarks of Lady Conway that her memory is so bad that she cannot even recognize her own relatives and tells them to go away. Miss Marple suggests that this might be shrewdness rather than memory loss.

In February 1962 Judith and Graham went out to Baghdad for the winter, so that Graham could photograph the numerous artefacts Max had unearthed. Max raised the necessary funds for Graham's trip through a college bursary. Judith accompanied her husband through Agatha's generosity. Graham recalls that Agatha wanted him and Judith to experience 'the beauty and romance of the desert' so she could relive, through them, the early days of her marriage to Max 'when she had been so happy and in love'.

They stayed at a house in Baghdad that had been acquired by the British School of Archaeology in Iraq in 1948. Graham spent numerous days at the Iraq Antiquities Department photographing the finds. Meanwhile Judith talked to the local archaeologists and was shown the city sights by Iraqis who shared her love of art. The couple were thrilled by the Middle East; they even enjoyed roughing it in the archaeological camps in the desert, including Mosul, where the best view of the breath-taking terrain was from the seat of the hillside lavatory which had three walls and no door.

Judith and Graham had unexpected confirmation that Max's rela-tionship with Barbara was as serious as ever when Graham called at the Mallowans' Swan Court flat in London before leaving for Baghdad. Max was furtively ensconced there with Barbara, having made the mistake of forgetting that he had asked Graham to drop by to receive instructions about photographing the Nimrud collection. Although Judith and Graham knew that Agatha was aware of the affair, they never men-tioned the lovers' tryst to her, because they knew of her anxiety at the prospect of another divorce.

There were, however, soon to be reminders of the past from which no one could protect her. Archie, the great love of her life, died on 20 December 1962. He was seventy-three, and the sinus problems that had dogged his earlier flying career had led in more recent years to asthma and bronchial-related complications. He was not religious and requested no flowers and no funeral or burial service.

There was further upset when Agatha belatedly heard that her childhood home in Torquay was going to become the site of a housing development. She acted fast, but it was too late to save Ashfield. Judith recalls watching Agatha weep inconsolably after hearing that the house had been pulled down. Ashfield had more than just childhood mem-ories; it was where she had courted Archie and given birth to Rosalind. If Agatha had known Max would betray her she would never have allowed herself to be persuaded to sell Ashfield all those years before.

Agatha was by now the world's best-selling author in the English language. Would-be biographers constantly pestered her with requests for assistance in their research into her life and works. Her refusal to help was adamant, because she dreaded the thought of the disappear-ance being dredged up after so long. This motivated her to finish the final chapters of her autobiography in October 1965; she suspected that a number of biographies on her would appear after her death and she wanted to ensure that people could read her own posthumous account of her life. She ended her memoirs by saying that at seventy-five she wished to thank God for her good life and for all the love that had been given to her.

Agatha revised her memoirs throughout 1966. She refused to give in to suggestions that they should be published during her lifetime; she was not interested in the publicity and she knew people would want to know why she had left out her disappearance. Despite being over five hundred pages long, the post-war years were crammed into thirty-odd pages; sig-nificantly, there was no mention of Archie's death. Nor, obviously, was there any hint of Max's deficiencies as a husband. Instead she concen-trated mainly on recalling her pleasure at the opening night of the play *Witness for the Prosecution* and over the archaeological discoveries she made with Max. History had always fascinated her and it pleased her that in a small way she had contributed to its understanding. Despite its omissions, the autobiography is a very enjoyable read, attesting to the considerable pleasure she got out of life.

The publication in 1966 of Max's study of his life's work, *Nimrud and Its Remains*, established him as one of the foremost authorities in his field. Agatha's pride in seeing her husband fêted was undermined by her knowledge of his affair, but the writer consoled herself with the fact that the mild stroke Max had suffered five years earlier had not taken him from her altogether. She increasingly relied on him to protect her privacy from over-zealous journalists and fans, and he was always a stalwart support in this respect.

The fans Agatha found least troublesome were those who wrote for her autograph; those who requested a photograph were firmly turned down. She continued to regret the loss of her youth. In her memoirs she refers to the fact that on several occasions in her later years the oppor-tunity had arisen for her to meet up with an unnamed beau from her past. This was Amyas Boston, and the reason she declined to see him was because she knew he would remember her as a lovely young girl at a moonlight picnic at Anstey's Cove, and she was anxious that he should not see how the passing of time had changed her.

As Agatha grew older her detective stories revealed more of her personal tastes and opinions. This was partly because she no longer plotted her stories so tightly and because the use of a dictaphone led to a more verbose style. Her opinions on such diverse topics as lavatory plumbing, comfortable armchairs for the elderly, household linen and the availability of proper muffins come across clearly in her 1965 novel *At Bertram's Hotel*, while her views on the dress of the young are even more apparent in her 1966 novel *Third Girl*. Although Agatha considered that young girls went out of their way to look dirty and unattractive, she regarded 1960s' men more indulgently because they had the appeal to her of 'Van Dyke portraits with curled hair and their velvets and their silks'. Her later books are all the more fascinating for revealing the views of their aged creator.

Her romantic ideals had changed little from the time she had cast Archie as the Leader of the Vikings in her poem 'The Ballad of the Flint'. One of the young male characters in her 1967 novel *Endless Night* describes the temptress as a glorious and sexy Valkyrie with shining golden hair, the most lovely creature he had ever seen: 'She smelt and looked and tasted of sex . . .' The book conveys the message that love cannot prosper on betrayed innocence.

As people grow older they often lose touch with the younger generation. But *Endless Night,* one of Agatha's best and most unusual later books, is proof that this did not happen with her. However, the world had changed, and she was disturbed by the increasing violence apparent in British society: 'Sometimes I'm almost afraid to live in this country,' she said, 'because I feel there is a tendency here to enjoy cruelty for its own sake.'

In 1967 Gordon Ramsey, an American academic, produced *Agatha Christie: Mistress of Mystery,* a complete bibliography of her work and an affectionate assessment of her writings. Agatha's literary advisers had urged her to cooperate with him since they were having considerable difficulty keeping up with her prolific output. Initially she had allowed him to visit her in London and had also welcomed him to Greenway, but she had restricted their talks mainly to her books so that there was very little discussion of more private aspects of her life. Agatha had soon tired of helping him with his research and had become so acutely defensive that she had even objected to him mentioning the two unpublished books she held in reserve from the 1940s: *Curtain: Poirot's Last Case* and *Sleeping Murder: Miss Marple's Last Case*.

Her reaction to his raising the subject of the novels was extraordinary, since she had already mentioned their existence to Francis Wyndham in a rare interview for the *Sunday Times Weekly Review* on 27 February the previous year. What Agatha was most unhappy about was a reference in the bibliography to when she went missing in 1926, although Gordon Ramsey summarily dismissed the notorious episode in half a page by explaining that the authoress had amnesia at the time of her disappearance.

In 1968 Max was knighted for his services to archaeology. Agatha had the satisfaction of knowing that he would never have achieved such success if she had not financed his expeditions. Moreover, becoming Lady Mallowan meant she had achieved her own childhood ambition of becoming 'Lady Agatha', and her title helped her mask her identity from her fans even more effectively than had 'Mrs Mallowan'. Meanwhile Barbara remained in the background, making herself as indispensable as ever to Max, and Agatha stoicly turned a blind eye to their relationship.

The authoress remained acutely sensitive to references to the disappearance. For instance, when an American publisher asked her to complete an outline for a plot begun by Franklin Roosevelt about a man who successfully plans his own disappearance, she refused to cooperate on the project. Stella Kirwan, Agatha's secretary at the time, meanwhile had enormous difficulty persuading the producer of the television series *This Is Your Life* that there was nothing Agatha would hate more than to have her personal history presented to her on television in front of an audience. Privacy was paramount to Agatha, and she was greatly displeased at being shown unauthorized aerial photographs of Greenway that had been taken for a magazine.

The closest Agatha ever came to mentioning her past was when she relaxed her guard with the sympathetic journalist Marcelle Bernstein in a much-publicized interview that appeared in the *Observer* on 14 December 1969: 'I married at 24; we were very happy for 11 years. Then my mother died a very painful death and my husband found a young woman. Well, you can't write your fate: your fate comes to you. But you can do what you like with the characters you create.'

Agatha had good reason to idealize her first marriage. During the painting of her portrait that year by Oscar Kokoschka, the famous artist noticed her habit of tapping her fingers, which were then badly afflicted with psoriasis, on the arms of her chair. She was still upset over Max's relationship with Barbara, which showed no sign of abating. To make things worse, an anonymous journalist – unaware of her marital problems – had attributed the following quote to Agatha: 'The advantage of being married to an archaeologist is that the older you get the more interested he is in you.' Agatha hated the quote and always denied having said it.

26

THE TWILIGHT YEARS

AGATHA WAS AT the peak of her fame in the 1970s and to those fans who eagerly awaited each new 'Christie for Christmas' it seemed as if she had brooked no serious rival for years. The decade began with the publication of *Passenger to Frankfurt*, which became a best-seller in Britain and the United States. Initially, however, her UK publishers had hesitated over whether to publish it at all and had only done so on condition that she subtitle it 'An Extravaganza' and include an introduction to explain why she had written it.

In *Passenger to Frankfurt* Agatha had produced an international thriller involving terrorism, hijacking and an attempted resurgence of Nazi Germany by the son of Adolf Hitler. Although the plot was extremely unusual for a Christie novel, it is interesting to note that the book centres on the successful hunt to recover Project Benvo, the code-name for a drug, which, when injected into man, effectively eradicates violent impulses by inducing a permanent state of benevolence. Readers who do not like this book often fail to realize just how concerned she had become about the violence she felt she saw, initially in Britain, and latterly as a world-wide epidemic.

Despite Max's continued relationship with Barbara, the authoress's self-esteem rose when she heard she was to be made a Dame of the British Empire in the 1971 New Year's Honours list. Agatha was an ardent monarchist, so she was delighted by such a titled bestowed by the Queen. Not even the attention of the press could prevent her from attending her investiture at Buckingham Palace, although she declined to be interviewed by journalists.

Her new book, *Nemesis*, which marked a return to the domestic whodunits for which she was famous, was begun in January 1971, and next to her name above the title in her notebook she added the initials DBE. The plot deals with the depravity that can result from thwarted love and supplies one of the most emotionally compelling motives for crime in her literary canon.

In June she was treated for a broken hip at Nuffield Orthopaedic Hospital in Oxford after falling at Winterbrook and hobbling about painfully for a week. Judith and Graham had advised her to get her injury examined straight away. Agatha dismissed the idea, thinking she was just bruised, but it turned out to be more serious.

Meanwhile Max was concerned about their finances. In addition to Greenway and Winterbrook, there was the upkeep of his new Mercedes and the Swan Court flat in London where he would spend time with Barbara. It angered Judith and Graham that he did so little to ensure Agatha's comfort: the hall light at Winterbrook came crashing down one day, the roof leaked and the house was in urgent need of general maintenance and repair. Although Agatha was a wealthy woman, much of her money had been distributed in trusts for her family in anticipation of her death. The only immediate money at hand came from Agatha Christie Ltd. The fact that Max was keeping Barbara added to his financial anxieties, recalls Graham.

Agatha's self-esteem received a boost that year when Madame Tussaud's expressed a desire to model a wax effigy of her. She gave her permission with pleasure, as she had always enjoyed visiting London's waxworks museum as a child.

In 1972 Michael Parkinson, the television chat-show host, compiled *Michael Parkinson's Confessional Album – 1973*, in which famous people were asked to record their likes and dislikes. It was unusual for Agatha to respond to a public questionnaire, but she was happy to oblige on this occasion because filling in family confessional albums had been an enjoyable pastime in her youth. She gave her ideal of beauty in nature as 'a bank of primroses in spring', cited Elgar, Sibelius and Wagner as her favourite composers and named T.S. Eliot's *Murder in the Cathedral* as the play she most admired. Her favourite quotation came from Sir Thomas Browne: 'Life is a pure flame, and we live by an invisible sun within us'; while she gave as her motto Dr Johnson's 'The business of life is to go forwards.' She stated that the qualities she most liked in men were 'integrity and good manners'. When asked who her heroes were in real life, she wrote: 'None. I am not a hero-worshipper.' This complete volte-face from her intensely romantic outlook during her first marriage revealed how much she had changed over the years. She did, however, cite her favourite heroines in real life as the 'Little Sisters of the Poor'.

When the publishers of the *Guinness Book of Great Moments* wrote asking for her permission to reproduce a corrected proof of a page from *Nemesis*, she agreed. It was a distinct feather in her cap, for a woman whose grammar and literary style had often been, with some justification, derided by her critics. They usually made the mistake of judging her as a novelist, when she was really a great story-teller. She was particularly good at writing about children and had the ability to be equally convincing when writing in the first person as either a man or a woman. In fact, Agatha frequently belittled her writing, calling herself 'a good honest craftsman'. What is not in doubt is that she had become a literary legend in her lifetime.

As Agatha's health began to deteriorate, her daughter made increasingly frequent visits to her mother's side. In Rosalind's absence Agatha's most devoted companion was a Manchester terrier named Bingo, who had been so terrified as a puppy that he used to bite everyone on sight. The one person he did not attack was Agatha. Mistress and dog adored each other, and Bingo slept at the end of her bed. Max's ankles became a mass of scars and visitors to Winterbrook soon fell victim to Bingo's jaws, for he was adept at lying in wait. Agatha would joke with Max that the reason Bingo bit him every time he picked up the telephone when it rang was because he thought the devil was inside it. Notwithstanding, he was a good guard dog, for he gave the alarm one day when a burglar erected a ladder outside Agatha's bedroom window and escaped with just two rather moth-eaten old fur coats.

Agatha's 1972 novel, *Elephants Can Remember,* concerned a love triangle that ended in triple tragedy. There is a veiled reference to Agatha's *alter ego* in Harrogate when one of her characters remarks that the ill-fated Lady Ravenscroft had spoken before her death about starting a new life connected with St Teresa of Avila, the nun who became a saint through her reform of the convents. The remark is intriguing, for it in no way propels the plot or leads to an explanation of Lady Ravenscroft's death.

Agatha felt tired and worn out and her last book, *Postern of Fate*, which was published in 1973, was written in a mood of resentment and defiance. She wanted to be left in peace but felt obliged to deliver her annual manuscript to Agatha Christie Ltd on time. She complained to Mrs Thompson, her housekeeper at Greenway, that her publishers were waiting on every word she wrote. As is common in elderly people, Agatha's thoughts turned increasingly to the past, and the home into which Tommy and Tuppence Beresford move in *Postern of Fate* is modelled on her beloved Ashfield.

While the exposition was a gem of inspiration, the rest of the novel was disappointing, since, unusually, Agatha had started off without a preconceived conjuring trick with which to dazzle her readers. Max determined to salvage the novel by editing it himself, with the help of Agatha's then secretary, Daphne Honeybone. His editing and that of Agatha's publishers lacked due care and attention: the ages of the Beresfords' grandchildren are given as fifteen, eleven and seven – despite the fact that two of them are meant to be twins. Judith and Graham recall Max cajoled Agatha into completing *Postern of Fate* because he was worried about their finances 'and that Parker woman'.

The writer's most significant publication that year was *Poems*. The volume includes nearly all the poems that had appeared in *The Road of Dreams*, as well as more recent ones. 'A Choice' shows the authoress's futile attempt to put the regrets of the past behind her in order to live in the present. Significantly, not one of her love poems celebrates the unqualified joys of love. They express the darker side of yearning, trepidation, despair, abandonment and loss. In 'What Is Love?' Agatha bemoans the fact that love is not like a tree, 'rooted in time – for all eternity'.

Written in anticipation of the fact that she might die before Max, Agatha seems to suggest in 'Remembrance' that he will forget her, although her love for him would remain undiminished after her death.

When it became apparent that there would be no new novel for 1974, Collins released *Poirot's Early Cases*, which was a collection of short stories she had published in *The Sketch* in the 1920s.

In October that year Agatha had a heart attack and was confined to bed. She passed the time by rereading her Mary Westmacott novels. '*Unfinished Portrait* I think is one of the best after *Rose and the Yew Tree*,' she told Edmund Cork. When once asked by the detective novelist and critic Julian Symons why she had used a pseudonym for her romance novels, she replied, 'I think it is better to keep the two sorts of book separate. I like keeping them to myself, too, so that I can write exactly what I like. You can write a bit of your own life into them in a way, if nobody knows it's you . . . I would like to have written all sorts of different books, tried all kinds of different things. But of course detective stories supported me and my daughter for many years, and they had to be written.' It was an extraordinary epitaph for a writing career the success of which was based on detective stories. Agatha also reread her autobiography and had copies sent to Max and Rosalind, two of her sternest critics, for approval.

The medication Agatha took for her heart left her frail and thin. She regressed more and more into the past. She was more lucid some days than others; sometimes she would get so confused she would panic because she thought she had to pack for Baghdad, recalls Judith. Agatha was under no illusions that she was nearing the end of her life, and one day she pinned all her brooches on her dress to wear one last time. Max and Rosalind meanwhile looked after her as best they could with the help of a night nurse. Judith and Graham felt that Max was impatient for Agatha to die so that he could marry Barbara.

Agatha was outwardly uncomplaining when Max's mistress came each weekend to relieve Max of his caring duties. But one day Agatha took up a pair of scissors and cut off her locks of white hair. When someone mutilates their appearance it is often a sign of deep emotional disturbance. Agatha had every reason to feel resentful at being nursed by her husband's mistress. Her act may have been a cry for help or a deliberate attempt to shock and startle Max and Barbara into a belated sense of guilt. I would suggest that Agatha most likely confronted the fact that she was no longer a beautiful woman and cut off her hair in preparation for meeting God. She had, after all, had a strong religious faith for many years. At any rate Max and Barbara behaved more distantly to each other in Agatha's presence after this and treated her even more attentively.

A visit to Winterbrook House by Lord Snowdon, the royal photographer, led to a series of photographs of Agatha and Max appearing in the *Sunday Times,* heralding the arrival in the cinema of *Murder on the Orient Express.* With her crumpled pink-and-white rose-leaf complexion, white hair and shrewd, kindly eyes Agatha looked more than ever like many of her fans' popular conception of Miss Marple.

Agatha met Lord Louis Mountbatten in November 1974 at the glittering film première of *Murder on the Orient Express.* He had written to her over forty years earlier with an idea for a story that she had incorporated into her most famous novel, *The Murder of Roger Ackroyd.* The occasion was attended by other members of the Royal Family, and she insisted on rising from her wheelchair when she was presented to the Queen and the Princess Royal. Agatha's pleasure at being presented to royalty left her incandescent with happiness. Not even the presence in the background of television cameras could diminish her elation. Later there was a lavish supper party at Claridge's Hotel. The stars of the film each came to pay their respects at her table, and it was well after midnight when Lord Mountbatten wheeled her from the ballroom to her waiting car to an enormous standing ovation. It was to be her last major public appearance.

The film's release spread her fame throughout the world, but how sensitive she remained to references to her disappearance may be measured from the fact that when the publisher Otto Penzler asked her to approve her entry for the *Encyclopaedia of Mystery and Detection* in mid-1975 she was upset by two allusions to her 'attack of amnesia'. Meanwhile, since there was no new novel for that year it was decided for her that *Curtain: Poirot's Last Case* would be released.

One evening, towards the end of her life, when a young boy came to see her, a calm and serene Agatha presented him with a quotation that encapsulated her own philosophy of life:

I have three treasures,
Guard them and keep them safe.
The first is love.
The second is never do too much,
The third is never be the first in the world.
Through love one has no fear.
Through not doing too much one has
amplitude of reserve power.
Through not presuming to be the first in
the world one can develop one's talent
and let it mature.

When she finally caught a cold during the last winter she murmured: 'I'm going to meet my Maker.' She died quietly not long after this as Max was wheeling her in her chair from lunch at Winterbrook House on 12 January 1976. Death had released her from the bizarre and agonizing love triangle to which she had allowed herself to be subjected for nearly thirty years. The world lost a literary legend and, ironically, her death became a media event. The thousands of moving tributes that appeared from around the world confirmed Agatha as the greatest of all the Golden Age detective writers – and nearly all recalled how she had become famous by disappearing.

The writer had always kept on her bedside table her mother's copy of Thomas à Kempis's *The Imitation of Christ,* and beneath 'Agatha Mallowan' she had written on the flyleaf part of St Paul's Epistle to the Romans:

Who shall separate us from the love of Christ?
Shall tribulation, or distress, or persecution or famine, or nakedness,
    or pen, or sword?
I am persuaded that neither death, nor life, nor angels, nor
    principalities, nor powers, nor things present,
    nor things to come, nor height nor depth, nor any other creature,
    shall be able to separate us from the love of God,
    which is in Christ Jesus our Lord.

Graham recalls that it was only 'at the end that she had grown tired of religion and had felt let down by the whole thing'. Having adhered to her wedding vows to Max, for better and for worse, Agatha was buried, in accordance with her request, with her wedding ring in Cholsey grave-yard. Her fortune and Greenway were bequeathed to her daughter. Winterbrook House and 22 Cresswell Place had been made over to Max long before she died.

Max married Barbara the following year. His autobiography, which was published the same year, dismissed Agatha's eleven-day disappear-ance in a single sentence as resulting from 'a loss of memory'. Max went to great pains to impress on readers how happy his marriage to Agatha had been. He died from a heart attack in August 1978 and was buried with Agatha in Cholsey. His widow, Barbara, continued to live in Wallingford. She died in November 1993. It was her private wish to be buried with Agatha and Max. Her request was denied.

A clause in Max's will stipulated that a sum of money be set aside each year to allow members of the British School of Archaeology in Iraq to drink a toast at their annual lecture in memory of him and Agatha.

The posthumous publication of Agatha's autobiography merely com-pounded the greatest mystery of her life. Agatha had once referred to Hercule Poirot, with whom she maintained a love–hate relationship, as 'the Old Man from the Sea', claiming he was a millstone round her neck throughout her life. The same was true of the disappearance.

27

Unforeseen Ripples

After Agatha's death the wall of silence she had built around herself during her lifetime remained inviolate. Biographers and journalists seeking to penetrate it were frustrated. Yet since her death sales of her works have trebled; she has sold in excess of two billion copies of her books, thus ensuring continued speculation over the truth behind her disappearance so many years ago.

Those close to Agatha and Nan, who know the truth of what happened on Friday 3 December 1926, have always refuted tales of an extraordinary encounter between Agatha and a journalist in the lounge of the Harrogate Hydro on the afternoon of her discovery, Tuesday 14 December, which first surfaced two weeks after her death. According to Ritchie Calder, the former *Daily News* reporter, there was no melodrama when he walked up to Mrs Teresa Neele and addressed her as Mrs Christie. She was not flustered, and when he asked her how she had got there she said she did not know and that she was suffering from amnesia, whereupon she retired to her room for the rest of the afternoon. The *Daily News* report the following day, in breaking the news of Archie's identification of Agatha in the hotel, never mentioned such an encounter taking place, and Lord Ritchie Calder, as he later became, only wrote of the incident eight years before his death in an article, 'Agatha and I', that appeared in the *New Statesman* on 30 January 1976.

In the article he advanced the opinion that '"Amnesia" was much too clinical a word for someone supposedly surprised into conversation, and if, as her doctor later suggested, she had an identity crisis, well, there was no Theresa [*sic*] Neele lurking in the self-possessed woman I met.' Ritchie Calder said he had been in Harrogate because he had been sent there to assist the *Daily News*'s night reporter Sidney Campion.

Two separate researchers, Kathleen Tynan and Gwen Robyns, seeking to establish the veracity of the encounter, have told me that Ritchie Calder repeated to them how he had immediately followed Sidney Campion by train to Harrogate to help him cover the story. However, before his death in 1978 Sidney Campion, who knew Ritchie Calder in later life, told Kathleen Tynan in a letter dated 27 September 1976: 'I am very mystified that I never met Ritchie Calder on the Harrogate story. When two or more of the staff were on the same assignment, it was the rule for them to get together and work out any necessary plans for success. I called at the Manchester office, and there was never any mention of Ritchie Calder, and until the death of Agatha Christie I never heard of Ritchie Calder being on the Harrogate story.'

This information has not been public knowledge till now, since the research Kathleen Tynan undertook during that period was not incorporated into the fictional screenplay she was commissioned to write for the 1979 film *Agatha*, whose opening credits ran a disclaimer to the effect that what followed was an imaginary solution to an authentic mystery. Family and friends rightly dismissed this film as a distortion of the facts. Indeed, Agatha Christie Ltd and the publishers Collins vigorously fought two unsuccessful court cases in the United States to prevent it from being distributed.

There has been further confusion about an alleged 'fourth letter' Agatha is said to have written before she disappeared that has intrigued and tantalized her fans. The late Deputy Chief Constable Kenward's daughter, Gladys Kenward Dobson, gave Gwen Robyns to understand in her 1978 unauthorized biography, *The Mystery of Agatha Christie,* that a 'fourth letter' had been written by Agatha on the night of the disappearance and that in this communication she had appealed to Deputy Chief Constable Kenward for help because she was in fear of her life. Gladys Kenward Dobson's account of what her father is supposed to have done after receiving this letter on the morning of Saturday 4 December is unequivocal: 'He received it in the 10 a.m. mail on Saturday and brought it to our home nearby to show me before going over immediately to inform the Sunningdale Police Station and begin investigations.'

Sunningdale falls between the counties of Berkshire and Surrey and it was policed until the early 1990s by the Surrey Constabulary, who have confirmed that there was no police station there in 1926 and that the village did not get one until the early 1960s.

Gladys Kenward Dobson claimed that the reason she knew about the letter was because she had spent 'many years of active service in the police force as her father's secretary'. After an extensive search, however, the Surrey police have been unable to find any records of her alleged police career, although they were able to confirm that from the early 1970s until her death in 1980 she presented a cup and runner-up prizes, in memory of her father, at the Surrey Constabulary's Annual Bowls Match.

Former Police Constable Eric Boshier remembers her in the mid-1920s as as a friendly, outgoing young woman, since his duties often took him to the Woodbridge Road headquarters. She was a familiar sight around the police yard. He also maintains that Deputy Chief Constable Kenward did not have a secretary. He states there were no secretaries in the Surrey force in those days, least of all female ones, and he recalls that the first one was a male officer who learned shorthand shortly before the Second World War.

Gladys Kenward Dobson also told biographer Gwen Robyns that she burned all her father's papers after he retired from the police force in 1931, including the 'fourth letter'. She gave Gwen Robyns to understand that she had personally destroyed the letter Agatha had left for her secretary Charlotte, when, in fact, this letter, the only surviving document in the case, was held by the Berkshire police and subsequently returned to Charlotte after Agatha's discovery.

Gladys Kenward Dobson always asserted that the strain of the case led to her father's early death in 1932 at the age of fifty-six, although medical records show that his death was the result of a chronic degenerative condition of the heart muscle. Her testimony must be in doubt, as no one close to Agatha has ever confirmed the existence of a 'fourth letter'. Gladys Kenwood Dobson made the same misleading claims to Kathleen Tynan about the letter. The policeman's daughter felt deeply resentful of the attacks the press made on her father and repeatedly told Kathleen Tynan: 'They crucified you in those days.'

Ironically, following the public release of the existing Home Office police records from the case, it was discovered that Deputy Chief Constable Kenward himself had tried to play down the scale of the search. Although he had given Arthur Dixon of the Home Office the impression in a telephone conversation on 9 February 1927 that the search of the Surrey Downs had only been carried out over two days, Kenward indirectly admitted in his report, written later that day, to having searched for five days. Yet one of his most loyal officers, Tom Roberts, who, after he had risen in the ranks from Police Constable to head of the Surrey CID years later, unwittingly revealed in his autobiography, *Friends and Villains*, that he personally had spent nine days on the search.

Understandably, Deputy Chief Constable Kenward's report on 9 February made no reference to a 'fourth letter', since Agatha had never written to him. The police officer was quick to point out, however, the failure of the Berkshire police to locate Agatha: 'As for prosecuting enquiries in other parts of the country, this was entirely a matter for the Berkshire police, in whose district Mrs Christie disappeared from.' He went on to point out with justification that the number of police said to have been engaged had been greatly exaggerated and to confirm that he had received 'invaluable assistance' from the public and 'innumerable special constables (unpaid)'.

Official police figures for 1926 show that the Surrey police force was made up of 356 regular officers, and there can be no doubt that the press misinformed the public over the number of regular policeman engaged on the search, citing 600 in one instance. Tom Roberts came to his mentor's defence in his autobiography by blaming Deputy Chief Constable Kenward's most dismal hour on the sensational press coverage; he also understates the number of police involved. He mentions in his book the 'many' press cuttings in his career scrapbook in which photographs reveal no more than twelve policemen at any one time involved in the search of the downs. I have been shown his scrapbook at Camberley Police Station by a member of his family and the press cuttings alluding to Agatha's disappearance amount to a total of three articles. Before he died Tom Roberts privately admitted that, to his knowledge, as many as 250 police officers were involved in the combing of the Surrey Downs.

Obviously Deputy Chief Constable Kenward found himself in an unenviable position after Agatha was located. He would have been open to criticism if he had not searched the Surrey Downs for the crime writer, especially if her body had later been found, but because he had actively sought to find her he became a target for criticism for having wasted people's time and the taxpayers' money.

Former Police Constable Eric Boshier has confirmed that Deputy Chief Constable Kenward later suffered for his conviction that her body would be found: 'He made an ass over it. The word of mouth among police officers was that Kenward was convinced she would be found at Newlands Corner. The press had a good laugh at him when she was found elsewhere. But he solved a lot of cases in his time. He was a very good chap.'

Additional confusion over why Agatha was in Harrogate has arisen from contradictory claims made by the literary critic Eric Hiscock about his former employer, Sir Godfrey Collins, who died in 1936. Although Sir Godfrey had instructed his publishing staff during the disappearance not to speculate to the press on Agatha's possible whereabouts, Eric Hiscock discussed the issue in his 1970 autobiography, *Last Boat to Folly Bridge*: 'I have always believed that Sir Godfrey knew, and that he wasn't the least bit surprised when she was ultimately discovered holed up in a Harrogate hotel.' However, on 19 April 1980, in *The Bookseller*, Eric Hiscock asserted that on the morning after Agatha had disappeared Sir Godfrey had instructed him not to talk to the press about the matter because 'she is in Harrogate, resting'.

While Agatha certainly became a household name as a result of media interest in the disappearance, claims of an alleged 'fourth letter', together with ones of an 'encounter' and 'prior knowledge' of her whereabouts, have confused commentators ever since, including Agatha's authorized biographer.

In her 1984 biography, *Agatha Christie*, Janet Morgan mistakenly claims that, on the night of her disappearance, Agatha left Styles around 11 p.m. Janet Morgan's hypothesis is that Agatha may have missed a crucial gear change at Newlands Corner and incurred amnesia after running her car off the road. In her reconstruction, which incorrectly identifies the chalk pit into which the car almost crashed, Janet Morgan has Agatha travelling from Guildford in the direction of Shere. She suggests that the missed gear change came after Agatha drove over the crest of the hill and that the car ended up on the left-hand side of the hill, about half-way down the A25 Dorking Road where there is a small quarry, which, according to Janet Morgan, is so steeply embanked that this seems to her to be the only place where a car might run off the road.

Water Lane is, however, on the right-hand side of the descending A25 Dorking Road, and the fact that Alfred Luland's refreshment hut (which has since been replaced by Barn's Café) is on the left-hand side of the road, along with the gravel pit described by Janet Morgan, makes her reconstruction impossible; after spotting the car on the morning it was discovered the witness, Frederick Dore, crossed *over* the road to the refreshment hut to ask Alfred Luland to take charge of it while he told the police about his discovery.

Janet Morgan goes on to suggest that Agatha caught a penny bus into Guildford on the morning of Saturday the 4th and that after proceeding by train from Guildford to London she caught 'either the Pullman leaving King's Cross at 11.15 a.m. or the 11.45 a.m. from St Pancras'. Railway records show none of the trains departing for Harrogate left at these times.

It may well be that the immediate family allowed the biographer to infer that Agatha consulted a psychiatrist and a Regius Professor of Pastoral Theology at Oxford to recover her memory, but there is no evidence of this whatsoever. Janet Morgan also tells readers that Agatha left for the Canary Islands in February 1928, instead of five weeks after the disappearance in January 1927. Her suggestion that Agatha may have disappeared because she was a 'somnambule', capable of hypnotizing herself at will, is no more credible than her contention that unrelated 'recent work' in this field 'suggests a useful line of thought for those who are interested in Agatha's case'.

The disappearance has captured the imaginations of more people than anyone could ever have imagined, and it is perhaps ironic that in March 1993 the creators of the London Weekend Television series *Agatha Christie's Poirot* unwittingly blended fiction with history. In a scenario that was never envisaged by his creator Hercule Poirot finds his investigation of 'The Jewel Robbery at the Grand Metropolitan' hampered by the public – who are convinced he is the newspaper creation 'Lucky Len', for whom there is a ten-guinea reward for recognizing him from his newspaper photograph.

Epilogue
A Realm of Her Own

THE PUBLICITY THAT arose from the disappearance shook Agatha until her dying day and, although her continued friendship with Nan helped sustain her in its aftermath, Agatha always regretted having staged it with her friend's help. Moreover she never got over the loss of Archie. Walter Savage Landor's lines perhaps most poignantly encapsulate her lifelong heartbreak: 'While the light lasts I shall not forget, and in the darkness I shall remember.'

After Agatha's death, her writing case was opened and found to contain her wedding ring from Archie, together with letters from him, some mementoes and a cutting of Psalm 55, verses 12, 13, and 14:

> For it is not an open enemy, that hath done me this dishonour: for
> then I could have borne it.
> Neither was it mine adversary, that did magnify himself against me:
> for then peradventure I would have hid myself from him.
> But it was even thou, my companion: my guide, and mine own
> familiar friend.

Love was the most important thing in Agatha's life: she had been raised to 'await her fate' and for her the true symbol of success in life was being a married woman. It is indicative that when she booked into the Harrogate Hydo she accorded herself the title of a married woman. How important this status was to her was reinforced when she created her fictional counterpart Mrs Ariadne Oliver, since there was never any mention in the books of Mr Oliver or what had become of him. Marriage, for better and for worse, was essential to Agatha's existence, for, as she once told Max, she was like 'a dog that needs to be taken for walks'. Moreover, as a result of the humiliating public scrutiny she endured in 1926, the extraordinary fame that later came her way never went to her head.

By not mentioning the disappearance in her autobiography Agatha's intention was not to mislead or confuse her fans. She simply wanted to forget the episode, something she had unsuccessfully tried to do all her life. If Max had not been unfaithful to her she would have been less afraid of her future. Agatha loved Archie far more than she ever did Max, and so Max was never able to hurt her as deeply as Archie. One of the most painful lessons Agatha learned from the breakdown of her marriage to him was to love others as much for their faults as for their virtues. The reason her autobiography omitted the unpleasant episodes in her life was because she intended it as a hymn to God for all the good things that had befallen her.

Agatha spent much of her life hiding from her public. This makes it all the more important to know what happened during the disappearance, because only then can one appreciate how she exorcized her pain over the episode and her subsequent divorce in her writings. She used her poetry to reveal her anxieties about whether she was loved or would ever find love. The short stories 'The Edge', 'Harlequin's Lane' and 'The Man from the Sea' reveal the chaotic aspects of her marriage to Archie. Her Mary Westmacott novels include some of her most eloquent expressions of Archie's impact on her life. 'The Dressmaker's Doll' and *The Burden* reveal her mixed feelings about Max's mistress Barbara, while *Verdict* was a brave, if unsuccessful, attempt to reconcile herself to Max's infidelity. When the love of both the men in her life failed her, Agatha was not without hope for most of the time because she found forgiveness and love in the eyes of God.

She cared passionately for the rights of the innocent. It is significant that she did not see evil as a social organism; rather, as a deviation springing from the heart of the individual. Such individuals were, in her view, like derelict ships that drift in the darkness and wreck the sound seaworthy craft. She came to identify closely with the Arab proverb which states that the fate of each man hangs around his neck but that there is always an alternative, if hidden, route that can be taken.

Agatha was destined to be known as the disappearing novelist in more ways than one; much of the world she knew and wrote about has almost completely vanished: a world of chauffeured Daimlers and Bentleys, solvent aristocracy and stately homes. Many of her loyal readers hanker for this bygone age. Her detective stories are civilized and elaborately plotted versions of her 'Gun Man' dream; in them anyone can turn out to be the killer. The more chaotic her life became the more she made her fictitious world neat and orderly.

The reason she never admitted the full extent of her pain to her fans was because she did not want our pity. She wanted for herself what she had long wished on others: 'The peace of God which passeth all understanding.' Her detective stories endure because they nourish in her readers the hope that good will always triumph over evil, and the charm, good humour and humility with which she imparts her message make her fans love her all the more.

Perhaps her greatest achievement is to represent to each successive generation a nostalgic link with a way of life that disappeared along with the British Empire.

One knows that a writer has been well loved if, when he or she dies, fans wish there was one more book left for them to read, and no one is more deserving of such an accolade than Agatha Christie.

WORKS OF AGATHA CHRISTIE

The following comprehensive list of works published in the UK makes clear how well known Agatha Christie was at the time of her disappearance. Note that short stories designated * were collected in *Poirot Investigates*, those marked † were collected as *The Big Four*, while those marked ‡ were collected as *Partners in Crime*.

1920
The Mysterious Affair at Styles (Bodley Head)

1922
The Secret Adversary (Bodley Head)

1923
The Murder on the Links (Bodley Head)
'The Affair at the Victory Ball', March, (*The Sketch*)
* 'The Curious Disappearance of the Opalsen Pearls', a.k.a. 'The Jewel Robbery at the Grand Metropolitan', March (*The Sketch*)
'The Adventure of the King of Clubs', March (*The Sketch*)
* 'The Disappearance of Mr Davenheim', March (*The Sketch*)
'The Mystery of the Plymouth Express', April (*The Sketch*)
* 'The Adventure of the Western Star', April (*The Sketch*)
* 'The Tragedy at Marsden Manor', April (*The Sketch*)
* 'The Kidnapped Prime Minister', April (*The Sketch*)
* 'The Million Dollar Bond Robbery', May (*The Sketch*)
* 'The Adventure of the Cheap Flat', May (*The Sketch*)
* 'The Mystery of Hunters Lodge', May (*The Sketch*)

'The Clue of the Chocolate Box', May (*The Sketch*)
'A Trap for the Unwary', a.k.a. 'The Actress', May (*Novel Magazine*)
* 'The Adventure of the Egyptian Tomb', September (*The Sketch*)
'The Clue of the Veiled Lady', October (*The Sketch*)
'The Kidnapping of Johnnie Waverly', a.k.a. 'The Adventure of Johnnie Waverley', October (*The Sketch*)
'The Market Basing Mystery', October (*The Sketch*)
* 'The Adventure of the Italian Nobleman', October (*The Sketch*)
* 'The Case of the Missing Will', October (*The Sketch*)
'The Submarine Plans', November (*The Sketch*)
'The Adventure of the Clapham Cook', November (*The Sketch*)
'The Lost Mine', November (*The Sketch*)
'The Cornish Mystery', November (*The Sketch*)
'The Double Clue', December (*The Sketch*)
'The Adventure of the Christmas Pudding', December (*The Sketch*)
'The Le Mesurier Inheritance', December (*The Sketch*)
‡ 'The First Wish', a.k.a. 'The Clergyman's Daughter', a.k.a. 'The Red House', December (*Grand Magazine*)

1924

The Man in the Brown Suit (Bodley Head)
Poirot Investigates (Bodley Head)
The Road of Dreams (poetry) (Geoffrey Bles)
† 'The Unexpected Guest', January (*The Sketch*)
† 'The Adventure of the Dartmoor Bungalow', January (*The Sketch*)
† 'The Lady on the Stairs', January (*The Sketch*)
† 'The Radium Thieves', January (*The Sketch*)
† 'In the House of the Enemy', January (*The Sketch*)
† 'The Yellow Jasmine Mystery', February (*The Sketch*)
† 'The Chess Problem', February (*The Sketch*)
† 'The Baited Trap', February (*The Sketch*)
† 'The Adventure of the Peroxide Blonde', February (*The Sketch*)
'The Girl in the Train', February (*Grand Magazine*)
† 'The Terrible Catastrophe', March (*The Sketch*)
† 'The Dying Chinaman', March (*The Sketch*)
† 'The Crag in the Dolomites', March (*The Sketch*)
'The Passing of Mr Quinn', a.k.a. 'The Coming of Mr Quin', March (*Grand Magazine*)
'While the Light Lasts', April (*Novel Magazine*)
'The Red Signal', June (*Grand Magazine*)
'The Mystery of the Blue Jar', July (*Grand Magazine*)
'The Mystery of the Second Cucumber', a.k.a. 'Mr Eastwood's Adventure', August (*Novel Magazine*)
'Jane in Search of a Job', August (*Grand Magazine*)
‡ 'Publicity', a.k.a. 'A Pot of Tea', a.k.a. 'A Fairy in the Flat', September (*The Sketch*)
‡ 'The Affair of the Pink Pearl', October (*The Sketch*)

‡ 'Finessing the King', a.k.a. 'The Gentleman Dressed in Newspaper', October (*The Sketch*)
‡ 'The Case of the Missing Lady', October (*The Sketch*)
‡ 'The Adventure of the Sinister Stranger', October (*The Sketch*)
‡ 'The Sunninghall Mystery', a.k.a. 'The Sunningdale Mystery', October (*The Sketch*)
'The Shadow on the Glass', October (*Grand Magazine*)
‡ 'The House of Lurking Death', November (*The Sketch*)
‡ 'The Matter of the Ambassador's Boots', November (*The Sketch*)
‡ 'The Affair of the Forged Notes', a.k.a. 'The Crackler', November (*The Sketch*)
‡ 'Blind Man's Buff', November (*The Sketch*)
'Philomel Cottage', November (*Grand Magazine*)
‡ 'The Man in the Mist', December (*The Sketch*)
‡ 'The Man Who Was Number Sixteen', December (*The Sketch*)
'The Day of His Dreams', a.k.a. 'The Manhood of Edward Robinson', December (*Grand Magazine*)

1925

The Secret of Chimneys (Bodley Head)
'Traitor Hands', a.k.a. 'The Witness for the Prosecution', January (*Flynn's Weekly*)
'A Sign in the Sky', July (*Grand Magazine*)
'Within a Wall', October (*Royal Magazine*)
'A Man of Magic', a.k.a. 'At the Bells and Motley', November (*Grand Magazine*)
'The Fourth Man', December (*Pearson's Magazine*)
'The Benevolent Butler', a.k.a. 'The Listerdale Mystery', December (*Grand Magazine*)

1926

The Murder of Roger Ackroyd (Collins)
'The House of Dreams', a.k.a. 'The House of Beauty', January (*Sovereign Magazine*)
'S.O.S.!', February (*Grand Magazine*)

'Magnolia Blossom', March
    (*Royal Magazine*)
'The Rajah's Emerald', July (*Red Magazine*)
'The Lonely God', July (*Royal Magazine*)
'Swan Song', September (*Grand Magazine*)
'At the Crossroads', a.k.a. 'The Love
    Detectives', October (*Flynn's Weekly*)
'The Under Dog', October
    (*London Magazine*)
'The Soul of the Croupier', November
    (*Flynn's Weekly*)
'World's End', November (*Flynn's Weekly*)
'The Voice in the Dark', December
    (*Flynn's Weekly*)
'Wireless' (*Sunday Chronicle Annual 1926*)

After the disappearance Agatha Christie
re-established her usual prolific output in
a relatively short time.

1927
The Big Four (Collins)

1928
The Mystery of the Blue Train (Collins)
Alibi (play adapted by Michael Morton *from
    The Murder of Roger Ackroyd*)
    (Samuel French)

1929
The Seven Dials Mystery (Collins)
Partners in Crime (Collins)
The Sunningdale Mystery (Collins)
The Passing of Mr Quinn (book of the
    film adapted by G. Roy McRae from
    the short story) (London Book
    Company)

1930
The Mysterious Mr Quin (Collins)
The Murder at the Vicarage (Collins)
Giant's Bread (Mary Westmacott)
    (Collins)
Chimneys (unpublished play based on *The
    Secret of Chimneys*)

1931
The Sittaford Mystery (Collins)

1932
Peril at End House (Collins)
The Thirteen Problems (Collins)
The Wasp's Nest (unpublished play)

1933
Lord Edgware Dies (Collins)
The Hound of Death (Odhams)

1934
Black Coffee (play) (Alfred Ashley)
Murder on the Orient Express (Collins)
The Listerdale Mystery (Collins)
Why Didn't They Ask Evans? (Collins)
Parker Pyne Investigates (Collins)
Unfinished Portrait (Mary Westmacott) (Collins)

1935
Three Act Tragedy (Collins)
Death in the Clouds (Collins)

1936
The ABC Murders (Collins)
Murder in Mesopotamia (Collins)
Cards on the Table (Collins)
Love from a Stranger (play adapted by
    Frank Vosper from the short story
    'Philomel Cottage') (Collins)

1937
Dumb Witness (Collins)
Death on the Nile (Collins)
Murder in the Mews (Collins)

1938
Appointment with Death (Collins)
Hercule Poirot's Christmas (Collins)

1939
Murder Is Easy (Collins)
Ten Little Niggers (later retitled *And Then
    There Were None*) (Collins)

1940
Sad Cypress (Collins)
One, Two, Buckle My Shoe (Collins)
Peril at End House (play adapted by Arnold
    Ridley) (Samuel French)

1941
Evil Under the Sun (Collins)
N or M? (Collins)

1942
The Body in the Library (Collins)
Five Little Pigs (Collins)

1943
The Moving Finger (Collins)
Ten Little Niggers (play later retitled *And Then There Were None*) (Samuel French)

1944
Towards Zero (Collins)
Absent in the Spring (Mary Westmacott) (Collins)

1945
Death Comes as the End (Collins)
Sparkling Cyanide (Collins)
Appointment with Death (play) (Samuel French)
Hidden Horizon (play a.k.a. *Murder on the Nile* based on *Death on the Nile*) (Samuel French)

1946
The Hollow (Collins)
Come, Tell Me How You Live (Agatha Christie Mallowan) (Collins)

1947
The Labours of Hercules (Collins)

1948
Taken at the Flood (Collins)
The Rose and the Yew Tree (Mary Westmacott) (Heinemann)

1949
Crooked House (Collins)
Murder at the Vicarage (play adapted by Moie Charles and Barbara Toy) (Samuel French)

1950
A Murder Is Announced (Collins)

1951
They Came to Baghdad (Collins)
The Hollow (play) (Samuel French)

1952
Mrs McGinty's Dead (Collins)
They Do It With Mirrors (Collins)
A Daughter's a Daughter (Mary Westmacott) (Heinemann)
The Mousetrap (play) (Samuel French)

1953
After the Funeral (Collins)
A Pocket Full of Rye (Collins)
Witness for the Prosecution (play) (Samuel French)

1954
Destination Unknown (Collins)
Spider's Web (play) (Samuel French)

1955
Hickory Dickory Dock (Collins)

1956
Dead Man's Folly (Collins)

1957
4.50 from Paddington (Collins)

1958
Ordeal by Innocence (Collins)
Verdict (play) (Samuel French)
Towards Zero (play written in collaboration with Gerald Verner) (Samuel French)
The Unexpected Guest (play) (Samuel French)

1959
Cat Among the Pigeons (Collins)

1960
The Adventure of the Christmas Pudding (Collins)
Go Back for Murder (play based on *Five Little Pigs*) (Samuel French)

1961
The Pale Horse (Collins)

1962
The Mirror Crack'd from Side to Side (Collins)
Rule of Three (three one-act plays: *The Rats, The Patient, Afternoon at the Sea-Side*) (Samuel French)

1963
The Clocks (Collins)

1964
A Caribbean Mystery (Collins)

1965
At Bertram's Hotel (Collins)
Star Over Bethlehem (poems and children's stories) (Agatha Christie Mallowan) (Collins)

1966
Third Girl (Collins)

1967
Endless Night (Collins)

1968
By the Pricking of My Thumbs (Collins)

1969
Hallowe'en Party (Collins)

1970
Passenger to Frankfurt (Collins)

1971
Nemesis (Collins)

1972
Elephants Can Remember (Collins)
Fiddler's Three (unpublished play a.k.a. *This Mortal Coil* a.k.a. *Fiddler's Five*)

1973
Postern of Fate (Collins)
Akhnaton (play written in 1937) (Collins)

Poems (Collins)

1974
Poirot's Early Cases (Collins)

1975
Curtain: Poirot's Last Case (Collins)

1976
Sleeping Murder: Miss Marple's Last Case (Collins)

1977
An Autobiography (Collins)
A Murder Is Announced (play adapted by Leslie Darbon) (Samuel French)

1980
Miss Marple's Final Cases (Collins)

1981
Cards on the Table (play adapted by Leslie Darbon) (Samuel French)

1992
Problem at Pollensa Bay (HarperCollins)

1993
Murder Is Easy (unpublished play adapted by Clive Exton)

1997
While the Light Lasts (HarperCollins)

1998
Black Coffee (novel based on the 1930 play; adapted by Charles Osborne) (HarperCollins)

1999
The Unexpected Guest (novel based on the 1958 play; adapted by Charles Osborne) (HarperCollins)

2000
Spider's Web (novel based on the 1954 play; adapted by Charles Osborne) (HarperCollins)

SELECT BIBLIOGRAPHY

Many books have been written about Agatha Christie and her literary creations. Those marked with an asterisk are generally regarded as major works.

Adams, Tom, *Agatha Christie Cover Story*, Limpsfield, Surrey: Paper Tiger, 1981

Bargainnier, Earl, *The Gentle Art of Murder: The Detective Fiction of Agatha Christie*, Bowling Green, Ohio: Bowling Green State University Popular Press, 1980

*Barnard, Robert, *A Talent to Deceive: An Appreciation of Agatha Christie*, London: Collins, 1980

Behre, Frank, *Get, Come, and Go*, Stockholm: Almqvist and Wiksell, 1973

Behre, Frank, *Studies in Agatha Christie's Writings*, Stockholm: Almqvist and Wiksell, 1967

Bryan, George B., *Black Sheep, Red Herrings and Blue Murder: The Proverbial Agatha Christie*, Bern: Peter Lang, 1993

Cotes, Peter, *Thinking Aloud: Fragments of Autobiography*, London: Peter Owen, 1993

East, Andy, *The Agatha Christie Quiz Book*, New York: Pocket Books, 1981

Escott, John, *Agatha Christie: Woman of Mystery*, Oxford: Oxford University Press, 1997

Feinman, Jeffrey, *The Mysterious World of Agatha Christie*, New York: Grosset and Dunlap, 1975

Fido, Martin, *The World of Agatha Christie*, London: Carlton Books, 1999

Fitzgibbon, Russell H., *The Agatha Christie Companion*, Bowling Green, Ohio: Bowling Green State University Popular Press, 1980

*Gerald, Michael C., *The Poisonous World of Agatha Christie*, Austin, Texas: University of Texas, 1993

*Gill, Gillian, *Agatha Christie: The Woman and Her Mysteries*, New York: Free Press, 1990

*Gregg, Hubert, *Agatha and All That Mousetrap*, London: William Kimber, 1980

Haining, Peter, *Agatha Christie's Poirot*, London: Boxtree, 1995

*Haining, Peter, *Murder in Four Acts*, London: Virgin, 1990

Hart, Anne, *The Life and Times of Hercule Poirot*, London, Pavilion Books, 1990

Hart, Anne, *The Life and Times of Miss Jane Marple*, London: Macmillan, 1985

Hiscock, Eric, *Last Boat to Folly Bridge*, London: Cassell, 1970

Kaska, Kathleen, *What's Your Agatha Christie IQ?*, Secaucus, New Jersey: Citadel Press, 1996

*Keating, H.R.F. (ed.), *Agatha Christie, First Lady of Crime*, London: Weidenfeld and Nicholson, 1977

Langton, Jane, *Agatha Christie's Devon*, Bodmin: Bossiney Books, 1990

Light, Alison, *Forever England: Femininity, Literature and Conservatism Between the Wars*, London: Routledge, 1991

Maida, Patricia and Spornick, Nicholas, *Murder She Wrote: A Study of Agatha Christie's Detective Fiction*, Bowling Green, Ohio: Bowling Green State University Popular Press, 1982

*Mallowan, Max, *Mallowan's Memoirs*, London: Collins, 1977

*Morgan, Janet, *Agatha Christie: A Biography*, London: Collins, 1984

Morselt, Ben, *An A–Z of the Novels and Short Stories of Agatha Christie*, Paradise Valley, Arizona: Phoenix Publishing Associates, 1985

Murdoch, Derrick, *The Agatha Christie Mystery*, Toronto: Paguarian Press, 1976

*Osborne, Charles, *The Life and Crimes of Agatha Christie*, London: Collins, 1982

*Palmer, Scott, *The Films of Agatha Christie*, London: Batsford, 1993

Ramsey, Gordon, *Agatha Christie: Mistress of Mystery*, New York: Dodd, Mead and Co., 1967

Riley, Dick and McAllister, Pam, *The Bedside, Bathtub and Armchair Guide to Agatha Christie*, New York: Frederick Ungar, 1979; revised edition, New York: Frederick Ungar, 1993

*Rivière, François, *In the Footsteps of Agatha Christie*, London: Ebury Press, 1997

Roberts, Tom, *Friends and Villains*, London: Hodder and Stoughton, 1987

*Robyns, Gwen, *The Mystery of Agatha Christie*, New York: Doubleday, 1978

Ryan, Richard T., *Agatha Christie Trivia*, Boston: Quinlan Press, 1987

Sanders, Denis and Lovallo, Len, *The Agatha Christie Companion: The Complete Guide to the Life and Works of Agatha Christie*, New York: Delacorte, 1984; revised edition, New York: Berkley Books, 1989

Saunders, Peter, *The Mousetrap Man*, London: Collins, 1972

Shaw, Marion and Vanacker, Sabine, *Reflecting on Miss Marple*, London: Routledge, 1991

Sova, Dawn B., *Agatha Christie A–Z: The Essential Reference to Her Life and Writings*, New York: Facts on File, 1996

*Toye, Randall, *The Agatha Christie Who's Who*, London: Frederick Muller, 1980

Toye, Randall and Gaffney, Judith Hawkins, *The Agatha Christie Crossword Puzzle Book*, London: Angus and Robertson, 1981

Tynan, Kathleen, *Agatha: The Agatha Christie Mystery*, New York: Ballantine Books, 1978

*Underwood, Lynn (ed.), *Agatha Christie Centenary Booklet,* London: Belgrave Publishing (HarperCollins), 1990

Wagoner, Mary, *Agatha Christie,* New York: Twayne Publishers, 1986

Wynne, Nancy B., *The Agatha Christie Chronology,* Santa Barbara, California: Ace Books, 1976

Although numerous articles have been written about Agatha Christie she gave few interviews; the most significant are marked with an asterisk.

Atticus, 'Men, Women and Memories', *Sunday Times,* 13 and 20 February 1949

*Bernstein, Marcelle, 'Hercule Poirot is 130 – But Then Agatha Christie Is 79', *Observer,* 14 December 1969

Calder, Ritchie, 'Agatha and I', *New Statesmen,* 30 January 1976

Christie, Agatha, 'Agatha Christie Pleads for the Tragic Family of Croydon', *Sunday Chronicle,* 11 August 1929

Christie, Agatha, 'Does a Woman's Instinct Make Her a Good Detective?', *The Star,* 14 May 1928

Christie, Agatha, 'How I Became a Writer', *Listener,* 11 August 1938

Christie, Agatha, 'Mrs Agatha Christie: Her Own Story of Her Disappearance', *Daily Mail,* 16 February 1928

Herald and Express (Torquay), 'The Agatha Centenary' (three souvenir supplements issued by the *Herald and Express*), 5, 6 and 8 September 1990

Hicks, Rosalind, 'Agatha Christie, My Mother', *The Times Saturday Review,* 8 September 1990

Hiscock, Eric, 'Personally Speaking', *Bookseller,* 19 April 1980

*Knox, Valerie, 'Agatha Christie at 76 Is Still Plotting Murders', *The Times,* 1 December 1967

Ramsey, Gordon C., 'A Teacher Meets Agatha Christie', *Worcester Academy Bulletin,* Spring 1966

Snowdon, Lord, 'The Unsinkable Agatha Christie', *Toronto Star,* 14 December 1974

*Symons, Julian, 'Agatha Christie Talks to Julian Symons About the Gentle Art of Murder', *Sunday Times,* 15 October 1961

*Winn, Godfrey, 'The Real Agatha Christie', *Daily Mail,* 12 September 1970

*Wyndham, Francis, 'The Algebra of Agatha Christie', *Sunday Times Weekly Review,* 27 February 1966

Anon, 'One Woman's View of a Great English Scandal', *San Francisco Chronicle,* 14 August 1976

Anon, 'The Queen's: *The Claimant*', *The Stage,* 18 September 1924

Anon, 'Stories That Thrill', *The Herald* (Melbourne), 20 May 1922

Anon, supplementary material from the *New York Times* News Service and the

Associated Press, 22 September 1978 (Because of a newspaper strike, the *New York Times* was not printed at that time, but records were kept, including an article to the effect that a federal judge, Lawrence W. Pierce, had refused to block distribution of a movie and novel based on Agatha Christie's unexplained disappearance in 1926. Two lawsuits had been brought by the late writer's estate and by her only child, Rosalind Christie Hicks, and named in the suit as defendants were Ballantine Books, Casablanca Records and Filmworks, First Artist Corporation and Warner Brothers Inc. The film *Agatha*, starring Vanessa Redgrave and Dustin Hoffman, a fictional speculative account of the disappearance, was subsequently released in 1979.)

INDEX